——— **To Make a** ———

Long Story Short

What others have said...

If you don't know the plot-line of the Bible -- and even if you do -- I thoroughly recommend this epic retelling of the one story that everybody needs to know. It is respectful yet readable, insightful and invigorating. Best of all, it makes you want to read the original!

Revd. Canon J. John - international speaker and author.

Justyn Rees has reduced the story line of the Bible to a gripping tale, told with wit and warmth. This is the spinal cord of the world's oldest and most influential book, the story line from which the many branches of its doctrines, promises and privileges extend. It will be revealing to those who do not know the story, refreshing to those who do, and renewing to those who once knew, but have neglected it.

Charles Price - pastor of The Peoples Church, Toronto, and TV and radio host of Living Truth

I was gripped! From the beginning of creation to the end of Revelation I just couldn't wait to read more! Justyn has conveyed the Best Story Ever in up to date, everyday language. He has captured the drama, the wonder and the life changing impact of the Bible in a way that will make it a treasured book to receive, and to give away.

Julie Sheldon - international speaker, author and ballet dancer.

At last a book that simply tells the story – and just the story! It's brilliant! Now ordinary people, like me, can understand the Old Testament and how it links with the New; and realize how utterly fascinating, funny and relevant the bare-bones of the Bible's story actually is!

Jennifer Larcombe - author, conference speaker and Bible teacher.

Justyn Rees is a brilliant storyteller. The first line of each story engages the reader, and gently takes us into a world of wonder and exploration. Justyn exposes the emotion of each moment with subtle details that form a new picture in one's mind, capturing the moment with fresh understanding. One could imagine sitting near a quiet brook listening intently to every word, while Justyn unravels the next episode of this eternal story.

Richard Dodding - founder of Missions Fest Vancouver and director of the International Teachers Institute in Ukraine and Kazakhstan

There are not many books that are a 'Must Read' for everyone - but this book is. I don't know any other book that will make the Bible come to life like this does.

Max Sinclair - author, speaker and founder of Christian Vision for Men, UK (CVM)

Justyn Rees as a consummate story-teller has captured the essence of the Bible—true to the text, true to the Spirit, eminently readable. It captures our hearts and draws us into God's story so that it becomes our story, the very thing God had intended when God inspired people of old to write the sacred text. Take and read and you won't be able to put it down. Best of all, your faith will grow.

R. Paul Stevens - Professor Emeritus, Marketplace Theology, Regent College, Vancouver, BC.

Other books written by Justyn Rees:

TO MAKE AN OLD STORY NEW
The Epic Saga of the Bible's Old Testament Retold with Colour and Warmth

HONEST DOUBT, REAL FAITH
A story of faith lost and recovered

LOVE YOUR NEIGHBOUR, FOR GOD'S SAKE
How to introduce Jesus to your friends and neighbours

CONTACT JUSTYN REES:
www.justynrees.com
jrees@upstream.ca

To Make a

Long Story Short

A COMPELLING RETELLING
THAT MAKES THE BIBLE'S NEW
TESTAMENT DANCE WITH LIFE

Justyn Rees

WESTBOW
P R E S S
A DIVISION OF THOMAS NELSON
& ZONDERVAN

WestBow Press books may be ordered through booksellers or by contacting:

WestBow Press
A Division of Thomas Nelson & Zondervan
1663 Liberty Drive
Bloomington, IN 47403
www.westbowpress.com
1 (866) 928-1240

ISBN: 978-1-4908-3792-5 (sc)
ISBN: 978-1-4908-3791-8 (hc)
ISBN: 978-1-4908-3790-1 (e)

Library of Congress Control Number: 2014911548

Printed in the United States of America.

WestBow Press rev. date: 7/11/14

Table of Contents

1

The Child

As his eyes gradually grew accustomed to the darkness, the old man made out the square bulk of the altar, silhouetted against the light from the lamp stand. The place had a musty smell, cut off as it was from the light of day and the fresh air of the big world outside. But this was the closest place to heaven, a thin place, if ever there was one, a mere membrane separating him from the realm beyond.

All his life he had prepared for this moment, when he would stand alone in the presence of God to present the requests of his people. He had never been there before and never would be again. This was a once-in-a-lifetime opportunity, afforded him by the flip of a coin, the roll of a dice, and this morning he had won the lottery. Finally, it was his turn. Today was his big opportunity to express to God what was in his heart.

At first, he followed the script, praying for his people. Then he added other requests: It sure would be nice if the Messiah would make his long-promised appearance before much longer. A bit of a break from foreign oppression and endless taxes wouldn't go amiss. And, oh yes: "God bless King Herod and Emperor Augustus in Rome."

Then a thought crossed his mind. His greatest disappointment in life was that his wife had never given him a son. They had often brought their request to the Almighty, but he had never seen fit to answer. So what better moment to add his own personal request to his official prayers than right now? "Lord, 'tis me, Zac, doing the talking today. If I might be so bold as to add a personal PS on behalf of Elizabeth and myself. A child of our own—"

The words had barely passed his lips when a voice from the darkness startled him: "Zechariah, your prayer has been heard."

No one was permitted to be in that Holy Place but himself, so what some stranger was doing eavesdropping on his prayers, Zechariah couldn't imagine. Then he made out a figure standing to the right of the incense altar, a silhouette in the darkness.

"Don't be afraid, Zechariah. God has heard your prayer, and Elizabeth will give you a son. You are to call him John. He will be great in the Lord's sight and will be filled with the Holy Spirit right from birth. Many will be led to faith in the Lord God because of him. In fact, he will be like Elijah to this generation, turning fathers to love their children and rebels to right living. He will prepare people for the coming of the Christ."

Surprise was perhaps an understandable reaction, but scepticism, and from a man of the cloth? "How do I know you are telling me the truth? I am just an old man, and Elizabeth is long past childbearing."

"Perhaps I should introduce myself," said the stranger with a hint of offence. "My name is Gabriel. I spend every day standing close to God in heaven. And it was God himself who sent me to deliver to you this message. Dumb you are to doubt and dumb you shall remain till my words come true."

It took him awhile to pull himself together, but eventually Zechariah realised that he was alone again. He groped his way back through the curtains and, pushing open the massive double doors, stood squinting in the bright afternoon sun before the expectant congregation in the temple outside. There he was, with the news for which the world had been waiting, but when he walked up to the lectern to make the great announcement, he couldn't say a word. Dumb!

When his duty was done, Zechariah hurried home. His greeting may have left something to be desired, but his body language was eloquent enough, for at the end of the month, Elizabeth found herself to be pregnant.

———————————

Some seventy miles to the north, in the region of the country now known as Galilee, was the small town of Nazareth, where lived a teenager, Mary, engaged to be married to a local tradesman, Joseph. Though the match had been made by their parents when they were both children, they had recently agreed to the plan, meaning they were now formally engaged and legally committed to the marriage, which would be solemnised a year later.

They were blue-blooded Jews, both of them able to trace their ancestry back to King David and beyond.

Six months after his appointment with Zechariah, angel Gabriel paid a second visit to the human race, this time to Mary in Nazareth.

"Good evening, Mary. God be with you."

But Mary was terrified.

"There's no need to be afraid," assured Gabriel. "You are the object of God's great favour. Soon you are going to give birth to a son whom you are to call Jesus. He will be great, Son of the Most High. He will inherit the throne of David and reign over Israel forever."

In preparation for her marriage, Mary had heard the talk about the birds and the bees. "How can I get pregnant since I am a virgin and have never slept with a man?"

"The child will not be son of any human father. The Holy Spirit will come upon you, and the power of the Most High will envelop you, so the child will be God's Son."

Mary didn't make the same mistake as had Zechariah, requesting proof, but the messenger gave it to her without her asking: "If you want clear evidence that this will happen, you have only to ask your aunt Elizabeth, who, you may be surprised to learn, is six months' pregnant. Nothing is too hard for God."

"I am the Lord's servant. May it happen to me just as you have promised." Simple acceptance of the extraordinary.

Mary didn't sleep much that night, but when she woke the next morning, she wondered if it had all been a dream. Who could she talk to about it? Joseph? Certainly not! Mother of the Son of God? Get real! But what if down the road she really did find herself to be pregnant but hadn't told Joseph up front? Would he believe her then?

The only person who might possibly believe her would be Elizabeth – that is if she was herself pregnant. But Elizabeth had never been able to conceive and, in any case, was now far too old to give birth. Yet what if she *was* pregnant?

The only way to find out was to pay her a visit. So, with the blessing of her parents and the reluctant consent of her fiancé, Mary joined a caravan of travellers and headed towards Jerusalem.

As she approached Elizabeth's house, uncertainty dogged her steps. Would she be able to tell if Elizabeth was in the family way? Did it show at six months? And if she was not pregnant, would Mary dare bring up the subject of her angelic encounter? But then if Elizabeth wasn't pregnant, none of it was true, so nothing would need to be said.

Mary stepped through the open door: "Anybody home?"

A slight cry came from the kitchen, like someone had been kicked. "Well, bless my soul. Is that you, Mary?" Wiping her hands on a towel, Elizabeth came into the hall, round as a basketball. "This sure is a blessing! Just what have I done to deserve a visit from the mother of my Lord?"

"It's only me," blushed Mary.

"Do you know," continued Elizabeth unabated, "as soon as I heard your voice, the child in my womb leapt for joy?"

"So you really are pregnant, then?" Well, Elizabeth might just have put on weight.

"Oh yes, I most certainly am. But how did you know?"

Mary explained her visit from Gabriel.

"Wonderful that you at least believed what he said! Not like others I could mention," she added as Zechariah came into the room. Apart from giving her a hug, Zechariah didn't offer her much of a greeting; in fact, he said not a word.

Mary, on the other hand, could not contain her spontaneous overflow of praise. She had been unable to say anything to anyone since she had met Gabriel and was fair bursting to let it all out. "My soul glorifies the Lord, and my spirit is bubbling over with joy in God my Saviour. Do you know, Aunt Liz, I am a nothing, a nobody, but from now on, everyone will call me the most blessed of all women who ever lived? The Mighty One has done this for me. Isn't he kind?"

There was much to be said between the two women, and even more so when it became clear that Mary was also pregnant. They chatted away about babies till Zechariah must have wished he had been struck deaf as well as dumb.

Three months passed in a flash, and it was time for Mary to start the long journey home before her pregnancy made travel difficult. Scarce was Mary out of the door when Elizabeth's labour pains began. To no one's surprise, she gave birth to a boy.

When the circumcision party was held a week later, everyone crowded into the home to share their joy. The natural assumption was that the boy would be called Zechariah, after his dad.

"Absolutely not," Elizabeth insisted. "He's going to be called John."

"You can't call him that. No one in the family has ever been called John." So they asked Zechariah what he thought. Getting no reply, they passed him a writing slate.

"His name is JOHN!" he wrote. Then in a clearly audible voice, he said, "My son is to be called John."

Pandemonium, tears, and applause followed.

It was as though a dam had burst. Zechariah, who had been unable to utter a word for nine months, let it all fly. "Praise the Lord!" he shouted. "It's happening at last. The Lord is coming to save his people, and salvation is coming from the royal line, exactly as he promised David. What's more, his promise to Abraham is not forgotten. Now we can serve the Lord with confidence. The sun is rising, dispersing the shadows and lighting up the path of peace."

Then turning his attention to the tiny infant nestled in his arms, he continued: "And you, my little lad, you will be a prophet, a forerunner to announce the coming of the Christ, to declare salvation, to promise forgiveness, and to assure people of God's kindness."

The child grew to be a rugged outdoorsman, much like the prophet Elijah had been. He loved the solitude of the wild places and spent days exploring the crags and ravines of the wilderness to the south.

But meanwhile, Mary travelled back to Nazareth. Her three-month belly was beginning to show, but that might have been put down to her aunt's culinary skills. Eventually the truth would have to come out. Would she be believed? What would Joseph say?

Mary's worst nightmares were realised when Joseph didn't believe a word of her tale. From his perspective, it was obvious what had happened. She had gone down to the big city, got pregnant, her religious uncle had filled her head with God talk, and now she was blaming the whole shameful affair on the Almighty.

But the question remained: What was he to do? The Scriptures demanded a ruthless resolution – stone her as an adulteress. But Joseph loved Mary and dismissed that option without a second thought. A quiet divorce seemed the best course of action. An engagement was a legally binding contract and could only be ended with the help of lawyers. So be it.

Joseph never was quite clear whether he was awake or dreaming, but that night, he found himself face-to-face with an angel: "Joseph, son of David, don't hesitate to make Mary your wife because she is telling the truth. The child really is conceived by the Holy Spirit. You are to call him 'Jesus' because he will save people from their sins." He could have added that the sins from which Joseph himself might need saving included those of being a stubborn, unbelieving, hard-hearted husband, ready to divorce or stone his bride.

Instead, Gabriel quoted the words of Isaiah: "'A virgin will become pregnant and the child will be called "Immanuel," which means *God with us*.'"

Then Joseph was left alone with his thoughts. "A virgin will become pregnant"? *A virgin?* So Mary had not cheated on him. She was still a virgin. And the child would be "God with us"? *God?* Not illegitimate, but God himself?

The wedding went ahead on schedule, but before the town gossips had time to question Mary's figure, Caesar Augustus way off in Rome spared the newlyweds embarrassment by ordering a census to be taken throughout his empire. To have their names appropriately registered involved Mary and Joseph returning to their ancestral home in Bethlehem. In the fields around Bethlehem, their very great grandmother Ruth had gleaned grain, then married the farmer, Boaz. There David had been born and raised on that same family farm. And that's where Joseph and Mary headed to keep Caesar happy.

They left early so they could make the journey in easy stages, bearing in mind Mary's delicate condition. They may have made a temporary home with Zechariah and Elizabeth and their nine-month-old baby John. But as the census day approached, they were required to travel the last few miles to Bethlehem to register. The trouble was that everyone else had to be there that same day, and the town was jammed with relatives from all over the country. They tried to get a room at the inn, but it was booked solid, so they spread out their bedrolls and made do with the open air.

It may have been the hard ground, or it may have had something to do with the prophesy of Micah: "From you, Bethlehem in the land of Judah, will come someone who will rule over Israel. Then the girl who is in labour will give birth to he who is from ancient times." Sure enough, she who was in labour did give birth. No surprise – it was a boy and just in time to be enrolled in a Roman census, giving him an official entry in the human history books.

But what *was* a surprise was the unexpected arrival of a group of nervous-looking shepherds. Self-consciously, they admitted they were looking for a newborn baby, and not just any baby, specifically they had in mind one that was wrapped in rags and bedded in a manger. Now it just so happened that in the absence of a crib and the baby clothes that Mary and Elizabeth had so diligently knitted, the little fellow had been wrapped in rags to keep out the cold and laid on a pile of hay in a convenient animal-feeding trough. Those shepherds were ecstatic. They shared that they had been out in the fields watching their flocks when suddenly they had been scared spitless by the appearance of what could only have been an angel. "No need to be frightened," he had assured them. "I have very good news for you fellows and, in fact, good news for all people everywhere. This very day, just over there in Bethlehem, a Saviour has been born. He is the Lord Christ." The shepherds, being uneducated workingmen, had little notion of "Saviours" and "Christs," so the angel explained, "Here's how you will recognise him. He'll be wrapped in rags and laid in a manger." Now rags and a manger were closer to where those shepherds lived! Then apparently the whole night sky had lit up with myriads of angels all singing glory to God and celebrating peace on earth.

"So naturally we had to come for a look-see. Pardon the intrusion," they explained.

By morning, everyone in town knew about the child. Those fellows just couldn't keep quiet!

Once the formalities of the census were squared away, the family headed back to Elizabeth and Zechariah's home. There the child was circumcised and officially named "Jesus," on Joseph's specific instructions. Zechariah, who always did everything according to the book, reminded them of their duty to present the child to the Lord in the temple at Jerusalem. So five weeks later, Mary and Joseph, with their baby, headed into the big city.

They climbed up the steep hill to a group of half-reconstructed buildings, pulsing with pilgrims and priests – Herod's temple.

Herod, "King of the Jews," as the Roman senate titled him, had first been appointed to public office by Julius Caesar. Following his unfortunate assassination, the good will of Rome still shone on Herod, thanks first to Anthony, then Octavius, or Caesar Augustus, as he became known. However, Roman admiration for Herod was not shared by the Jews, who took a dim view of having a ruler foisted on them who was not of pure Jewish blood, and certainly not from David's royal line. Herod did his best to compensate for this by concentrating his considerable genius for construction on the rebuilding of the temple. Its predecessor, built by the returning exiles some five hundred years earlier, had suffered the ravages of time and politics. Surely a rebuild of that historic structure would endear Herod to his subjects and make him worthy of their respect as king of the Jews, in the grand tradition of King Solomon?

As instructed by Zechariah, Joseph and Mary threaded their way through the confusion of building blocks and scaffolding, and headed for the altar, where they presented to the duty priest their meagre offering: a couple of pigeons. They could not afford the lamb that the rich folk might have offered.

Just then, a very old man came up and stood for a moment, staring at the child. "Madam," he said. "Might I be permitted to hold your baby, just for a moment?"

"Why, please sir," she replied, passing her precious bundle into his shaky old arms.

The look on the old man's face was that of a man reborn. He had waited for this moment all his life, now here was the Christ, cradled in his arms.

"Now Lord, I can die in peace. With my own eyes I have seen your salvation." Mary and Joseph were amazed. Then the old man blessed them, and turning specifically to Mary, he said, "You know, things are not going to be easy. It is how people will respond to this child that will determine their destiny, up or down, for better or worse. Many will speak out against this little boy, and thereby lay bare the secrets of their own hearts." Then he hesitated, and for a moment he looked very sad. In a whisper that only Mary could hear, "One day it will be as though a sword will pierce your own soul also." Collecting himself, he handed the child back to his mother's arms.

The awkwardness of the moment was covered by the arrival of another admirer: Anna. She was eighty-four years old and had been living for the arrival of the Messiah ever since she had been widowed, well over half a century earlier. But from now on, she would be unending in her proclamation of the good news that the Messiah was alive and well in Israel.

Mary and Joseph made their first home in Bethlehem. As a carpenter, Joseph was not long unemployed, and soon they found themselves right at home among their many relatives, who still lived in the family hometown.

Jesus was a toddler when the foreigners came knocking. Exactly where they came from, no one knew, but it must have been from somewhere way east of there, for their accents were thick. And just who they were remained a mystery. The rumour around town was that they were royalty, perhaps even kings, but no one was in any doubt that they certainly were very wise.

They explained that they had seen an unusual star back home and had followed its leading, convinced that it presaged the birth of a king. So when the star had come close to Jerusalem, they had abandoned the star in favour of common sense and headed straight for the palace.

"Where is he who has been born king of the Jews?" they had demanded.

King Herod had been very upset, since he himself was king of the Jews, a title conferred upon him by Rome. And any child born to be king of the Jews would have to be one of his own, and since he had had no recent additions to his family, he was understandably mystified. After consulting his advisors, he had concluded that the only possible alternative would be the long-foretold Christ King, who, according to the prophet Micah, would be born in Bethlehem. So very graciously he had pointed them five miles down the road to where they now were.

Clinging to Mary's skirt was a little boy, and when these gentlemen saw him, they immediately fell to their knees and bowed to him in worship. Generous to a fault, they then pulled from their treasure boxes a most expensive set of gifts, fit for a king: items of gold, a bottle of incense, and a jar of myrrh. Perhaps of little immediate practical value in and of themselves, but the price of these gifts would tide the family over the lean years that were about to overtake them. Mary, who treasured special things, may perhaps have laid aside the myrrh for when it might be needed in years to come.

Hospitality was naturally offered but declined, the visitors insisting that God had warned them in a dream not to make the return journey through Jerusalem and to avoid Herod at all costs.

And that night, Joseph had a similar dream. Before it was light, he packed his bags and led his family on the road south. Which was as well, since scarce were they gone when a group of horsemen came clattering into town and massacred every little boy two years old and younger.

Mary, Joseph, and Jesus travelled down to Egypt. And there they stayed till once again the angel disturbed Joseph's slumber, telling him it was now safe to return home.

Hearing that Herod the Great was dead and that his ruthless son Archelaus was king of Judea in the south, they chose to return to Nazareth in Galilee, under the more benign rule of Herod Antipas. So there they settled in their old neighbourhood, able to pick up the threads of Joseph's construction business.

In the obscurity of a no-account village in the southern hills of Galilee, the toddler grew to a teenager, surrounded by his younger brothers and sisters.

A great adventure altered the routine of life soon after Jesus' twelfth birthday. His parents took him with them on the annual Passover pilgrimage to Jerusalem: such a contrast to his home village, where everyone knew each other. Thousands of pilgrims jostled through the narrow streets to get to the temple, still in the throes of renovation. After a week, he was beginning to get his bearings, but it was now time to head for home. Somehow, he got separated from the family in the crowd. Now what to do, who to ask, where to go?

He elbowed his way through the forest of grownups to the temple. Surely his parents were bound to show up there sooner or later, the obvious place to look. But they didn't. Figuring that the temple court would be as safe a place as any, he curled up in a corner and passed a chilly night. Next day, there was still no sign of mom and dad. To pass the time, Jesus listened in to some of the seminars that were hosted by the teachers of the law. As he got more confident in these theological circles, he ventured to ask a question. This was no childish enquiry, but an intelligent contribution to the discussion. Bit by bit, as the crowd ebbed and flowed, he edged closer to the centre of the circle, till he was sitting right in the front row. Soon he was involved in the conversation, not merely asking questions but venturing observations, stunning even the most learned of the teachers with his insight and perspicacity.

Three thrilling days passed before his parents found him. "Why have you behaved like this? Your father and I have been worried to death," Mary scolded.

"But why did you not realise that the obvious place to find me would be in my father's house?" The irony of the slight emphasis on *"my father"* was perhaps lost on his worried parents. But later when Mary thought back on the incident, she made a mental note of his exact words.

So it was back to Nazareth for all of them, and there Jesus grew towards manhood, taller and wiser every day, loved by God and man alike.

2

The Man

Some years later, word spread through the country that one of the old-time prophets was preaching down by the Jordan River. Apparently, he was a wild man, clothed in leathers, living off the land, eating bugs and honey. It was John, Zechariah and Elizabeth's son, all grown up.

His message was straight from the shoulder: "Repent, for the kingdom of heaven is close."

From far and wide, crowds flocked to hear what he had to say. It was amazing that he was so popular, since his message did little to appeal to anyone's ego, especially to the religious set. Perhaps that was why ordinary people loved him.

"You bunch of snakes!" he shouted at a group of Pharisees in the crowd. "What makes you think you will escape the coming judgement? Don't just *talk* about repentance: *do something!* And don't imagine for one moment that just because you are descended from Abraham you will somehow be exempt from the coming judgement. Fruitless trees God cuts down with his mighty axe and burns them."

"So what should we be doing?" someone asked.

"Share what you have with others."

"And what about us?" called out a tax collector.

"Don't collect a penny more than is owed."

Not to be left out, a group of soldiers asked what repentance would look like for them. "Don't be violent with people but treat them fairly." Then he added one more thought: "And be content with your pay."

John was not satisfied merely to deliver the message God had burned on his heart. He had to *know* that the people were getting it, responding, doing something about it. He called them to be baptised and then plunged those who responded under the water, symbolically washing all the old ways down river.

"I am only washing you with water," he told them, "but someone is about to come who will purify you with fire. It is he who will baptise you with the Holy Spirit. Don't look at me as though I were something special. I am not even worthy to undo his boot laces."

"Well, who exactly are you, then?" enquired a delegation of priests and Levites from Jerusalem. "Do you think you are the Christ?"

"Absolutely not."

"Then are you the prophet Elijah that Malachi told us to expect before the Christ would come?"

"No."

"Well, how about the prophet that Moses foretold?"

"Wrong again. But keep guessing!"

"No. You give us an answer so we can pass it on to those who sent us. What do you have to say about yourself?"

"Very well. I am the voice that calls out in the desert, 'Make way! Move the mountains. Raise the valleys. Straighten the bends. Smooth the rough. Prepare a highway for our God. Salvation is coming.'"

It was in the middle of a busy day, with many people crowding into the water for baptism, when John suddenly recognised the next in line. It was his cousin from Nazareth, Jesus. Nobody knew who this young man with a northern accent was. But John knew all about him, since his parents had told him ever since he was a child. This was the one he had been talking about for the past months, and now here he was, wanting to be baptised along with everybody else.

"Wait just a moment," John said. "The shoe is on the wrong foot here. Surely it is you who ought to be baptising me, not the other way round."

"No, John. This will prove a significant moment when the fulfilment of righteousness begins."

So John plunged Jesus under the water, just as he had countless others. But as he came up, it was totally unlike anything John had ever seen before. A shaft of bright light shone through a tear in the clouds, and a white dove fluttered down alighting on the crown of Jesus' head. A voice echoed clearly from above: "This is my dearly loved Son. I am so proud of him."

Afterwards, John would confess that this was not actually the surprise it might have been, since God had told him to expect just such an occurrence: "The one on whom you see the Spirit descend and remain, he is the one who will baptise with the Holy Spirit." What shreds of doubt John might have retained were immediately eradicated: "I saw it with my own eyes and give witness without any doubt that this really is the Son of God."

John continued to proclaim his message, but Jesus returned to obscurity, to what turned out to be something akin to boot camp in the desert. For six weeks he fasted, eating not a crust. Then the devil himself came calling. The old snake had rarely shown his face since luring Adam and Eve to take the forbidden fruit, way back at the birth of the human race. Of course, that didn't mean he hadn't been active, for someone had been successfully carrying on his business during all that time. But now here he was, in person.

"Since you are the Son of God, why not tell this rock to become a loaf of bread?"

"There's more to life than bread," Jesus replied. "Obeying God's word! That is where life comes from." Yes, and Satan well knew that disobeying God's word had cost Adam and Eve their lives and all their children after them.

Jesus left the solitude of the desert and wandered into Jerusalem. He climbed to the top of one of the towers of the temple, from where he got a bird's eye view of the crowds below. Suddenly, there he was again: "Since you are the Son of God, jump! Prove it in front of all these people. God won't let you fall, will he?"

"It is not right to put God to the test like that."

Still weak with hunger, Jesus hiked up to a high mountain peak. It was as though he could look out on the whole world from that vantage point. "I could give you all that, you know," said the devil. "All you have to do is bow before me, just for one second."

"Go away," said Jesus, turning his back. "It is written, 'Worship only God!'"

With that, the devil was gone, and Jesus was left alone.

Back down in the Jordan Valley, John was intensifying his message of a coming Saviour. The evolution of his "One day soon" to "Any day now" made the crowd glance over their shoulders. But then one afternoon, John spotted Jesus in the crowd: "He is right here, ladies and gentlemen, standing among you!" Now the people were looking at each other. Any stranger could be him.

The following day, John was chatting with a couple of his followers when he broke off midsentence and stared beyond them. "There he is, guys. That is God's sacrificial Lamb, who will take away the sin of the whole world."

Quite who or what they expected to see as they turned to look is anyone's guess. An animal, perhaps? A ghostly apparition? What they did see was an ordinary-looking man strolling along the trail beside the river.

The two left John and followed the stranger, half expecting him to evaporate before their eyes. He led them up river, away from the crowd. Following as they were at a discreet distance, they thought they might have lost him for a moment, so hurried round a corner to catch up. And there he was, standing in the middle of the path, smiling at them.

"Hi fellows. What are you looking for?"

"Well, teacher," they stammered, "we were just wondering where you are staying."

"Come and see."

So they walked together for a while. Introductions were exchanged, and Andrew, one of the pair, told Jesus about his fishing business and his family, particularly about his hot-headed brother, Simon.

As soon as they could reasonably take their leave, Andrew ran to find Simon. "Hey Si! You'll never guess who we just met." He couldn't. "The Messiah. We just met the Messiah!"

Well, who believes his brother when he comes up with a tale like that? So Andrew dragged him to the place Jesus was lodging. Andrew made the introductions, arguably the most profoundly important thing any man ever did for his brother.

"So you are the famous Simon, son of John, that I have heard so much about. I think I will call you 'Peter'." That's all it took, and Simon Peter was hooked, to use a good fishing analogy.

Next morning, Jesus was up with the larks. He told them he was heading north to Galilee. Since that was home to Andrew and Peter (as he was called from then on), they agreed to travel with him. En route they met Philip, a buddy from the fishing community on the lake of Galilee. They might have passed him by had not Jesus called out: "Follow me!" And he did.

As soon as they arrived at the lake, Philip ran off to find his buddy, Nathaniel Bartholomew. He found him taking a siesta in the shade of a fig tree.

"Hey Nate, wake up." Nathaniel hovered in the twilight zone of consciousness, reluctant to abandon a vivid dream in which he had seen a glimpse of heaven with angels coming and going and God looking down at him. To dream of God had been amazing, but it left him feeling unworthy, almost deceitful under God's all-seeing gaze. Perhaps Jacob had also felt that way when he had woken from a similar dream? But Nathaniel's dream was fading fast as Philip's nagging voice persisted: "We have found the person Moses and the prophets wrote about, the Messiah. His name is Jesus. He's from Nazareth."

"From Nazareth, you say? Nothing good ever came from that godforsaken place," he said irritably.

"Well, come and meet him for yourself."

Reluctantly, Nathaniel got to his feet and followed his excited friend.

"That's him," whispered Philip as they approached Jesus.

"Here comes a true son of Jacob," said Jesus. "Not a trace of deceit in him."

"Have we met before?" Nathaniel asked, taken aback. He had just been dreaming about Jacob. "How do you know me?"

"I saw you sleeping under that fig tree."

No one had been there. Nathaniel had been alone with his dream. The colour drained from his face, and he went weak at the knees. "You really must be the Son of God, the King of Israel," he exclaimed, to everyone's astonishment.

"You haven't seen anything yet, Nathaniel. You are going to see heaven opened and the angels of God, but not in your dreams; for real next time."

Jesus was due at a wedding in the little village of Cana, not far from his hometown of Nazareth: "You guys are welcome to tag along." So they all went.

The wedding was a huge success, a riot of fun. The bride and groom were close friends of Jesus' family, so his mum was closely involved in the catering. The celebrations went on for several days, which was not unusual. If you are going to have a party, then why not make it a good one? So much fun was had by all that the wine ran out.

Red faced, the headwaiter confided this embarrassment to Mary. This was a crisis of the first order for the young couple, at the very beginning of their lives together. Could this be a bad omen of troubles to come in their marriage?

Mary went to find Jesus, who was at the centre of the festivity: "Son, a word in your ear." Jesus followed his mother. "We have run out of wine."

"My dear, what do you think I should do about it? Is it my time, do you think?" Perhaps the moment was right for Jesus to show his true face. God had first displayed his likeness through the union of a man and a woman, so a wedding was the fitting place for God's work of restoration to begin.

Mary turned to the headwaiter: "Just do whatever he tells you."

He turned to Jesus for instructions: "For a start, fill those water jars." The jars were there for the purposes of hygiene, a convenient opportunity for hands to be washed before eating. To take care of ablutions may not have seemed like a priority in the current crisis, but those waiters did it anyway. It took some time, since there were six jars containing close on two hundred gallons between them. But eventually it was done.

"Now dip some out and take it to the best man," Jesus instructed.

The headwaiter held his breath as he poured water into the wine glass and then closed his eyes as he waited for the cry of outrage that would inevitably follow the first sip. But none came.

"Excellent bouquet," the best man remarked appreciatively. Then he called across the table to the groom, "How come you kept the best wine till last, old man?"

Andrew and Peter, Philip and Nathaniel had watched all this, wondering what was going on. But gradually it dawned on them that, for the first time in their lives, they had witnessed a real-life miracle, one that they could actually taste. Who was this man?

Since they were close to Jesus' home, they headed up the road into Nazareth, where the new friends got acquainted with Jesus' family. Joseph had been dead some years by then, so the family was led by the matriarch, Mary. With Jesus off wandering round the countryside, the family business had fallen to his younger siblings to run: James, Joseph, Simon, and Jude. Their sisters helped their mother run the home.

As was the custom, they all went off to the synagogue on Saturday morning for the Sabbath service. Jesus was invited to read the Scripture. The lesson was from the writings of the prophet Isaiah. Something in the way he read those well-known words made them live. It was as though they were his own words, not merely a record of what Isaiah had once said, years before.

"The Spirit of the Lord is on me. He has anointed me to preach good news to the poor, to heal the broken-hearted, to free the captives, to give sight to the blind, to deliver the oppressed, and to proclaim the year of jubilee."

When he had finished, there was a silence. Then he quietly closed the book and gave it back to the attendant. Instead of returning to his seat, he addressed the congregation: "Ladies and gentlemen, this day you are witnesses to the fulfilment of this prophesy. It was written about me." A buzz went round the room.

"Who does he think he is? He's just a carpenter's son, isn't he?" The buzz rose to a roar of disapproval, and soon, they were all on their feet, shouting.

"The old adage that says 'a prophet is never accepted in his own hometown' certainly seems apt here," Jesus called, trying to make himself heard above the noise.

Soon, the polite congregation had become an angry mob, and they jostled him out of the building, then drove him right out of town till they came to a cliff top. Jesus' family and followers were sure he was going to be pushed over, but then he calmly turned and faced the mob. There was quiet. The crowd parted, and he walked through unmolested.

So now where was he to go, unwelcome as he was in his own hometown? He headed down to the lake of Galilee to the little fishing community of Capernaum. There Jesus found lodgings and made it his home from then on.

It was in Capernaum that Jesus began his preaching, taking up the refrain from his wild cousin John: "Repent, for the kingdom of heaven is very near." Recognising the theme, many were drawn by his words and his gracious way of expressing things. He took to giving his lectures on the beach, and the people would flock down there to hear what he had to say.

One morning, the crowd was so thick that he was in danger of being elbowed into the water. He noticed Peter and Andrew, who by then were back to work. They had just finished the night shift fishing and were cleaning the weed out of their nets by their boat, which was pulled up onto the sand.

"Push out a little, would you, Pete. I need to talk to these folks for a while." It was the perfect amphitheatre, with the audience sitting on the beach, and Jesus' words carrying over the still water from the boat.

When he was done, he turned to Peter and Andrew: "Row out a little farther, fellows. Let down your nice clean nets and see what you'll catch."

"We worked all last night and didn't catch a minnow. But if you say so …" Jesus did say so, and they did as they were told. Which, as it turned out, was just as well, since every fish in the lake chose that moment to be swimming past. The net was so heavy with fish that they couldn't pull it back into the boat. So they yelled to their partners, James and John, who were still on the beach. Between them, they had the best big fish story since the days of Jonah.

Up to his knees in flapping fish, Peter suddenly was overcome with a sense of awe. Who was this man who appeared to know more about fishing than he did? And who was he, Peter, to be in such company? He fell to his knees amongst the fish: "I am just an ordinary sinful man, Lord. I shouldn't be here with you. Perhaps you had better move on."

"Move on? Not on your life! You are going to follow me from this moment forward. I am going to make you a fisher of people, not just fish."

And follow him Peter did, and not just Peter, but Andrew as well and the other guys they had found earlier. Now James and John were added to the group. They were a rowdy couple of lads, brothers who were in business with their father, Zeb. Jesus nicknamed them "Sons of Thunder."

Next Saturday, it was back to the synagogue. Word had not reached Capernaum about the debacle in Nazareth the previous week, so Jesus was invited to deliver the sermon. But to everyone's astonishment, this was no ordinary talk, no mere rehash of what the commentators had to say. He delivered his message with authority and conviction. But halfway through, there was an interruption. A young man, who was well known in town to be a brick or two short of a load, jumped to his feet and started to heckle. But what he had to say had an eerie feel to it.

"Ha!" he shouted. "Ha! What do you think you are doing here, Jesus from Nazareth? Do you think you are going to destroy us all? I know full well who you are. You are God's Holy One."

The ushers stepped forward to take him out, but Jesus pre-empted them. "Be quiet!" he barked. Then: "Come out of him!" The man convulsed, screamed, and then lapsed back into his chair, looking dazed.

The normally subdued after-service conversation was all a-buzz: "What is this?"

"Some new kind of teaching, if you ask me."

"Not like the usual boring stuff."

"He even tells the evil spirits where to go."

"Yes, and they obey him!"

Peter invited Jesus home to lunch, bragging about his mother-in-law's cooking. But when they arrived at the door, there was no mouth-watering smell emanating from the kitchen. The good lady, it became apparent, was sick in bed with a high fever.

"Let me go and see her," offered Jesus, and a moment later, the two appeared at her bedroom door, Jesus supporting her arm.

"I'm fine now," she said, shaking him off. "Just let me get back into my kitchen."

Around teatime, after the afternoon nap, there was a knock at the door. "It's for you, teacher." There was a lady with a migraine, wanting to know if Jesus had a cure. She was the first of a steady stream of people with a variety of maladies. The grapevine had been active, following what had happened in the synagogue, and now everyone wanted Jesus' magic touch.

Next morning, he was nowhere to be found. When eventually they tracked him down outside of town, he told them that he had to be moving on. "There is good news to share and lots of people who need to hear it. So pack your bags, and let's be on our way."

They hadn't got far before they met a leper, ringing his bell so people would keep clear of his contagion. He was an ugly sight, riddled with the wretched disease. As he drew nearer, it was clear that he was on a mission, striding purposefully along. When they asked him what was his hurry, he told them he was looking for the healer. He was pathetically pleased when they pointed to Jesus. He threw himself down at Jesus' feet. "If you want to, I am sure you could heal me, like I heard you did those people yesterday."

Up to that point, the healings had all been relatively minor: headaches, paralysed arms, mental illness. But leprosy was a different matter.

A smile creased Jesus' face. "Why yes, of course I want you to be healed." He reached out and did the unthinkable. He touched the man, kindly putting his arm round his shoulders. No one had touched him since he had first been diagnosed. "Be clean!" Instantly the disfigurement was gone, and his skin was unblemished as a newborn baby.

"Now don't you tell anyone about this," Jesus instructed the man. "But you will have to go to the priest to get certified healthy, just as the Scriptures require."

But there was no way he could keep that a secret. Soon the word was out, and Jesus' anonymity was a thing of the past. Crowds met him everywhere. So when he came back to Capernaum, he had to arrive under cover of darkness.

The rumour mill started turning early next morning, and before breakfast was done, the crowds were already gathering at Andrew and Peter's house. Very soon, the furniture had been pushed back, and the place was packed tight with people, eager to meet the man from Nazareth. Even a group of scribes had turned up, insisting on the comfortable seats. Others were outside, craning to get a look in the windows and doors, desperate at least to hear what he was saying. Jesus told them amazing things, using stories to illustrate his meaning.

But the quiet attention of the crowd was distracted by sounds coming from the ceiling above their heads. Then there was a definite banging, and soon dust and masonry were falling into the room. A moment later, there were shafts of daylight slanting down on them from above. Gradually, the hole widened and four anxious faces could be seen peering down. A bundle began to emerge through the hole, a heavy bundle judging by the grunts from above. It turned out to be a lad wrapped in his sleeping bag, suspended by a rope. He was lowered into the room, right where Jesus had been standing. The young man crumpled to the floor and lay there, a distorted ragdoll. Everyone knew who he was: one of the local teens who had suffered a mishap that had left him paraplegic.

"Serves him right," some of the older people mumbled. "Those louts should be more careful." But clearly those "louts" did care. They were peering anxiously through the hole in the ceiling, expectantly looking at Jesus, who returned their stares with just the ghost of a smile on his face.

Then he bent down to where the lad was lying. "Young man, I forgive your sins."

There was muttering from the back row: "Does this guy think he is God, that he presumes to forgive sins? This is blasphemy."

Jesus straightened up: "What are you gentlemen muttering about? Let me ask you something. Which do you think would be easier for me to do, heal this man or forgive his sins?"

Their silence suggested that they considered neither a possibility. Jesus continued, "Well then, so that you may know that I do indeed have the authority on earth to forgive sins ..." He looked down at the pathetic bundle on the floor, "Come on, fella, get up! Pick up your sleeping bag and go home."

The bundle moved for the first time, wriggled to a sitting position, then throwing aside his bag, got to his feet. Next moment, the lad was dancing around, yelling with joy. His buddies on the roof joined the jubilation, and everyone was clapping and shouting, "Hallelujah!"

"Now we've seen it all!" someone exclaimed.

By now, everyone in town knew something was going down. Jesus decided it would be smart to move the meeting to the open air, so he headed for the beach. On the way, he passed through the business district of town and noticed a man sitting in a dingy office, with his door open to let in the light. A sign hung over the open door: "Levi and Sons. Tax Collectors."

A sad-looking man glanced up as Jesus passed.

"Good morning, Matt," called Jesus. "This is the first day of the rest of your life. Come follow me."

Matthew jumped to his feet, flipped over the sign to display "Closed," slammed the door, and joined the crowd.

That evening, Matthew invited Jesus and his friends to supper. When they got there, the house was already full of all kinds of low-life men and women, predominantly Matthew's tax collecting cronies, but among them were known criminals of various stripes. However, the food was good and drink was plenteous.

Later, when some of the religious community criticised Jesus for the company he kept, Jesus responded, "Those who are in good health have no need of a doctor. I am not here to offer help to the righteous, but rather to give sinners a new start."

"But that's no excuse for gluttony. Even John's disciples fast, and the Pharisees certainly do. So why don't you?" Little did they know that Jesus had just completed six weeks with no food at all.

"A wedding is not a good time for a fast. Once the bride and groom have left, then fasting may be appropriate. But in any case, you can't force old traditions into a new paradigm, any more than you can sew a patch of new cloth onto an old garment, or pour new wine into an old wineskin. It just doesn't work."

"Okay, but there's another concern we have: hygiene. How come your followers flout the traditions of the elders by not washing their hands before they eat?"

"Perhaps it's because a man is not so much defiled by what he eats as he is by what he hatches in his heart. Corruption doesn't originate in the stomach, but in the heart."

The legalists dogged Jesus' footsteps. If his followers happened to snap off a couple of heads of grain on Saturday, that was working on the Sabbath. Sitting in the front row of the synagogue next week was a man with a deformed right arm. Would Jesus compromise the Sabbath by healing him? You didn't have to be God to know that this was a setup, but Jesus wasn't going to let this man go on suffering just to accommodate their twisted scruples. He walked to the front and beckoned to the man. "Come stand up here by me." Then he turned towards the best seats, where the scribes and Pharisees always sat: "Now tell me. Is it right on the Sabbath to do good or to do harm, to save life or to kill?" Of course, it was a rhetorical question, so not waiting for a reply, he turned to the man: "So reach out your hand." A strong arm grew from the shrivelled stump as he did so. "The Sabbath was instigated for the benefit of people, not to be a burden on them."

Of course the majority present was thrilled, but not so the Pharisees. This man was trouble and would have to be watched.

3

The Country

While Jesus' popularity was growing exponentially, he had in mind to pick a select few whom he could groom for future leadership. So he spent the night in prayer, and then in the morning, he invited his devotees to meet with him on a hill outside of town. From them, he chose just twelve men.

This group of course included those he had already specifically invited: Peter and Andrew, James and John, Philip and Nathaniel. Then he had added Matthew, the taxman. The others were Thomas, always a bit of a pessimist; James, not to be confused with Jesus' brother of the same name; Simon, not to be confused with Simon Peter. This Simon had previously been a political activist. Finally there were a couple of Judases, one of whom had a head for figures, so they made him the treasurer.

All these became his official Disciples – followers – but Jesus told them that they were soon to be his Apostles – emissaries. From then on, Jesus spent more and more time with just them alone, explaining in depth what he only hinted at before the wider public.

So that very day, he started his new programme. Aware that back in the valley, the crowds were thick on the ground, he gave his Disciples a whole day's private teaching session. They always referred to it later as "the Sermon on the Mount."

It was revolutionary stuff. He told them that the truly happy were the poor, sad, hungry, and persecuted, because the long-term gain would outweigh the short-term pain. He extolled the virtues of meekness, mercy, purity, and peace-making. He told them they were to be as salt in a corrupt world, light in a dark room. While he may have crossed swords with the legalists, he assured his Disciples that, far from undermining the Law of Moses, his intent was to strengthen it. Anger or insult were tantamount to murder; lustful looks were adultery in the heart; "remarriage" was generally a polite term for adultery.

"Speak plainly," he told them. "'Yes' or 'No' is all you need, not oaths or embellishments. If someone throws a punch, don't hit back; let them have another go. Sues you? Give them what they want. Begs or borrows? Go ahead and give it all away, since you can't serve both God and money anyway.

"Don't just love your friends; love your enemies too. Good is not good enough. Perfection! And words alone don't suffice. Practical obedience is what counts."

He taught them much about prayer, which he stressed was best done in private. "It doesn't have to be wordy or long winded. Just make your point, then trust God. God already knows what you need anyway."

He gave them a template for prayer, which he said should be addressed to "Our Father in heaven." They should request that his name be honoured, his kingdom realised, and his will done at ground level just as in heaven. Then they could go on to pray for daily necessities, forgiveness, guidance, and protection. "Persistent prayer is always answered," he assured them.

He finished by defining two clear choices: two roads that appear similar at the start but lead to radically different destinations; two foundations for life, rock or sand, obedience or negligence.

Though most of this had been directed to the Disciples, the crowds had gradually gathered around to listen in. "Blown away" is the best way to describe their reaction to such revolutionary ideas.

When eventually he came back down the mountain into Capernaum, he was met by a group of city fathers. Trouble, the Disciples imagined. But it was not as they thought. These elders had come on behalf of the local Roman centurion, a well-respected man who was a generous benefactor of local culture and religion by all accounts. It seemed his much-loved servant was seriously sick. These elders knew on which side their bread was buttered, so they begged Jesus to come and heal the man. The centurion himself stepped forward at this point, an imposing figure in uniform, with a military bearing and a foreign accent.

"My Lord," he addressed Jesus. "I am not worthy to have you come into my home. I know all about giving and receiving orders, so I realise that all that is required is for you to give the command, and it will be done."

Jesus was impressed. Turning to the city fathers, he said, "I have to tell you, that in all my travels in this country, I have never encountered such great faith." Then he turned back to the centurion: "Go on home. Let it be done just as you have believed."

And somewhere in the unseen world, someone saluted. "Yes sir!"

With his new entourage of Disciples identified, it was now time to go walk about. But the crowds were not ready to be left behind, so hundreds followed, and hundreds more were added to that number as they passed through the communities along the way. They headed south and were approaching a border town called Nain when they noticed another crowd emerging from the town gates. At first, they thought it would be more hangers-on, but as they drew closer, it was plain that this was a sombre procession: a group of mourners carrying a coffin. The two processions drew closer, one led by Jesus, full of joy and laughter, exuding life and vitality. The other moved slowly, unwillingly, with grief-leaden footsteps, weighed down by death. At the front, by the coffin, was a distraught woman.

By the time the two groups met, Jesus' procession had lapsed into respectful silence. Jesus walked up to the woman, who was now standing still beside the casket. One of the mourners murmured that the deceased was her only son and that her husband had also died recently.

"Courage, lady. Don't cry," Jesus said, touching her arm. Then he stepped up to the open casket, placed his hands on the side, and looked down into the face of the dead boy. For a moment there was silence, a face-off between life and death. Then Jesus spoke clear words of command: "Young man, get up!"

There was a gasp from the mourners at this outrage, but then the body stirred and the boy sat up, rubbed his eyes, and looked around. "Hello Mum. What's happening? Where am I?"

Jesus helped him out of the box and down to the ground. What a way to end a funeral!

Rather than continue south into Samaria, they swung north, and skirting Nazareth, since they weren't welcome there, they came to Cana, the village where Jesus had famously turned water to wine. While they were there, a finely dressed man hurried up to them, breathless. He was royalty, a member of Herod's court, and had travelled all the way up from Capernaum, specifically to find Jesus.

"It's my boy," he panted. "He's dying. Please come immediately and heal him."

"I have heard it said that seeing is believing," replied Jesus. "But do you actually need to see me touch him before you will be able to believe in his healing?"

"Sir, I beg you. Come quickly before my son dies."

"No," said Jesus. "You go! Your son will live."

The conflict was written all over the man's face as he turned to leave. Jesus was his last remaining hope, so could he really walk away with nothing but a promise? But he did.

Halfway home, his servants met him, jubilant. The boy was fine.

"When did he turn the corner?" the man asked.

"The fever left him yesterday just after lunch, I'd say around one."

That was the precise time when Jesus had said, "Your son will live."

Others were also trying to track Jesus down. A couple of anxious-looking young men hurried up next afternoon. Andrew, who had previously been one of John's disciples, recognised them immediately and made the introductions.

But the news was not good. John was in prison. Apparently, he had been outspoken about King Herod's recent marriage to Herodias. She had previously been married to Philip, Herod's brother, but Herod had gone ahead and married her anyway. John had tactlessly denied the validity of the marriage, calling it "adultery." The upshot was that John had been arrested and thrown in jail.

When the pleasantries had been exchanged, John's disciples explained to Jesus their mission: "John has sent us to enquire if you really are the one he has been talking about, or if we should be on the look-out for someone else."

Jesus didn't answer their question right away but invited them to stick around for a while and watch. What followed was a typical afternoon: healings, exorcisms, and sight given to blind people. Jesus' Disciples were growing used to this kind of thing, just a normal day at the office. But John's followers were flabbergasted. Eventually, Jesus called them over. "Go on home now and tell John what you have witnessed." Then he quoted a paragraph from Isaiah's writings: "'The poor have good news preached to them, the broken hearted are healed, the blind see, the dead are raised.'" Possibly the only phrase of the quotation that was omitted was the part that John must most have longed to hear: "Freedom for the captives." It must have been tough for an outdoorsman to be locked away from the sunshine.

As soon as they were out of earshot, Jesus addressed the crowd: "Why did you all flock out to the wilderness? Was it a nature walk, perhaps? Or was it the latest fashions you were checking out? You wanted to see John's fine clothes, right?" Everyone who remembered the leathers roared with laughter. "So why did you go? Because you knew he was a prophet, didn't you? Actually, he was more than that. Despite his denial, he really was the one Malachi told us all to expect, the Elijah figure. There never was a greater man than John, but it's even better to actually enter the kingdom, than merely to foretell it."

---------------------------------- 4 ----------------------------------

The City

Now around then, Jesus and his Disciples joined the throngs heading to Jerusalem for the Passover celebrations. It was expected that all able-bodied male adults should attend, but in any case, no one wanted to miss the fun.

As it turned out, it wasn't all fun. For a start, as soon as they got into town, Jesus caused a bit of a ruckus in the temple by disrupting the market. He didn't approve of conducting business in a place of worship. But if that irritated the authorities, worse was to come.

At the north end of the city, close to the sheep market, was a public pool known as Bethesda. Surrounded as it was by arches, it provided plenty of shade from the hot sun and so was popular with the public. There was a widely held superstition that, every so often, an angel would call by to heal one lucky person. But there was, of course, a catch. To qualify, the candidate had to be first into the pool the moment the water started to bubble, a sure sign that the healing angel was in attendance. In fact, the whole thing was a cruel joke, for the moment there was any hint of a bubble, the whole place would erupt with people, hobbling, crawling, rolling, elbowing each other out of the way so as to be first in. And in the confusion, was anyone actually healed? Who could tell? But at least it held out a faint hope to the otherwise hopeless.

On the first Sabbath afternoon of the festival, Jesus and his Disciples paid Bethesda a visit. The place was inundated with disabled folk: blind, lame, paralysed, all with the long-term look of hopeless resignation on their faces. One man caught Jesus' eye.

"Hello friend," Jesus greeted him. "How long have you been coming here?"

"Thirty-eight years, sir."

"So do you want to be healed?"

"Of course I do! Trouble is, I am paralysed, and no one ever helps me into the water when it is stirred up. Someone else always gets in before I do."

"Okay, so I am here to help you now. Get up! Roll up your bed and go on home."

The man stared at Jesus for just a moment, then waiting no longer, jumped to his feet and began to walk. Pandemonium! Jesus slipped quietly away and was swallowed up in the crowd before a queue could form.

The trouble was that this deed was done on the Sabbath, and the man was spotted carrying his mat home. To carry a bed was acceptable to the religious authorities, provided it was occupied, but this bed clearly lacked the required occupant.

"Hey, you! What do you think you are doing, carrying a load on the Sabbath?"

"Don't blame me! The man who just healed me told me to carry it."

"Who is this man?"

"No idea, I'm afraid. He didn't give his name."

Jesus was concerned for the man so sought him out, eventually tracking him down in the temple. "Good to see you up on your feet," he greeted. "So in future, no more sinning. We wouldn't want anything worse to happen, would we?" The man knew exactly to what Jesus was referring, though no one else did.

He headed straight for the authorities with the name of the man responsible for his Sabbath breaking. There's gratitude for you.

So now the authorities were on Jesus' case, both for the disturbance in the market and for inciting people to break the Sabbath.

"My Father works seven days a week, so I am just following his example," Jesus explained when they caught up with him. "You carefully study the Scriptures, don't you, because you think that by so doing you will gain eternal life. But you miss the whole point. The Scriptures are all about me. I am the one who gives life, not the book. The truth is that whoever listens to what I say and believes God who sent me, already has eternal life and will never be condemned." But that just made them mad.

The matter reached the ears of the ruling Council. This man was clearly trouble, and they would be wise to consider how to get rid of him before things got out of control.

But not all the Pharisees were so quick to judge. There was one member of the Council who felt that Jesus should be investigated more thoroughly, so Nicodemus took it upon himself to visit him personally. This was not an officially sanctioned investigation, so in order to cause no offence to his fellows, he sought a private meeting under cover of darkness. By process of discreet enquiry, he discovered where Jesus was lodging and arrived late at the door. His knock got him admitted to a simple room, just a couple of chairs and a candle on the table between them.

Nicodemus was an important figure in the capital, not merely a member of the Council, but one of Israel's foremost teachers. He was used to people being intimidated in his presence, so he graciously sought to put at ease this simple country preacher: "Rabbi, we realise that you must have God's blessing, for how else would you be able to do the extraordinary miracles that we have heard so much about."

"The plain truth is, Nicodemus, it is impossible to have any idea what the kingdom of God is about without being born again."

"What do you mean, 'born again'? You are not suggesting, I hope, that a grown man should seek to pass through his mother's womb a second time?" - this with an amused smile.

"The truth is that no one can get into the kingdom of God but that he is born again by the Spirit of God. Clearly, human wombs bear human beings, physical children, flesh and blood. But only the Spirit can give birth to spiritual beings, children of God. So you shouldn't be surprised when I tell you plainly that even you must be born again."

Nicodemus' face was a study. What was this man talking about? At that moment, a breath of air came through the open window, rustling the drapes and flickering the candle flame. "Did you see that, Nicodemus?"

"See what?"

"The wind."

"Of course not."

"But it did blow, didn't it?"

"Well, yes."

"But how did you know if you couldn't see it?"

"I could feel it, see the candle flame dance."

"Well, it's just like that with being born of the Spirit. You can't see the Spirit, but the changes he makes in a person's life are clear evidence of the rebirth he gives."

"Okay, so tell me how. How can this happen? How can a man be reborn?"

"I am amazed that you, Israel's foremost teacher, don't know this. So let me explain. You will be well familiar, are you not, with the occasion when the Israelis grumbled against Moses in the wilderness, and in consequence, a plague of snakes bit the people so that many of them died. So humour me! Tell me what Moses did."

Nicodemus, who could have easily recited the story without opening the book, patiently replied, "God told him to make a bronze model of a snake and to lift it high on a stake so that whenever anyone was bitten, all they had to do was express their belief in God's remedy by looking to the snake. Then they would live."

"Exactly. So in much the same way will I be lifted up on a stake so that everyone who believes in me may live. God loves this world so very much that he is giving me, his only Son, so that whoever believes in me won't die of the snake's venom of sin, but will live forever. God is not looking for an excuse to condemn people for what they will do to me, but rather his purpose is to save people."

The candle flame burned steadily on the table between them. "Light, Nicodemus, light has come. But there are many who choose to skulk in the shadows for fear they will be shown up for the frauds they really are. But those whose lives are genuine come to the light, so it will be plain that what they do is inspired by God."

On the way home, with his mind buzzing with the extraordinary things he had just heard, did Nicodemus stick to the shadows for fear of being recognised as having been in company with Jesus, or did he walk unafraid through the pools of light offered by the street lamps?

The return journey to Galilee, after the festival, might have taken them over the Jordan River near Jericho, then north, up the east bank of the river. The advantage of this route was that it avoided Samaria. "Samaria" used to be the name given to the capital city only, but now it encompassed the whole region extending from the Jordan River in the east to the Mediterranean Sea in the west. It effectively separated Galilee in the north from Judea in the south. The problem with Samaria was that it was full of Samaritans. Ever since the exiles had returned four hundred years previously, there had been mistrust of Samaritans. They were half-breeds, the products of mixed marriages between Israelis and the peoples transplanted there by the Assyrians. Despite their willingness to help Nehemiah and Ezra with the rebuilding of the temple, their offers had been turned down. So ever since, there had been this enmity between the two people groups.

Since they weren't welcome in Jerusalem, the Samaritans had built their own temple on the slopes of Mount Gerizim, and there they were content to pursue their own blended form of religion.

But to Jesus, prejudice was anathema, so ignoring the taboo, he took the direct route straight north through Samaria. A day and a half out of Jerusalem, they came to the village of Shechem, or Sychar, as the locals called it. This was a historic landmark. There Abraham had built an altar when first he set foot in the promised land two thousand years previously. Thirst had moved him on. His grandson Jacob had come back, purchased the real estate, and dug a well. So it was not thirst that caused Jacob to leave, but shame: the disgrace of his sons having slaughtered their neighbours. Another five hundred years had passed, then Joshua had stood there in the shade of the old oak tree, in the natural amphitheatre formed between two mountains. A million people had massed on the slopes of Mount Gerizim and Mount Ebal, all of them children of Abraham and Jacob. Joshua had challenged them to choose between the blessing of obedience or the curse of rebellion. But it had been the wrong choice that had eventually driven them far away, into exile.

Now into that same valley came Jesus and his Disciples. The only thing that remained was the well Jacob had dug. There were some scattered boulders that might once have formed Abraham's altar. And there were some gnarled old roots that possibly had given life to a once mighty oak tree. But Jesus was tired and thirsty, and it was lunchtime. So he sat down on a rock beside the well and sent his Disciples into town to buy some food. The sun was hot, and the well was deep, and there was no bucket. So he dozed and waited for someone to happen by – unlikely, since it was the hottest time of day, and who in their right mind would choose to carry water before the cool of the evening?

But his luck was in, and before long, a woman approached. She had a bucket and a length of rope.

"Excuse me, lady," called Jesus. "Would you give me a drink?" The woman was a little taken aback. For starters, etiquette forbade a man from addressing a woman without an introduction. And then there was that Samaritan/Jewish prejudice.

"I am surprised, sir, that you would ask a drink of me." Did he have something in mind other than water?

"If you had any idea who I am and what is the gift God offers you today, then it would have been you who would be doing the asking, and I who would be giving you living water."

"I can't see how you would be able to offer me a drink when you have no bucket, sir. And from where else do you imagine you would be able to get water if not from this well? Don't tell me that you are a better man that our forefather Jacob, who dug this well, drank from it, and provided for his family and livestock?"

"Everyone who has ever drunk from this well over the past two thousand years has got thirsty again. But whoever drinks the water I am offering will never be thirsty again. It will be as though he had a spring of water within him, bubbling up to give life without end."

"Great! Give me a drink of this water so I never will be thirsty again nor have to come back here to draw more." Thirst. *That was what had driven Abraham away.*

"I will, but first go get your husband and then come back here."

There was an awkward silence. "I don't have a husband, sir."

"I know, lady. I know. You have previously had five different husbands, but the man you are currently living with is not one of them." No wonder she chose the heat of the day as the best time to draw water – less risk of bumping into any women whose husbands she might have borrowed.

Shame! That was what had driven Jacob from this same well in Shechem.

When faced with one's own failings, it often helps to switch the topic to a discussion on religion. "So you must be some kind of a prophet. Okay, so tell me. My ancestors have worshipped God up there on Mount Gerizim for the past five hundred years, but you Jews insist that the place for true worship is in Jerusalem. So which is the right choice?" Choice! Joshua standing on that exact spot had challenged the nation to choose. *"Choose then this day whom you will serve, but I and my family will serve the Lord."*

"Lady, the question you should be asking it not 'where' but 'who.' 'Choose this day *whom* you will serve.' It is not geography that makes worship right or wrong, but whom you are worshipping. God is spirit, so true worship is always spiritual, and always truthful, no matter where it happens. You Samaritans have long groped around in the dark, looking for truth, but salvation is arising from the Jews."

"Yes, I have heard of the coming Messiah, whom you call 'the Christ.' I understand he is to be Jewish, just like you." Jesus remained silent, and the lady paused for a moment, a quizzical look on her face. "And, sir, I know that when he comes he will know all about us. He will be able to tell us all our secrets – just as you have done." Now the unspoken question was written all over her face: "You wouldn't by any chance be...?"

"You have it, lady. I am the one about whom you are talking."

Just then the Disciples came back, loaded with fruit and sandwiches. Embarrassed, the woman hurried off towards town, forgetting, in her haste, her precious bucket. She headed for the bar in the middle of town and burst in, breathless with excitement. "Hey, everyone. Listen up. I just met a man out by Jacob's well who told me my life story. Never met him before in my life, yet he knew all about me. Do you think this could be the Christ?"

Christ or not, anyone who could tell this lady's story would warrant a listen, so a crowd of them followed her back to the well. There, sitting around on the scattered stones of Abraham's altar, amongst the roots of the great tree of Moreh, around the well that Jacob dug, the whole town listened to Jesus' words and drank deep from the water of life.

Jesus' ability to know all about people without ever being told was a quality that amazed people on other occasions as well. He and his Disciples were invited to attend a dinner party, hosted by a well-respected Pharisee named Simon. All went well till a sex worker came into the courtyard where the meal was being served and stood behind Jesus' chair, tears streaming down her cheeks. Simon and his posh guests did their best to ignore the intrusion, but then things got really ugly. The woman got down on the ground behind Jesus and proceeded to weep anguished tears all over his feet, wiping them with her long flowing hair. The final abuse came when she started kissing his feet and rubbing perfume into them.

Jesus said nothing and neither did their host, but Simon thought plenty: *If this man was genuinely a prophet, as they say he is, then he would know what kind of woman this is who is pestering him.*

"Simon," said Jesus, raising his voice to address the head of the table. "I have a story that might amuse you."

"Then tell it, Teacher."

"A money lender had two defaulting debtors. One owed fifty thousand dollars, the other five thousand. The money lender, being a generous-hearted fellow as money lenders usually are [laughter rippled round the table], forgave both men their debts." The story thus far was a little difficult to credit, but the veracity of the story was not the point. "So tell me, Simon, which of the two do you imagine would love the money lender the most?"

"Well, I imagine it would have to be the one who was forgiven the most."

"Exactly right. Now, Simon, about this good lady behind me. When I arrived at your house this evening, you provided no water to wash my feet, but she has washed them with her tears and dried them with her hair. You didn't even shake my hand, but she is kissing my feet. You provided me with not so much as a bar of soap, but she has anointed my feet with perfume. The bottom line is that her sins, which are many, are all forgiven. Little wonder she loves so much. But the forgiveness of your sins, which you discount as but few, leave you with little heart to love."

Then turning for the first time to face the woman on the floor behind him, Jesus lifted her to her feet. "So your sins really are all forgiven, lady, just as you trusted they would be. Now go home in peace."

She was overjoyed, but Simon and some of his pharisaic friends were not so positive: "Who does he think he is, forgiving sins?"

5

The Lake

Back home in Capernaum, the beach continued to be a favourite venue for Jesus' meetings, and Peter's boat was, as often as not, his platform. The open air always allowed sufficient space for the ever-expanding crowds. For visual aids, he needed no chalkboard but used the natural things around him to illustrate his message: the lake and the farmland on the hills behind Capernaum. The local population was divided between fishers and farmers, and just because Jesus liked to do his teaching from a boat didn't mean he was ignoring the farmers.

"Whenever you farmers sow your seed, inevitably some falls on the hard-packed soil of the public footpaths, where it is quickly pecked up by the birds. Other seeds land on rocky ground; no depth of topsoil, so its growth spurt is short lived. Some farmers neglect to pull the weeds before sowing. So, though the seeds germinate, there is no harvest because the new growth is choked off before it can bear fruit. But happily, some seed falls into good deep topsoil, where it produces a return of thirty, sixty, even a hundred times your original investment.

"The kingdom of God is like the soil's natural ability to make seed grow. All you farmers have to do once the seed is in the ground is to sleep peacefully in your beds till harvest time (much laughter, particularly from the fishers).

"Or – you ladies would appreciate this – it is like tiny flakes of yeast that you sprinkle into the flour, making a world of difference to how the dough rises.

"Or you fishers might understand it better if I said that the kingdom of heaven is like a net full of fish. You have to keep the good fish but throw the junk back."

That evening, when he was all done, they were all too tired for small talk with the people on the beach, so Jesus suggested they head straight out across the lake. The Disciples were already in the boat, so they just pulled up the anchor and sailed lazily away on the flat calm water, with just a slight offshore breeze to give them way.

"So do you guys understand the illustration about the different types of soil?" Their reply was sufficiently noncommittal for Jesus to continue: "If you don't get this basic truth, you may well have trouble with all the other parables I tell.

"The seed is the word of God. The footpaths are the places where people regularly walk, and, as you know, familiarity always breeds contempt. So what God says just bounces off them and is snatched away by the enemy. The seed on the rocky soil is like those whose response is only shallow: immediate enthusiasm, but no real commitment. Trouble shrivels potential growth, like the midday sun. The seeds among the weeds are like people whose lives are full of stuff. They just don't have time or energy for anything else. But the good ground is like ploughed and harrowed topsoil, all broken up and receptive to the seed. That's where the seed can produce a bumper crop. Broken up lives tend to be the most open to what God is saying."

They were all quiet after that, and before long, the sound of gentle snoring told them that Jesus was enjoying a well-earned rest.

In the gathering gloom, they didn't notice the black clouds building up behind them in the west. With no warning, a wall of water hit them, driven by a furious squall. All was bedlam, sails ripping, spars breaking, sailors bailing, landsmen screaming. The boat was swamped and ready to take them all to the bottom of the lake. But Jesus slept on, oblivious.

"Hey Teacher," someone yelled. "Don't you care that we are all about to drown?"

Jesus sat up. He ordered the wind to quiet down and the water to be peaceful. Almost immediately, everything changed. The wind died to a whisper, and the waves shrank back to ripples, and there was a silence only broken by the drips from what remained of the rigging.

"So why were you all so terrified? Don't you trust me?"

"Who in the world is this man?" they asked each other quietly as they bailed the water out of the hull. "He speaks to the wind and the waves, and they obey!"

They headed on across the lake in the moonlight towards a stretch of the shore that they might have preferred to avoid, especially in the middle of the night. The cliffs were honeycombed with tombs and caves. Stories of the walking dead abounded. So when the boat eventually grounded on the beach, they were somewhat reluctant to alight. But Jesus shamed them all by jumping fearlessly over the side and crunching up the gravel. So they followed, bunching together, nervous of being left behind. Their footfalls were muffled when they reached the grass, so the silence of the place closed in on them.

"What was that?" someone gasped. There were sounds coming from all round them, grumblings and groanings. And with the tail of their eyes, they caught movements amongst the rocks. Was it their imaginations playing tricks with the moon-etched shadows?

Then all doubt was gone. A scream echoed down through the ravines, and they could just make out a creature in the moonlight, scurrying along the cliff top above them, silhouetted against the starry sky. It had lank straggly hair, long claws, and chains dragging behind it. Then it was gone for a moment, but they could still hear it panting as it scampered down over the rocks and through the scrub towards where they were standing. Then round a big rock it bounded and came to a skidding halt, not ten paces from where they all stood, tightly bunched behind Jesus.

It spoke in a rasping, semi-human voice: "What are you doing here, Jesus, Son of the most high God? I hope you are not here to give us trouble."

"Get out of him, you unclean spirit," barked Jesus. It was as though the man had been clubbed by a two-by-four. He fell to the floor and began to whimper.

"Do you have a name?" asked Jesus.

The creature looked up from where it was grovelling and, gathering what shreds of dignity it retained, replied in a voice that sounded like a multitude echoing from a long way off, "My name is Legion since there are thousands of us in this body."

The hair rose on the necks of the Disciples, but Jesus stood silently watching. Under his stare, the creature seemed to shrink back and cower into the ground. It began to moan, "No, please. Anything but that. Don't send us to the abyss. How about sending us into these pigs? But not the abyss!"

Pigs? What pigs?

"Go!"

Immediately, what they had taken for the rocks all around them, jumped to their feet, and stampeded along the steep bank, then they turned straight for the lake and hurled themselves into the water. The squealing and thundering of thousands of frenzied trotters was immediately cut off, and there was nothing but the dust in the moonlight to suggest that there had ever been an immense herd of pigs all around them.

"Well, don't just stand there gaping," Jesus said to his stunned Disciples. "This gentleman needs a bath and a shave. And get those shackles off him. Anyone got any spare clothes? We can't leave him stark naked."

By the time the sun was rising, the transformation was complete. Someone had a fire going, and breakfast was served on the beach with the guest of honour, whose real name they discovered but later forgot to record, sitting as sane as could be.

Further down the beach, a group of disconsolate farmers was wandering amongst the corpses that had washed up on the beach. They were none too pleased, by the looks of them, but then they shouldn't have been rearing pigs in the first place, since Moses had declared their meat non-kosher.

When they eventually recognised the liberated man and ascertained who was responsible for their financial ruin, they asked Jesus to leave. So the Disciples all climbed back into their boat and made to push off. "Let me come with you," begged the man.

"No. I need a representative on this shore. Go home and tell all your friends what God has done for you."

Back in Capernaum, there was great consternation over the fate of the fishermen in the storm the previous night. Their boat was still missing in the morning, so apparently they had not returned. So when the boat eventually docked around lunchtime, a huge crowd turned out to welcome them safe home. All the little waterfront cafes emptied out as people came down to the beach to see for themselves, the chief attraction being Jesus himself. There were relieved wives and children in the crowd.

But not everyone was relieved. There was one very worried looking gentleman: Jairus, the administrator of the local synagogue. He was anxious to see Jesus, so hurried up to meet him. "My little girl is dying," he gasped, falling to the ground at Jesus' feet. "Please hurry, for I fear we may already be too late. But just touch her, and she'll be okay. I'm sure of it."

"I am on my way," Jesus reassured him.

Now Jairus lived in a nice house on the outskirts of town, so they had a way to go. But progress was painfully slow, since the crowd was so thick. To make matters worse, there was an unexpected delay when some woman waylaid Jesus. Jairus vaguely recognised her as a member of the prenatal classes his wife had attended twelve years ago, before their "Little One," as they affectionately called her, had been born. Hadn't she lost her child, so dropped out of the class? Or had she perhaps terminated the pregnancy? Either way, she had been something of an outcast since that time, suffering from an incurable haemorrhage that had bankrupted her as she spent every penny she had to find a doctor who could cure her. But medical science just wasn't up to the challenge, so now here she was, seeking a miracle cure.

The woman had suffered private agonies of shame ever since the loss of her unborn child. She had heard all about the miracles that Jesus had been doing around town. But could she ever bring herself to come right out and ask him to heal her? What if he asked what was wrong? What if other people overheard?

Perhaps if I were just to touch him as he passes, she thought to herself. *No one needs to know.*

So as he had come up the road, she had got herself into a position where he was bound to pass close to where she was standing. In her extreme weakness, it was all she could do to remain upright as the crowd sought to jostle her out of the way. But she had stood her ground, and now here he was. She reached out, and her fingertips just brushed his sleeve as he passed. The change was immediate. She felt life flooding into her veins and knew she was healed.

But Jesus stopped and looked around. "Who was it touched me?" he asked.

"Hey, there's a crowd jostling you. Of course someone touched you," said one of his Disciples.

"No, someone touched my sleeve deliberately."

There was nowhere to hide, so the lady stepped forward and fell at his feet. As he bent down to hear what she was saying, she blurted out all her pain.

Jesus stood up and helped the lady to her feet. Then, holding up her hand, he said in a voice loud and clear so that the whole crowd could hear: "My dear daughter, you are a lady of great faith. Go in peace. You are whole."

So there she stood before the community, pronounced clean, a woman of faith. No more shame. No more doctors' bills!

It was at that exact moment that someone came up to Jairus with the news he had been dreading: "Little One is dead. No need to trouble the Teacher any more."

"Jairus," Jesus said, speaking through the man's grief. "Don't fear. Trust me!"

He excused himself from the crowd and, taking along just three of his Disciples, strode off to the fine house where the Jairus family resided. The funeral directors were already there, and the wailing of the professional mourners greeted them as they approached.

"What's all this noise about? You'll wake that sleeping child," said Jesus, annoyed.

"'Sleeping child?'" they mocked. "The kid's dead, you know. You can't wake the dead no matter how much noise you make." Laughter.

"Oh, get out of here," said Jesus.

After he went into the house, Jesus shut the door on all the hubbub outside and, taking only Jairus and his wife and the three Disciples, squeezed into the room where the child lay still on the bed. The little twelve-year-old was clearly dead: jaw slack, eyes open and staring, cheeks and lips drained of colour.

Jesus sat down on the edge of the bed, and very gently taking the limp hand in his, he spoke quietly to the lifeless little face. "Little One, it's time to get up."

Immediately, the mouth snapped shut, colour flared in the cheeks, and the child first sat up, then jumped out of bed. "When's breakfast, Mom? I'm starving!"

"Give her something to eat," said Jesus, chuckling.

Jesus' name was now a household word. Everywhere he went, people would flock to see him.

"Jesus!" a couple of blind men called out after him, stumbling along, desperately trying to catch up. "Help us, Son of David!"

"Well, do you believe I can restore your sight?" Jesus asked, stopping and turning to face them.

"Yes, Lord. We certainly do," they panted.

So he did.

Next was a man who could neither see nor speak. He could not call out for help as had the two blind men, nor could he find his way to Jesus. When Jesus recognised that this was the handiwork of a demon, he debunked the offending spirit. The man's vision was restored, and he praised God eloquently.

The crowds were thrilled. "This has got to be the Messiah!" they postulated, but the Pharisees were jealous.

"You want to know how he does all this?" they asked the people around them. "By the prince of demons he exorcises demons. He is possessed by the devil himself."

Jesus knew full well what they were saying: "Do you really think that even Satan would be stupid enough to fight against himself? I am here to plunder Satan's house, but you can't rob a strong man without first incapacitating him. But I must solemnly warn you to be careful what you are saying. Yes, say what you want about me. I am here to make forgiveness possible. But so long as you go on insisting that the wonderful miracles done by the gracious Spirit of God are in reality the work of Satan – that is over the top! You'll never find forgiveness down that road.

"Just as you can tell a tree by the fruit it produces, so you can discern in a man the kindness of God from the mischief of Satan. Who do you think is responsible for blindness? And who for sight? Common sense will be your judge, but beware lest your words one day testify against you."

"So give us a sign," demanded the Pharisees. "Something that will make us believe in you."

"It's a corrupt society that seeks to build its faith on signs. But if you must have something to believe in, how about Jonah and the whale? The corrupt citizens of Nineveh believed Jonah's story when he came to them after three days in the belly of the whale. And if you can believe that, then you will have no trouble when, after three days, I come back alive from the belly of the earth."

A woman in the crowd, probably in an attempt to encourage Jesus, shouted out, "How blessed is the woman from whose womb you were born!"

"Thank you for the thought, lady, but actually those who are truly blessed are those who both hear and obey God's word."

Someone else shouted, "Do you know that your mother and brothers are in town looking for you?"

Jesus did know that they had come to do what families are prone to attempt when they don't understand: to take charge. Seeing how pressured he was with the constant crowds around him, they were beginning to fear for his sanity.

"My family is already here," he said, indicating the people around him. "Whoever hears and obeys God's word is my mother, my sister, my brother."

And in truth, they were like one big family. Though the twelve Disciples were all male, there were also women who were very much part of the team. Some of them had amazing stories to tell, stories of deliverance, healing, and forgiveness. For example, there was a woman called Mary (to whom they added the suffix "Magdalene," to distinguish her from all the other Marys). She had been delivered from the tenacious hold of no less than seven demons. But not all the women were from the wrong side of the tracks. Joanna, in contrast, was the wife of one of King Herod's stewards. These good ladies made it their business to care for the financial and domestic needs of Jesus and his Disciples.

Jesus spent the next few weeks constantly on the go, moving from village to village, town to town. Everywhere he went, he healed sick people and proclaimed the good news of the kingdom. He never failed to be moved at the sight of yet another crowd of needy people.

One day, he said to his Disciples, "The harvest is ripe for the picking, but the reapers are too few. Time to ask the Lord of the harvest for reinforcements!"

Scarcely had they said "Amen" to this prayer when he turned to them all: "You are the answer to your own prayer! Harvest time and you are the reapers!"

He paired them up and then commissioned them to head off in half a dozen different directions to emulate what they had seen him doing: to heal the sick, to exorcise demons, and to preach good news. Before they left, he gave them specific marching orders:

"Travel light. Take no cash. Accept gratefully the hospitality you are offered, but move on quickly when you are not welcome. Trust God's Spirit to tell you what to say. Confess me before your fellow man, and I will confess you in the presence of God."

So off they went on their first solo.

King Herod had heard about Jesus but didn't know what to make of him. Certainly his conscience smote him, and with good reason, since he had recently murdered John the Baptist.

John had been in Herod's jail ever since he had been arrested for criticising the king for stealing his brother's wife. Herod used to bring John out of his cell, every so often, so he could listen to his lectures. It was a perverse kind of entertainment, since it always challenged his twisted conscience. His new wife, Herodias, was furious. She hated the wretched preacher and wanted him executed for his temerity in speaking against the king.

Then, on his birthday, Herod threw a party for his nobles. The entertainment that evening included a seductive dance by his new stepdaughter. In his inebriated elation, Herod rashly offered her "anything you want, up to half my kingdom!"

After a hasty consultation with Herodias, her mother, the young dancer approached the throne. "I would like, here and now, the head of John the baptiser on a plate."

Everyone had heard his promise to the girl, so Herod couldn't refuse.

Ten minutes later, a soldier returned with the grisly reward, which he presented to the young lady, who passed it on to her mother.

Little wonder then, that when Herod heard of the new preacher on the loose, he assumed it was John's ghost, come back to haunt him.

After a few exciting days, the Apostles came back to tell Jesus all about their adventures. Their joy was somewhat dampened when they heard the tragic news of John's demise.

"Come on," said Jesus. "Let's go and have a break for a few days."

So they sailed away in Peter's boat to Bethsaida at the north end of the lake. It was safely out of Herod's jurisdiction, just in case he might get some unpleasant ideas.

But "there's no peace for the wicked," as Isaiah once said, and in their case not much peace for the righteous either. Crowds saw them leave and crowds ran along the shore, watching where they made landfall. Things were made worse by the season. It was the run-up to Passover again, and those choosing to take the route to Jerusalem along the east bank of the Jordan had to travel round the lake head to get there. The upshot was that when they arrived for their away-from-it-all retreat, there were a few thousand people waiting to meet then. The Disciples groaned, but, as usual, Jesus was moved at the sight of so many needy people. He spent the rest of the day talking to them till late afternoon.

"Time to send the folks away so they can buy themselves some supper," the Disciples suggested.

"No," said Jesus. "You feed them."

"If we blow all the money in the kitty, that won't give them more than a few crumbs each."

"Philip, you're a local. Where can we get food for all these people?" Jesus asked.

Philip was at a loss to know what to say, but Andrew came up with a suggestion.

"Master, there is a kid here, offering his lunch."

"Has he got a boat load of food?" someone asked cynically.

"No, but he has five buns and a couple of fish."

"There must be five thousand hungry people here at the very least. So what good would a couple of sandwiches do?"

Jesus gratefully accepted the child's offering, then, as the people sat down on the fresh spring grass, he held up the little basket of food. He didn't beg or plead for more, but confidently thanked God for enough. Then he started to hand out the food for the Disciples to share round. When everyone had eaten enough, there were still a dozen baskets crammed with leftovers, one for each of the Disciples to have for lunch next day!

Jesus made them carry all the food down to the boat. "You guys go ahead, and I'll meet you tomorrow back in Capernaum."

To say that the way to a man's heart is through his stomach is one thing, but when five thousand male stomachs are satisfied, then the heart response can be astonishing. The crowd was ready there and then to vote Jesus their new king, but somehow he slipped away and hiked up into the hills, where he enjoyed a quiet evening alone with his Father.

The Disciples, meanwhile, were rowing hard. They didn't have far to go to get back to Capernaum, but the wind was ornery and blew nose on, no matter how they tacked. They soon realised that they were actually losing ground, so they lowered the sail and resorted to rowing. But the waves were steep, and progress was painfully slow. It was pitch dark. They were cold, drenched to the bone, and longing for bed. Matthew, the taxman, was feeling a little green, in danger of bringing up his share of the five buns and two fish.

Peter assumed his captain's position, clinging to the mast for support and encouraging his colleagues to row harder, or to bail quicker. "Matthew, if you have to do that, move to the lee side of the boat!"

It must have been around four in the morning when Peter let out a yell. Everyone looked to where Peter was pointing, the hair rising on their scalps when they saw what was upsetting him. A shaft of moonlight was shining through the scudding clouds, illuminating the silvery form of a ghost floating over the waves.

Apparently conscious of their cries, the ghost stopped. "Don't be afraid!" came a distant shout through the gale. "It's only me!"

Was that Jesus out there? Peter's mouth recovered before his common sense, and before he could stop himself, he shouted back, "Lord, if that really is you, then let me walk out to meet you on the water."

"Okay. Come on, then."

Now what was he to do, step out at the invitation of what was most likely a figment of his imagination, or stay in the boat with his friends?

He moved reluctantly to the edge of the boat and sat for a moment on the gunwale, with his feet in the water.

"Go for it, Pete," urged his friends.

"Get back in the boat," demanded his better judgement.

"Come!" invited the ghost. So he went and, to his utter amazement, didn't sink.

The applause from the boat helped him for the first few steps, but the farther he got from the boat, the more his courage began to blow away in the storm. The waves were menacing, the wind screamed in his face, and he had nothing but a ghost for company.

Faith borne of desperation forced a cry from his lips as he felt the water giving way beneath his feet. He was going to drown. "Help! Save me!" Such is the eloquence of the prayer of last resort, and such is the substance of a straw to a drowning man whose grasp is a prayer that reaches for a loving God.

Immediately, Jesus was right there, catching his flailing arms and pulling him back up out of the water. "Why did you doubt, Peter? You were doing so well." But from then on, Peter knew from personal experience that, even though he should doubt again, he would always be safe in the grip of his faithful friend.

Jesus kept his arm round him till they were both safe back in the boat. For some reason, the wind seemed to behave itself after that, and they were home in time for breakfast.

But still they got no peace. Some of the crowd had followed them back to Capernaum. "It's not me you want, is it?" Jesus challenged as they met the people on the beach. "You are just after another free meal. But I could give you food that will satisfy you forever, but you would have to work for it."

"What would we have to do, exactly?"

"Believe."

"Show us a sign, and we will believe. Moses gave our forefathers bread in the desert. Something like that might convince us."

"It wasn't Moses who provided the bread, you know. It was God who did it."

"Whatever. But from now on, give us this bread you talk of – every day!"

"I am the bread of life. Whoever comes to me will never be hungry again, and whoever believes in me will never be thirsty. I am the living bread from heaven."

"From heaven? We thought you came from Nazareth!" Guffaws of derisive laughter.

"The plain truth is, that unless you eat my flesh and drink my blood, you are as good as dead. But whoever eats my flesh and drinks my blood has everlasting life, and I will raise him up at the last day."

This was too much for many in the crowd. There was to be no meal ticket, and now the preacher was talking nonsense. Most of the crowd just wandered away. Even some of his most ardent supporters turned back and from then on gave up following Jesus.

"Do you also find this offensive?" Jesus asked his Disciples. "Are you going to leave me too?"

Peter spoke up for all of them: "How could we leave you, Lord? You speak words that give life. We have not the slightest doubt that you are God's Holy One."

This thinning out of his admirers gave Jesus the opportunity to travel, unencumbered by crowds of people. He took the opportunity to withdraw from Capernaum once again and headed northwest, up into the coastal region of Phoenicia, Syrian territory. He found lodging for himself and the gang, planning to take the time to teach his Disciples. However, his fame had preceded him, and it wasn't long before a young woman tapped at the door, requesting to see the teacher. When the landlady ushered her into the living room and pointed to Jesus, the woman threw herself down at his feet, babbling in her native Greek. Some of the Disciples, who understood the language, recognised that she was concerned for her demon-possessed daughter and urgently wanted intervention.

"The children must first eat their fill before the dogs can have the scraps," Jesus said in her tongue.

"True, Lord," she replied, surprising the Disciples by her form of address, "but even us Gentile dogs are permitted to lick up the crumbs that fall under the table."

"Well said, lady," Jesus chuckled. "Go on home. Your daughter is free."

They didn't stay long by the Mediterranean coast but headed back into Galilee. Peter couldn't bear to be separated for too long from his precious boat, so they all helped him push it off the beach and then jumped aboard. A smooth crossing graced their progress this time as they sailed across the lake to the Decapolis on the east bank, near the place where Jesus had commissioned Legion, the wild man, to be his representative. Like it or not, the man must have done a stalwart job, because it wasn't long before a small crowd approached. The object of their concern appeared to be a shy young fellow who seemed reluctant to speak for himself. The reason for his silence became obvious when others explained that he was deaf and had a debilitating speech impediment.

Sensitive to the lad's self-consciousness, Jesus led him quietly away from the crowd. There was no point in talking to him, since he couldn't hear, and no point in asking questions, since he couldn't reply, even if he wanted to. So nonverbal communication was the way forward. First, Jesus put his fingers in the young man's deaf ears. Next, he wet his fingers with his own spittle and touched his tongue. Then, looking towards the heavens, he sighed. Finally, looking the young man in the eyes, Jesus spoke for the first time: "Be opened!"

Slowly a smile spread over the previously blank face. "Thank you, oh, thank you," he said, speaking clearly and plainly.

Despite Jesus' urging that they should keep this miracle to themselves, those Decapolisians simply could not keep quiet, especially the young man himself, who had a lifetime of talking to catch up on. So crowds gathered from all over the region, thousands of curious people.

Jesus talked to them all day long, in fact for three long days. But the ear can only absorb what the stomach will sanction, and the crowds, whose food stocks were by now seriously depleted, were getting restless.

"I'm concerned for these dear people," Jesus confided to his Disciples. "We can't send them home with no food in their bellies, or they'll faint along the way."

The landscape was desolate, no market in any direction. "What supplies have we?" asked Jesus. They did the tally and came up with a mere seven loaves and a handful of small fish.

Jesus had the people sit and then gave thanks. Just as on the previous occasion, there was no begging or pleading, just confident gratitude. He broke the loaves and began to pass out the food. When every stomach was well satisfied, the Disciples gathered the leftovers and garnered seven full baskets.

Leaving their new friends on the shore, they sailed away over to the west side of the lake. There in Dalmanutha, he was again quickly recognised, and a delegation of aggressive Pharisees headed him off.

"We have heard about you," they announced darkly. "Since seeing is believing, why not show us a sign?"

Evidently, this disappointed Jesus: "Signs! Signs! You people are always demanding signs, yet you never seem to see them, even when they stare you in the face.

"Listen. Whenever you see clouds in the west, you take that as a sure sign of rain. And when the wind is from the south, that is a sign of hot weather. So if you can interpret the signs in the sky, how come you are so slow to understand the signs of the times?"

Back into the boat they climbed and headed north up the lake.

They drifted along in silence for some miles, each alone with his own thoughts. Eventually Jesus broke the spell. Still grieving over his latest brush with those who ought to have known better: "You know, you need to be on your guard against the yeast of those Pharisees. Such negative thinking could spread through society like leaven through a lump of dough."

Yeast! Yes, that was a reminder that they were getting hungry and all but one loaf from the seven baskets they had hauled into the boat the previous day were gone.

There was another long silence. Then someone murmured, "We should have got supplies back there in Dalmanutha."

But Jesus spoke up: "Hey fellows, you just don't get it, do you? Is it that your minds are dull or that your hearts are hard? Can't you see what is in front of your noses or hear plain speech? Or is it that you just have short memories?" They all shifted uncomfortably under this tongue lashing.

"So let me remind you," Jesus continued. "When I broke the five loaves for the five thousand, how many baskets of scraps did you gather up?"

"Twelve," they chorused like a bunch of schoolchildren learning their tables.

"And when seven loaves fed four thousand, how many baskets of leftovers?"

"Seven."

"So? Don't you get it? What was the common denominator?"

Some of them were apparently working out the equation on their fingers, others mouthing the numbers, but from their blank expressions, it was evident that the penny had not dropped. They were still working on the riddle when the boat ground on the beach in Bethsaida late in the evening, and the common denominator jumped onto the sand.

Next morning, it was back to work. A blind man was brought to him for his special touch. Still smarting over the Dalmanuthans' insistence on seeing a sign, he took the man's arm and led him out of the village to a secluded spot, well away from prying eyes. Jesus spat on his hands and rubbed the man's sightless eyes. Then, turning him around, Jesus asked him, "So what do you see?"

The man was clearly excited: "I can see!"

"Yes, but *what* can you see?"

"It's hard to tell. It might be trees, but they are moving around like people."

Jesus turned the man back to face him and then held his head between his two hands and placed his thumbs on his closed eyes. After a moment, he released him. "Now look again," he said. "Look carefully. What do you see?"

But this time there was no mistake: 20/20 vision.

"Go straight home," he told him. "Let's keep this between ourselves. Okay?"

"Signs!" Jesus muttered as he walked slowly back to the Disciples. "People don't see the wood for the trees."

6

The Mountain

From there, they left the lake behind and hiked north along the trail beside the Jordan River, round Lake Huleh and on towards the snow-capped peak of Mount Hermon. There, in the foothills of the great mountain, they wandered. No crowds, no sick people, no religious bigots – just Jesus and his Disciples. Resting on a ridge looking down on Caesarea Philippi, Jesus raised the big question: "So what's the word? Who are people saying that I am?"

"Elijah," suggested someone.

"Jeremiah or one of the old-time prophets," someone else threw out.

"John the Baptist ... with his head back on, that is!"

"But what about you?" Jesus said when the laughter had died down. "Who do you say that I am?"

Without a moment's hesitation, Peter came back with: "You are the Christ, the Son of the living God."

There was silence for a moment, then a big smile spread over Jesus' face. "Well, good on you, Simon son of John. You didn't get that from books or any human source, but my Father in heaven told you. You are rightly called 'Peter' – *Rocky* – for that is the rock on which I will build my church, the force that will buckle the very gates of hell, the key that will open the kingdom of heaven on earth."

Then he turned to the whole group: "What you have just heard is not yet for public ears. There are tough times to be endured first. We have to go to Jerusalem, and there I will suffer at the hands of the religious leaders and be killed. But on the third day, I will be raised back to life."

Peter was off in a daydream, enjoying an inflated sense of his own importance, still basking in Jesus' high praise about him being like a rock. He missed the part about the resurrection altogether and blundered right in to interrupt what Jesus was saying: "Now hold on a moment! Did you say 'killed'? Never! This will never happen to you!"

"Be gone, Satan!" Jesus roared, looking over Peter's shoulder. Everyone was shocked by this unexpected outburst. Then to Peter: "You are getting in my way, Peter. You are looking at this from a human perspective. That's not how God sees it at all."

Turning back to the whole group, he continued, "If any of you really means business about being my Disciple, and you plan to follow me all the way, then you will need a cross, for I am headed to the place of total self-sacrifice. If you want a cushy life, then go home now. But if you want real life, then let's go. What have you got to lose? The whole world would be a poor trade for your life, don't you think?"

They stayed around for a week, and then Jesus announced his intention to climb the big mountain next day. So very early in the morning, Jesus led Peter, James, and John out of their camp, leaving the others sleeping, and started the long climb towards the summit. All morning, they trudged slowly up hill. Up and up they went. They were mushing through patches of snow before they reached the summit around noon. The view was breathtaking. They threw themselves down and ate the sandwiches they had brought along. The last thing they were conscious of as they dozed off in the warm sun was that Jesus was praying.

Something startled them back into consciousness. They were no longer alone, but while they were sleeping, they had been joined by a couple of strangers. And something was funny about the light. They might have imagined that it was the brilliance of the sun reflected from the snow, but as they looked more closely, they became aware that Jesus himself was the source of the light. The radiance of his face and his clothes made even the snow seem dull. The recognition of the new arrivals was instinctive, for how else would they have been able to identify them as Moses and Elijah? The three Disciples were too afraid to speak at first, so they listened to the conversation, which had something to do with Jesus' mission in Jerusalem.

After a while, it became apparent that Moses and Elijah were getting ready to leave, so with little notion of what he was going to say, Peter blurted, "Wow, Lord. This is special. What a privilege to be here with you. Couldn't we keep this going a little longer, you know, make camp for a while? Us three would gladly erect three shelters, one for each of you guys."

Just at that moment, a cloud swept up the mountainside and obliterated everything. They found themselves lost in a brilliant swirling mist. Then a voice that seemed to come from all around them spoke: "This is my Son, whom I love very much. I am so proud of him. Listen to what he tells you."

They were terrified and buried their faces in the snow. But when they eventually dared look again, the cloud had gone, and there was Jesus, smiling at them. No one else. Only Jesus.

"Come on," he said. "Let's go down to join the others."

They stumbled along behind him towards a valley that could never be quite the same after such an experience. "What you have just witnessed is our secret," Jesus told them. "Keep it under your hats till after I am raised again from the dead."

This reference to "rising from the dead" was a puzzle to them. They had heard Jesus speak of it before, but they could not imagine what he was talking about. But that suggested another question.

"So that was Elijah back there, right?" Peter asked. "How come the scribes teach that Elijah must come before the Messiah to restore justice?"

"Yes, the scribes are right. But Elijah did come, and they didn't recognise him. And since they treated him so badly, it should be no surprise to you when they treat me the same way."

They finally cottoned on to the fact that he was talking about John the Baptist.

The sound of angry voices was the first indication of trouble as they approached the other Disciples. A crowd had gathered around them, and there was a lot of shouting and pushing going on. As they drew closer, it became apparent that some kind of religious argument was taking place.

"Look! There he is," someone shouted when they saw Jesus approaching. The crowd turned and surged towards him. They were evidently amazed that he should turn up at that precise moment.

"So what's going on here?" Jesus demanded.

"It's my son, Teacher," a man called out. "I brought him to you, hoping you could help him. But since you weren't here, your Disciples had a go, but … Well, no luck, I'm afraid."

"So what's wrong with him?"

"He has some kind of a dumb spirit. When he takes one of his turns, he collapses and foams at the mouth, grinding his teeth. Just look at him! He's wasting away, poor little lad."

"Where is your faith, guys?" Jesus asked, turning to his shamefaced Disciples. "How long is it going to take before you get it? Time is running out, you know. I'm not going to be with you forever. Bring the boy here."

His father led him towards Jesus, but as soon as he saw him, the lad collapsed, writhing on the ground.

"How long has this been going on?" Jesus asked the stricken man.

"Ever since he was a little kid. This thing seems bent on destroying him, even throws him into the fire or into the river to drown him. If you can do anything to help, we would be so grateful."

"If I can? If …? Faith knows no ifs! Anything's possible when you believe."

"But I really do believe," he choked through the tears that were now streaming down his face. And then, more honestly: "Well, most of the time, anyway." Desperation finally took over. He had no place else to go. "Please help me believe!"

All the while this was going on, more and more people were running up to see what was happening. So not wasting any more time, Jesus focused his attention on the boy. But it was not to the boy that Jesus spoke, but rather to his inmate: "You dumb spirit, get out of him and don't even think of coming back!"

The boy let out one terrible scream, convulsed as though wrenched by a violent force, then lay quite still – still as death.

"He's dead!" wailed someone.

"Nonsense!" Jesus said, taking his hand and lifting him to his feet.

"So why couldn't we cast that spirit out?" the Disciples asked later. "You gave us that authority, and we have cast out many demons in the past."

"It's not you who can cast out demons, but always the one who answers prayer. Never make the mistake of trusting in your own powers."

7

The Argument

Jesus' cover was blown, and their peaceful holiday was at an end, so they headed back into Galilee. But all the while, Jesus kept warning the Disciples of what lay ahead of him in Jerusalem: suffering, death, but resurrection on the third day. No matter how many times they heard it, they just didn't get what he was saying. Yet they didn't like to show their ignorance by asking, so they held their peace.

Back in Capernaum, someone had stopped Peter in the street to ask him if Jesus paid his taxes. "Of course he does," Peter had retorted, indignantly.

"So Peter, what do you think," asked Jesus, back at the house. "Do kings levy taxes from their own family or from others?"

"From others, of course."

"So since this tax you were asked about is to support the building of the temple, my Father's house, should not I, his Son, be exempt?"

Peter didn't know what to say to that. So Jesus continued, "But there's no sense in causing unnecessary offence, so go, throw a hook into the lake, and the first fish you catch will pay our taxes, yours and mine."

Taking his fishing pole, Peter headed to the beach and did what he loved most. A good tug told of a fair-sized fish on the line, which he landed with skilled ease. An impressive catch, maybe, but there was no way it was going to be worth enough to pay two men's taxes. But when Peter went to extract the hook, he found a coin in the fish's mouth. Exactly the right amount! If only paying tax was always that easy!

Arguments, like taxes, have a bad habit of disrupting the peaceful rhythm of life, and even in the company of Jesus, arguments erupted with monotonous regularity between the Disciples. Inevitably, it was when Jesus was talking to them about sacrificing his own life that they would start to dispute which of them should be regarded as the most important.

"Now listen here, guys," Jesus interjected as tempers were about to boil over. "See this little child?" Children often came close to Jesus when he was talking. "If you want to be great in the kingdom, then become like this little chap. Never deter children from coming to me, for the kingdom belongs to them. In fact, unless you humble yourself to be like a little child, you'll never even enter the kingdom, let alone be considered the greatest in it. To welcome a child is to welcome me. But for a man to prevent a child from coming to me, well, he'd be better off taking a swim with a millstone for a life ring. Never ever despise a child, for their guardian angels have direct access to the throne of God. A sheep farmer who loses even one little lamb will search and search till he finds it. How much more will God be unwilling for even one child to go missing."

The Disciples were still out of sorts, still smarting from their argument. So Jesus continued to build on a teachable moment: "Look, if you feel you have been wronged by a brother, don't let it fester. Go talk to him, face to face. If he won't listen, then involve a couple of others as witnesses or arbitrators. And if even then he refuses to deal with it, it may be time to take the matter to the whole assembly. But if your brother still won't listen, then he really has no further share in the fellowship. What happens on earth effects what happens in heaven. How much better, then, if you can be reconciled on earth so that the echo can be felt in heaven. Agreement between two parties on earth has my Father's approval in heaven, and where even a small group of two or three are united in my name on earth, I'm right there! That's the kind of company I love to share.

"So now, what were you arguing about?"

Peter was never one to back down quietly. "Lord, just tell me this, how many times am I supposed to forgive my brother when he wrongs me? Seven times is enough, right?"

The atmosphere was tense. Hostile looks still flashed across the room.

"Not good enough, Peter. Multiply that number by seventy, and then some. Listen, the kingdom of heaven is much like a king attempting to get his accounts settled. There was one man who was deeply in the hole, owing some ten thousand dollars. So to settle the matter, the king ordered that he and his whole family be sold as slaves. But the man begged for mercy, pleading on his knees for more time. So the king took pity on him, simply cancelling the debt.

"As the man walked out, he bumped into one of his fellows, who happened to owe him ten bucks. 'Pay your debts!' raved the first man, grabbing the unfortunate man by the scruff and shaking him mercilessly.

"'Give me time and I'll pay,' the man choked. But no. His creditor had him thrown into the debtor's prison, where he would have stayed but for the intervention of his friends, who told the king what had happened.

"Understandably, the king was furious and summoned the man. 'You wretch! I forgave your debt because you asked me to, so would it not have been reasonable to expect that you would pass on the favour?' The king had the hard-hearted man jailed and instructed the torturers to do their worst till he paid up in full.

"Likewise, my Father is so perfectly compassionate that he cannot tolerate those who are themselves devoid of compassion. He will go to infinite lengths to change these people's hearts, and if even then they refuse to change, they will be forever banished.

"So, remind me again, what was your argument about?"

8

The Festival

The Feast of Booths was a party. Everyone loved it, and Jesus' family wouldn't have missed it for the world. So his brothers came down from Nazareth and met up with Jesus in Capernaum.

"This is the perfect opportunity to make the grand entrance," they told him. "No point in keeping who you are a secret. Let everyone see your miracles right there in the big city." There was more than a hint of cynicism in their suggestion, for even they were not yet convinced.

"No, you go ahead," said Jesus. "I have no intention of stirring up trouble before its time."

When they arrived in Jerusalem, their brother was the talk of the town. But the talk was in whispers, since the authorities were clearly opposed to all this nonsense. Still, people were saying all kinds of things about him: "I think he's great; a fine man."

"No way. He's a fraud; a con artist of the first order."

"Where is he, anyway? Has anyone seen him?"

The celebrations were well under way before Jesus finally showed his face. A crowd quickly gathered round him in the temple, and it wasn't long before some important-looking people joined the back of the pack. They listened carefully to what was being said and then muttered, "Where did this guy get all this from? He didn't attend any of our theological schools, did he?"

"So you are wondering where I was educated," Jesus said, raising his voice, apparently aware of what they were saying. "My teaching is from God who sent me. Anyone who does God's will, recognizes what I'm saying to be the truth. But to anyone who plans to disobey, my word makes no sense. Moses spelled out God's will: 'You shall not kill' was one of his commands. How comes it then that you are plotting to murder me? No wonder you don't appreciate my teaching."

"You are nuts! Who do you imagine is planning to kill you?"

"You are still upset because last spring I healed that lame man on the Sabbath, aren't you? Yet you constantly break the law in order to keep the law. You circumcise children on the Sabbath because the law says you are to do it on the eighth day after he is born. Well, that's working on the Sabbath, isn't it? Catch-22, eh? Yet you are angry with me for healing a whole man on the Sabbath."

This caused a buzz of animated discussion amongst the crowd. "Why don't they arrest him? Here he is, speaking publicly, yet no one lifts a finger to stop him."

"Perhaps the authorities are now convinced he really is the Christ."

"No, he can't be. When the Christ comes, no one will know where he's from, yet everyone knows that Jesus is from Nazareth."

"We have to do something, or people will get the wrong impression," said the important people at the back of the crowd, so they pushed forward with the vague idea of grabbing Jesus.

But the crowd was clearly in sympathy with him. "When the Christ comes, won't he be recognised by the miracles he does?" they said. "Everyone knows this man has done some impressive stuff." So the authorities, perceiving that perhaps discretion really might be the better part of valour, withdrew and reported to the Pharisees.

When they heard that Jesus was in town and actually right there in the temple, the Pharisees dispatched the temple security guards to arrest him. Those fellows made the mistake of pausing to listen to what Jesus was saying and were fascinated. No wonder everyone was talking about him.

In the end, the security men returned empty handed to find most of the Jewish Council assembled and waiting.

"So where is he? How come you didn't bring him?"

"You should hear him, sir! Never heard anybody say things like that."

"Don't tell us that you have been sucked in! Do you see any of your leaders, or any educated people, giving him the time of day? Sure, the ignorant peasants outside who know nothing of the law are being duped. They are stupid enough to believe anything."

Sitting among them, quiet up to this point, was Nicodemus. He understood exactly what the security men were talking about. He had heard first-hand what Jesus had to say. Did he believe? Well, he certainly didn't write it all off as nonsense. So he couldn't just sit there and say nothing.

He rose to his feet and motioned to the chair that he wanted to speak. "A point of order, Mr Chairman. Doesn't the law require that a man be given a fair hearing before being condemned out of hand?"

"I didn't realise that you were a Galilean," the chairman retorted with slimy sarcasm. "You have read the Scriptures, I presume? [This to a man who knew the whole book by heart!] Does it state anywhere that the Prophet will come from Nazareth, that God-forsaken town?"

On that sour note, the meeting was adjourned and they all went home.

A group of those who had been present at the Council met early for a breakfast meeting the following morning. Something had to be done about this Jesus fellow. They surmised that since he claimed to be a champion of the law, there might be some way they could trap him by using the law. The question of how this might be accomplished was solved for them by the arrest during the night of a despicable woman, caught in compromising circumstances, and not for the first time, either.

And there was the wretched teacher again, sitting in a corner of the temple courtyard, with his usual crowd of admirers around him.

A threatening group of councillors pushed its way into the circle, dragging with them the terrified woman.

"Teacher!" their spokesman interrupted. "This woman was caught in the very act of adultery. The law you so clearly uphold states that a woman guilty of this crime should be stoned to death. What do you thing we should do with her?" Surely that would back this know-it-all into a corner. As a champion of the law, he could hardly contradict what Moses had written, but were he to say, "Stone her," then what would become of his reputation as a man of compassion?

Jesus said not a word. He ignored them, doodling with his finger in the dust between his feet.

"Well, what have you got to say? … Should we do what the law demands or not?"

Eventually, Jesus looked up. He knew that it took two to tango, and the law demanded that both parties should share the punishment. He also knew that this woman had done the rounds. "If any one of you is without sin, then he may go ahead and throw the first stone." He resumed his artwork.

One by one, the crowd drifted away, oldest first, but all avoiding eye contact with each other as they went.

When Jesus looked up next, there was no one left, except the woman, standing there with her head down. "So where did they go?" asked Jesus. "No one left to condemn you?"

"No one, sir."

"Well then, neither will I condemn you. Go on home, but no more sinning, eh?"

The Festival of Tabernacles always included a Festival of Light, when the centrepiece would be a huge chandelier that would light up the whole temple area. The party would go on all night, till the rising sun would eclipse the brilliance of the chandelier. Then the people would stumble off home to sleep it off. Coming from the very spot where the light had stood came a clear voice: "I am the light of the world. Whoever follows me will never again have to stumble in the darkness, but instead will have the light of life." The authorities were none too thrilled when they recognised the source.

On the last day of the festival, the focus switched to water. All the people would mass in the great court of the temple and dance round the altar, waving tree branches and singing psalms. The climax came when a company of priests would exit the temple through the Water Gate and process down the steep hill to the Pool of Siloam, where they would fill pitchers with water. This water would be poured out on the dusty ground back in the temple by the altar, recalling the miracle when in Moses' time water had gushed from a rock.

"Is anyone thirsty?" That voice again! "Then come to me and drink. Whoever believes in me will experience streams of living water flowing from within."

Two such egotistical declarations simply could not be allowed to go unchallenged. So the Pharisees confronted him publicly. First, they tackled the question of his dubious origins. Since he was from Nazareth, there could be no possible way that he could claim to be the Christ. "What have you to say about that?"

Instead of producing his birth certificate to show that he had, in fact, been born in Bethlehem, with the official entry in the Roman census to prove it, he broadened the geographical context of the question: "As a matter of fact, I'm not from anywhere in this world."

"So exactly who are you then?" they demanded.

"When you have crucified me, then you'll know who I am and what I am talking about."

There were some in the crowd who shouted encouragement to Jesus.

"Stick with my teaching, if you want to be my genuine disciples," Jesus called back. "Then you will know the truth and the truth will set you free."

"But we *are* free," someone replied. "We are descendants of Abraham: no one's slaves."

"Oh, but you are slaves: slaves to sin, and you can't break free. But if I, the Son, set you free, then you will be really free."

"But we are already free. Like we just said, we are Abraham's children."

"Then why don't you act like your father? Why do you want to kill me? That's not the kind of attitude you inherited from Abraham. That sounds to me like it comes from a very different father."

"God is ultimately our father," they contended, seeking to raise the issue to a higher level.

"If God were your father, then you would speak his language, but you don't understand the language of truth, but only the language of lies. That's the devil's language. I speak truth, but you don't get it, since you don't understand that language. The devil speaks lies, and since you belong to his family, you speak the same language and use lies to do your family business: murder. 'You will not die!' he originally promised Eve, and with that lie, he has killed everyone ever since. You too will die because of that lie, unless you believe the truth that I AM."

"You are demon-possessed!" they exploded.

"No, I'm not. I give honour to my Father, but you dishonour me."

There was a pause in the debate, and then, with great sadness, Jesus added, "If you would only accept what I am saying, you would never see death."

But instead of grabbing the lifeline, they pounced on his words like a cat on a mouse: "Now we know for sure that you really are demon-possessed, quite mad. Abraham died and so did all the prophets, yet you claim that if anyone believes what you are saying, he won't die? Don't tell us you are greater than our father Abraham."

"Your father Abraham was thrilled when he saw me, the ultimate fulfilment of all the promises God had given him."

"Come on! You are not yet fifty, and you want us to believe that you have met Abraham?"

"The truth is that before Abraham lived, I AM."

It wasn't just the distortion of human grammar that incensed them, it was the final repetition of the name that was uniquely God that got to them: "I AM."

Their fury knew no limit. They cast around for rocks and brickbats and would have stoned him to a pulp right there and then, but when they turned back with their missiles in hand, he was gone, nowhere to be seen.

A blind youngster sat begging by the road. His senses registered a crowd of possible contributors approaching. When they came abreast of where he was sitting, they stopped and stood there, talking about him.

"Teacher, whose sin is to blame for this kid's blindness? Was it his parents who sinned or is it his own fault?" It was humiliating to be discussed, the object of mere theological debate.

Then a kinder voice replied, "Sin has nothing to do with it. Rather this young man was born blind so that God's power can be illustrated through him. Remember I told you that I am the light of the world? This young man doesn't even know what light is." So saying, he spat in the dust, bending down to mix it into clay. Then, taking the mud, he smeared it on the youth's eyes, just like the Creator, finishing the job.

"Friend, now go and wash that off, but you must do so in the pool of

Siloam, which, as I'm sure you realise, means 'sent.' And remember that the one who sent you promised not only water to the thirsty, but light to the dark world."

Anxious to get the grit out of his eyes, the young man scrambled to his feet and tapped his way down the steep hill, towards the pool.

Only one who has never experienced "blue" could have any notion of what burst into his perception the moment he saw the sky reflected from the water's surface. Green trees, brown faces, red flowers, and the brilliance of the sun. Light! So that's what everyone had been talking about!

It was difficult to find his way home, since he only knew it by feel, but when eventually he made it, he was greeted by a very mixed reaction in the neighbourhood. "Hey, isn't that the blind kid?"

"No. It's his twin brother. That guy can see."

"Excuse me, but I am the self same."

"So how come you can see?"

"A man whose name I believe is Jesus put mud in my eyes and told me to wash it out in Siloam. I did as he said and – voila! I can see!"

"Where is this guy?"

"I have no idea where anything is, least of all where *he* is."

"We had better report this to the authorities," they all agreed and steered him to the temple. The Pharisees were there in force, since it was the Sabbath. Someone explained what had taken place.

"So how did this happen?" a Pharisee asked.

"A man called Jesus put mud in my eyes, and when I washed it out, I could see."

"There we are," the Pharisee said, turning to his colleagues. "Clear evidence that this Jesus is not from God, for if he was, then he wouldn't desecrate the Sabbath in this way."

Another voice cut in: "How could a sinner perform such extraordinary miracles if he didn't have God's blessing?" Difficult to argue with that, so the first interrogator turned back to the young man.

"So what do you have to say about him, since it was to you he gave sight?"

"He has to be a prophet."

Well, that didn't suit their argument, so they had to find a way to discredit the boy, and quickly. Perhaps he'd never really been blind. So they sent for his parents and got them to identify him.

"Yes, he's our son alright."

"And was he actually born blind?"

"Yes he was, poor guy."

"Well, how come he can now see? Who is responsible for this?"

"That's the mystery, isn't it? We have no idea who did this or how he did it. He's old enough to speak for himself. Ask him!" It was well known that the Pharisees were threatening to excommunicate anyone who was in sympathy with Jesus, and mom and dad weren't going to run that risk.

So the inquisition was focused back on the cause of all the trouble: "Young man, you should give glory to God for your healing. But this Jesus fellow is undoubtedly a sinner."

"Well, I'm no judge of character, sir. All I know is that I have been blind all my life, but now I can see."

"But how?" the questioner pursued relentlessly. "What did he do to you?"

"I've already told you what he did. Why do you want to hear it again? Oh, I get it. You are thinking of joining his disciples!"

"Why, you little twerp! Don't you dare tar us with the same brush as yourself. We are disciples of Moses, and there's no doubt that God spoke through him. But as for this fellow, why, we don't even know where he's from."

"Well, sirs, if I may say so, that is remarkable! Everyone knows that God doesn't work through sinners, but only through good men. Yet this Jesus has given sight to someone born blind, an unheard-of feat, and one that only God could accomplish. Could this really have been done by a sinner?"

"You little scoundrel! How dare you lecture us!" They threw him out of the temple.

Word of this excommunication reached Jesus, who sought him out. He eventually tracked the lad down by the sheep pens, on the outskirts of town. He was leaning on a rail and gazing in amazement at the animals. Naturally, he didn't recognise Jesus as he approached, since he couldn't have recognised his own mother, but even amongst all the bleating of the animals, he discerned something familiar about the voice of the stranger who spoke to him. He knew he had heard that voice somewhere before.

"Do you believe who I am?" asked Jesus.

"Well, I would sir, but who exactly are you?"

"You recognise my voice, don't you, but now you can see me." Then the penny dropped. This was the voice that had told him to wash in Siloam.

"Lord!" he gasped in wonder, falling to his knees. "Yes, I do believe."

Some persistent Pharisees were hanging around. Jesus turned to them: "I have come to even things up a little so that the blind can see and the sighted can become blind."

"So do you think we are blind?" they asked.

"The point is that you don't know you are, but insist that you see clearly. It's that which makes you doubly guilty."

Just then, a strange high-pitched cry attracted his attention. A shepherd had come to the pens and was summoning his sheep. All those woolly beasts looked just the same to the casual onlooker, but several of them immediately detached themselves from the rest of the flock and came trotting up to him, expectantly.

"So did you see that?" Jesus said to the Pharisees. "Did you see how his sheep came running? It's his voice they recognise, you know. They'd never come to a stranger; in fact, his voice might cause the sheep to scatter."

The young man whose sight had just been restored understood the importance of voice recognition, for that was how he had been drawn to Jesus. The Pharisees, however, found that what he was saying grated on their nerves.

"I am like a shepherd to my sheep. By night, I sleep in the entrance to the pen to keep them safe from intruders, and by day, I lead them out into fresh pastures. Unlike those whose intentions are to steal or harm them, I am here to ensure that my sheep have the very best in life. I am ready to sacrifice my own life to that end. A mere hired hand would run to save his own skin when threatened by a predator.

"I know my Father, and he knows me, and I know my sheep, and they know me. That's how it all works. One day, there'll be other sheep somewhere out there who will recognise my voice when I call. I will bring them also to the safety of the pen, so there will be one flock cared for by one shepherd. And one day, I will give my life for the sheep. It won't be anyone taking my life from me. No. I will freely give it and then take it up again. That's what the Father has told me to do."

A couple of months went by, and Jesus was once again heading to Jerusalem, this time for the Feast of Dedication. They were taking the long route south via the east bank of the Jordan and then crossing the ford near Jericho and so up to Jerusalem. Somewhere on the winding road that took them up from the valley and into the mountains, a teacher of the law challenged Jesus with a test question: "What must I do to qualify for eternal life?"

"Well, what do the Scriptures say?" Jesus asked, responding question for question.

"Love God with all your heart, soul, mind, and strength, and love your neighbour as you love yourself."

"Yes, that just about sums it up. Do that and you'll qualify."

But the teacher wanted to have the last word, not willing to appear foolish before the crowd: "So who exactly is 'my neighbour'? And how do you define 'neighbour' anyway?"

In reply, Jesus told a story about a traveller on the same route as they were walking: the Jericho to Jerusalem road. In the story, the poor man was mugged and robbed by bandits. Other travellers, including a priest and a Levite, saw the wounded man bleeding by the roadside, but left him where he was. Finally, a despised Samaritan happened by, gave him first aid, and helped him to a nearby inn. There he got him settled and paid the tab for the man to stay till he would be strong enough to resume his journey.

"Now," concluded Jesus, "which of the three proved himself to be a loving neighbour to the wounded man?"

"The one who helped him, of course."

"So go, do likewise."

Just before they arrived in the city, they halted in the village of Bethany, on the east slope of the Mount of Olives. A woman named Martha offered them hospitality, which they gladly accepted. There was much to be done to prepare a meal for her crowd of guests: food to be purchased and prepared, and the table to be set. So Martha set to work, chivvying her two siblings, Mary and Lazarus, to give her a hand.

Jesus used the time to teach the waiting guests: "Suppose you have an unexpected visitor who arrives really late one night, and, unlike our hostess here, you have nothing to give him to eat. So you go next door to your neighbour's house and bang on his door. 'Could you lend me some bread?' you shout through the mail slot.

"'What are you thinking?' comes the bleary reply. 'It's gone midnight, the door's locked, and you're going to wake my kids. Go away!'

"Love for neighbour may not get that man out of bed, but persistent knocking will eventually do the trick. Prayer sometimes seems like a closed door, doesn't it, but when it does, keep right on asking; keep pursuing what you want; keep knocking on that door.

"Or think of it as a widow who persistently approaches the local magistrate, demanding justice against one who has wronged her. But what does the magistrate care? He's not motivated by fear of God or love for his fellow man, so he refuses to hear her case. But she doesn't give up, she just keeps presenting her petition. Eventually, he gives in. 'This wretched woman is wearing me out, and she's going to give my reputation a black eye in this town if I'm not careful. So I had better see she gets justice.'

"If an unjust judge would eventually give justice to the persistent, how much more will God come to the aid of his people who cry out to him day and night for justice. I'm not suggesting that your heavenly Father is slow to respond, but simply that you need to persist in prayer in the face of what may appear to you as slowness. Which of you fathers would refuse your children if they asked for food, or give them a snake instead of a fish, or a rock instead of a bun? Of course you wouldn't. So how much more can you trust your Father in heaven to give you good things when you ask."

With all this talk of fish and bread, the Disciples were getting hungry, and the smell of cooking from the kitchen was tantalising. But then the aroma was marred by the smell of burning, and the peace was disturbed by an increasing sound of clattering pots and pans in the kitchen. Eventually, Martha burst into the room, clearly distressed.

"Lord, doesn't it bother you that my dear sister has left me to do all the work on my own? Tell her, Lord! Tell her to help me!" Mary, who had started out well intentioned to help prepare the meal, had been eavesdropping on the story, and before she knew it, she was sitting in the front row, right at Jesus' feet, fascinated by what he was saying.

"Martha," said Jesus, "life can be really stressful sometimes, can't it? But the important thing is to get your priorities right. Mary seems to be on the right track, so don't distract her."

Word that Jesus was in town got around, and next morning, a huge crowd gathered outside Martha's house. So Jesus went out and talked to them. He told them all kinds of things: proverbs interspersed with stories. "Guard against hypocrisy. Secrets will always get out. Never fear people, since the worst they can do is kill you. The cure for stress is to know God loves you. If God cares for birds and flowers, then why would he neglect you? God knows everything you need; he even knows how many hairs grow on your head."

A man in the crowd shouted out, "Hey, Teacher. Would you please tell my brother here to give me my share of our family inheritance?"

"Since when have I been appointed executor of your parents' will? Judge for yourself what is fair. Better that than one of you winding up in debtors' prison."

Then addressing the whole crowd: "Guard against greed, for life is not about getting lots of stuff. Listen. There was this rich man who had lots and lots of stuff and no place to store it all. So he built bigger and bigger barns, smug in the assurance that he had more than enough to live out his days in luxury. But that night God told him, 'Your number is up. Your life is over.' Now who will get all his stuff?

"No point in hoarding stuff for the here and now, so let God take care of your heavenly investments. Concentrate on God's kingdom, and all you ever need will be provided. Sell what you don't need and give away the proceeds, and your investments in heaven will grow exponentially. Remember, your heart will always follow your fortune."

Jesus fell silent for a moment, and maybe the crowd feared that the day's entertainment was at an end, so someone called out, "So what do you think about old Pilate killing those guys from Galilee? And right there in the temple as well. They must have done something bad to cause that to happen, don't you think?"

"Just because a bad thing happened to them doesn't make them any worse than anyone else. So let me ask you something: what do you think about the eighteen people who were killed last week when that tower in Siloam collapsed on them? Were they worse sinners than all the other citizens of Jerusalem?

"Think of it this way: A man had a vineyard in which he planted a fig tree. Year after year, he came to get fruit from it, but nothing. Finally, he said to the man who tended the vineyard, 'Cut that tree down. It's a waste of space.'

"'Leave it one more year, sir, and I'll give it some TLC. If by this time next year there's no fruit, well fine. Then we'll chop it down.'

"Be sure the axe is not far away and judgement is definitely coming to everyone, so be quick and repent before it happens: before Pilate gets you or a tower falls on your head."

On Saturday morning, Jesus went to the synagogue with their hosts and was invited to give a word. He noticed in the crowd a woman bent almost double by some kind of deformity. He called her to the front: "Lady, you are now free from this thing that has been tying you down." Nothing happened till he put his hand on her bent back, and suddenly she straightened and stood up right.

"Praise God!" she shouted, and the whole congregation erupted in delight.

At this, the chief elder of the synagogue rose to his feet. "Order! Order!" he shouted. When the hubbub was stilled, he addressed the congregation: "Now listen up, you people. There are six days in every week when you can bring people to be healed. But this is the Sabbath!"

"Hear, hear!" chorused his fellow elders.

"You bunch of hypocrites!" retorted Jesus. "Don't you all untie your donkeys to lead them to water every Sabbath? So what's wrong with releasing this lady on the Sabbath, this daughter of Abraham whom Satan has had tied up for eighteen long years?" There was applause from the delighted congregation, but the elders felt humiliated.

Next day was the big day, the Feast of Dedication, so Jesus with his Disciples completed their journey into Jerusalem. The weather was predictably deplorable for December 25, so they huddled under the shelter of Solomon's Colonnade to keep out of the rain.

The ever-present Pharisees soon spotted him. "Back so soon? How long are you going to keep us in suspense? If you really are the Christ, then tell us so there'll be no mistake."

"I have told you already, but you didn't believe me. The miracles I do in my Father's name prove it. But like I said last time I was here, only my own sheep recognise my voice and follow me. I give them immortality, and no one can snatch them from my care or from my Father's care. You see, I and the Father are one."

The Pharisees were immediately right back where they had been three months earlier, enraged and ready to murder him. They picked rocks out of the mud and made to hurl them at him.

"Hold on a moment!" shouted Jesus. "I have shown you all kinds of miracles from the Father. For which of these are you about to stone me?"

"It is not for any miracle, but for blasphemy. You, who are just a man, are claiming to be God!" Those rocks were itching to be launched from their muddy hands.

But the Scriptures did not foretell the Christ being stoned to death, so Jesus knew he was safe. And it was in the Scripture that Jesus took refuge from the impending hail of missiles. "May I remind you, gentlemen, that in Psalm 82, God himself addressed an assembly of mythological 'gods,' calling them 'sons of the Most High.' They were all clearly humbugs, their actions anything but godlike. So why then are you upset with me when I say that I am the Son of the Most High? Are not my actions consistent with those of my Father? If the Scriptures call those ungodly frauds 'sons of God,' then the Scriptures must be wrong. So go ahead; stone the Scriptures!"

They dropped their stones but stepped forward to seize him. And once again, he just melted away into the crowd. Gone!

9

The Rich

J esus withdrew to a safe distance on the far side of the Jordan, to Perea, the very place that John the Baptist had used for his meetings. This was in King Herod's jurisdiction but relatively safe from the clutches of the religious boys in Jerusalem. Word spread that Jesus was around, and many flocked to meet him. Lots of them had happy memories of John's words in that place: "Everything John predicted about the coming one is fulfilled in this man. John never did any miracles, but this man certainly does." And there, in that quiet place, where John had so faithfully pointed the crowds towards Jesus, many now put their faith in him.

But Jesus never sought to ride on a wave of popularity, always probing for real commitment. He told those new believers the same thing he had told his Disciples up in Caesarea Philippi: "If you want to follow me, then bring along your own cross, for you will need it where I am headed. And don't expect cushy accommodation along the way. Foxes have holes and birds have nests, but I have no place to call home. And I'm not waiting for anyone; no time for good-byes or even for family funerals. You can't plough a straight furrow while looking over your shoulder.

"Think carefully before joining me. If you are planning to build a house and don't want to look stupid by getting nothing more than the footings in place, then first get all your estimates in. Consult the bank manager if need be. Or, if ever you are made king and plan to go to war, muster your troops first to ensure you have enough men to win the battle. If not, seek to make peace before the fighting starts.

"The bottom line is that unless you are ready to give up everything you own, don't even think about following me."

"So are you saying that in the end only a few people will actually be saved?" someone called out.

"Well, certainly the entrance gate is narrow and hard to find, but be sure you find it and get inside before the gate is closed and locked. You'd be so upset to see Abraham, Isaac, and Jacob and all the prophets being admitted while you were left standing out in the cold. People from all over the world will go through that door, but will you? First last and last first will be the order of admission."

Some Pharisees approached him, for once not picking a fight: "You had better move on to somewhere else. This is Herod's turf, and he is planning to kill you."

"You can tell that fox, if you see him, that for the time being I have work to do right here, but before long, I will be going to Jerusalem. So you see, I am quite safe here, for the Scripture nowhere predicts my death anywhere other than in Jerusalem."

On the following Sabbath, one of the leading Pharisees from that region invited Jesus and a number of important guests to his home for dinner. The religious set in Perea didn't seem to be as hostile as their counterparts elsewhere; nevertheless, as they took their places, Jesus was conscious of the careful scrutiny of his fellow guests.

Sitting directly opposite him was a man in evident discomfort. Jesus had noticed his lumbering walk on the way in. His legs and arms were severely swollen. To heal the man would hardly be politically correct in a Pharisee home and on the Sabbath to boot, but to sit there and watch him suffer was unthinkable. Had word reached this far out into the country about his Sabbath healings of the lame man and the deformed lady? Was this perhaps a trap? Maybe he could quietly reach out under the table and heal the man without causing a fuss, but that was not Jesus' way.

"Tell me," said Jesus raising his voice and addressing himself to the top of the table, where sat the leading Pharisees and teachers of the law, "does the law permit healing on the Sabbath or forbid it?"

All conversation round the table immediately died away. There was silence. No one replied.

"Well then, tell me this. If your son, or even one of your livestock, fell into a well on the Sabbath, would you leave him there till the Sabbath was over, or would you pull him out?" Again silence. "I'll take that as a 'yes' then," Jesus said, reaching over the table to grasp the man's swollen hand. Before their eyes, the swelling shrank, and the man rose from the table with a look of surprised wonder on his face. He turned and walked quickly out of the room, leaving a buzz of animated conversation behind him.

"I have some advice to offer, particularly to you gentlemen at the top of the table," Jesus said when the excitement had died down. "When attending a wedding reception, you would be smart not to grab the best seats, lest a more important guest than yourself comes along, and you are relegated to a lower position. Embarrassing, don't you think? Much better to take a humble position and have the honour of being moved up the table when your host notices where you are sitting. Remember, the man who promotes himself risks being humbled, while the humble man can only ever be promoted.

"And you, sir," he continued, addressing their host. "I notice that most people at this table are your friends and relatives, who will doubtless return the favour by inviting you to their homes, just to keep things even. How much better, then, to invite disadvantaged people to your dinner parties, people who can't repay you. That would be to your credit at the resurrection."

"Hear, hear!" agreed one of the guests. "What a privilege it will be to eat at the great feast in the kingdom of God."

"You'd think that everyone would be only too anxious to be there, wouldn't you? But the reality is that it's not quite like that.

"A rich man once threw a great banquet and invited many guests. But when the day came, they all made excuses. 'I have just completed a real estate deal and have to go to check it out.' Or 'I have just had delivery of five teams of plough oxen. Must get them settled in.' Or even – and this is the best excuse yet – 'I have just got married. Can't possibly leave the wife at home alone!'"

Laughter rippled round the table, easing the tension.

"As you might imagine, the would-be host was most upset," Jesus continued. "He sent his servants to find some other people to share his banquet. 'Go quickly into the street and bring in the homeless, the handicapped, the vagrants, and the misfits.' But even then there were still empty seats. 'Very well,' said the frustrated benefactor, 'go out onto the highway and drag in all passersby. I will have a full house!' he roared. 'And another thing,' he shouted at the backs of his retreating servants. 'Don't let in any of those so-and-sos who were on my original guest list!'"

Once again, there was restrained laughter, but some had the uneasy feeling that the story was directed at them.

One of the guests, who had disapproval written all over his face, leaned forward: "I notice that you are not exactly choosy about some of the company you keep. This is not the only dinner party you have attended in recent days, if I am not mistaken?" Jesus had indeed recently been guest in a very different home: that of a notorious taxman, attended by all manner of his low-life associates.

"Well, look at it this way. Suppose you own a hundred sheep and one goes missing. Wouldn't you leave the ninety-nine to go find the lost animal? And when you find it, wouldn't you be so thrilled that you'd throw a party to celebrate? Well, it's just like that in heaven when one sinner repents.

"Or think of a woman with ten silver coins and one rolls off the table and is lost. Wouldn't she spring-clean that house from top to bottom till she finds it? And when she finds it, my, but what a party she shares with the whole neighbourhood! The angels in heaven throw a similar celebration over even one sinner who repents.

"A man had two sons. The younger of the two asked his father for the share of the inheritance that would one day be his, and he wanted it right away. With the cash in his pocket, he left home and travelled abroad. There he blew it all, living it up with no restraint. Eventually, he ran out of funds and, finding himself homeless and hungry, took a minimum wage job feeding pigs. Finally he came to his senses, realising how much better off were his father's employees back home than he was, starving to death in this pigpen.

"'I'll go home,' he resolved. 'I'll eat humble pie, admit my mistakes, and ask Father for a job.' And that's what he did, or rather, that's what he set out to do. But when he was still some way from home, his father saw him coming. He ran to meet him and enveloped him in a big bear hug.

"When the boy could finally speak, he delivered his prepared speech: 'Father, I have sinned against heaven and against you. I am not worthy to be known as your son.' He would have continued with the part about needing a job, but the father was already turning back to the house, bellowing to his servants: 'Hurry! Prepare a banquet to celebrate my son's homecoming.' So the party began.

"Returned sons are always more cause for celebration than even returned sheep or coins, don't you think? But the story doesn't end there. You see, there was the older brother who was out in the field at the time of the homecoming. He heard the sounds of music and dancing and came in to find out what was going on. 'Your brother's home and your father has killed his prize calf to celebrate,' explained an excited servant.

"But excited the older brother was not. He refused to join the party, so the father went out to persuade him to come in.

"'See here, Father. For years I have stayed home, working like a slave, never rebelling or doing anything to displease you. Never once did you give me so much as a goat to celebrate with my friends. Then in walks this son of yours who has blown your money on prostitutes and wild living, and you kill the fattened calf in his honour.'

"'My dear son, your company is a constant joy to me, and everything I own is yours for the taking, not just a goat! But your brother is home, and that calls for a celebration. He was lost, perhaps even dead, but here he is, alive and well!'"

There was a pregnant silence for a moment and then he looked straight at the disapproving Pharisee: "Now what was that you were saying about the company I keep?"

Not far from the Jordan, in southern Perea, was the newly refurbished town of Livias, lovingly restored by King Herod. Jesus was invited to attend several dinner parties in the fine homes of the rich and successful in the area. He always had plenty to say on the subject of wealth, not all of it complementary.

"There was once a rich businessman who gave his manager notice of termination because of his financial incompetence.

"'Now what am I going to do?' wondered the poor man. 'I'm too unfit to dig ditches, and there's no way I am going to beg for charity. There must be some way I can use my final days as I work out my notice to ensure that I leave on good relations with my employer's customers.'

"So he contacted all those who had recently taken delivery of the commodities that his company supplied. They were all pleasantly surprised by the final statement: substantially less than they had expected. A conspiratorial wink and a handshake sealed the friendship!

"Far from being angry at this, the business man gave his ex-CEO a good reference, recognising him as a shrew operator.

"I'm not saying that dishonesty is commendable, but simply that the secular world of business has a thing or two to teach the religious community. Perhaps the very best investment of financial wealth is to use it to make friends with those around you. Money is soon gone, no matter how you use it, but how glad you will be one day when eternity dawns to have a whole group of people there ready to welcome you, because you invested your money in making friends with them.

"But as to the question of honesty, trust is earned little by little, starting with small amounts. Who would trust substantial sums to one suspected of stealing even the small change from the till? And how could you be trusted with eternal riches if you can't be trusted with worldly wealth?

"Always remember who is the real boss. You can't serve both God and money equally."

"What a load of tripe!" one of the rich Pharisees was heard to mumble. He had recently taken possession of his grand new home and was proud of the impression that this gave to his neighbours of God's obvious approval being upon him.

"You have it all wrong, sir," responded Jesus. "You think that wealth is a clear sign to others that you have God's favour. But God is not interested in your outward veneer of success. He sees your heart. Much of what is so highly favoured by people is abhorrent to God.

"Once upon a time there lived a rich man in a big house – the last word in luxury. It was at his gate that a beggar named Lazarus squatted, longing to get a taste of even the scraps from the rich man's table. He was covered in open sores and too weak to chase off the scavenging dogs that pestered him as he lay there. Inevitably Lazarus died, but ironically the rich man also died that same day. Lazarus joined Abraham in glory on the other side, but the rich man found himself in hell. What made the torment worse for the rich man was that he could see Lazarus in the distance, much as Lazarus had been able to see the rich man in the distance in their former lives.

"'Father Abraham, have pity!' shouted the once-rich man. 'Send Lazarus to give me a drink of water. I'm in agony in these flames.'

"'No, son,' replied Abraham. 'Fair is fair. Now your circumstances are reversed. But in any case, there is a huge chasm between us and you that none can cross, even if they want to.'

"'Then would you at least send Lazarus to warn my family back home to not make the same mistake as I did by coming to this terrible place.'

"'They can read all about it in the Scriptures, if they choose to.'

"'Yes, but it would be so much more convincing if someone came to them from the grave. They would be sure to repent then.'

"'Not so, my friend. If they won't believe what they read in the Scriptures, then they won't believe even a messenger risen from the dead.'"

In that same upscale neighbourhood, a well-dressed young man approached Jesus: "Teacher! Good Teacher! Please tell me. I want eternal life. What do I have to do to get it? Something good, presumably?"

"What's all this about 'good Teacher' and 'good deeds'? Good, good, good! Only God is good, you know."

"Yes I know, but what do I have to do to be worthy of eternal life?"

"You have to be as good as God, to keep all the commandments all the time."

"Okay, but which commandments are you talking about?"

"Love your neighbour, honour your parents, don't kill, don't commit adultery, don't steal, don't lie …"

"Yes, I know. I have kept all those," the young man said impatiently, cutting Jesus off midsentence. "But what am I missing?"

"Well, if you had let me finish you might have heard. I was going to add number ten from the list: 'Don't covet.' If you want to be perfect, as good as God, then don't covet. But you do, don't you? You need to go and sell all your precious stuff, give the proceeds to others in need, then you can come and follow me. But you can't bring all that junk with you."

The eager expression on the young man's face slowly dissolved to disappointment. "I can't do that," he stammered. He stood there for a moment, then turned on his heel and walked away. There were tears on his cheeks.

"Oh, how difficult it is for rich people to get into the kingdom. Easier to thread a camel through a needle's eye."

Even some of the Disciples shared the mistaken notion that financial success was a sign of God's approval. "Well, who then can get into the kingdom?" they asked.

"No one, actually. Only God can get people into his kingdom."

"Yes, but we have sacrificed everything to follow you. Surely that will help."

"What you have left behind is nothing compared to what you will one day gain. All the scores will be evened then, and those at the top of the heap may wind up at the bottom, and those at the bottom may find themselves on top, the first last and the last first. Everything made fair.

"It will be a bit like a fruit grower who goes to the job centre at crack of dawn and contracts a group of labourers to work on his land for a flat rate of one hundred dollars for the day. Midmorning, he returns to the job centre and finds more willing workers doing nothing. He sends them to join the others. Same thing at lunchtime, and again an hour before quitting time: more workers to whom he promises to pay a fair wage. At knocking-off time, they all line up to be paid, with the last ones in, first in the line. To their delight, they receive a full one hundred dollars, as do those who had worked since lunchtime. Seeing their delight at their employer's generosity, the early birds were getting excited, anticipating more than they had originally expected. But no. All they get was the agreed wage: one hundred dollars.

"'That's not fair,' they grumble. 'We have been here all day, and these guys have only put in barely an hour.'

"'One hundred dollars was the agreement, wasn't it?' asks the employer. 'Do you resent my generosity to others?'

"The point is that those who are at the top of the heap may wind up at the bottom, and those at the bottom may find themselves on top, the first last and the last first. Everything will be made fair, not based on what is deserved, but based on God's generosity."

Later, when the crowds had gone home and the Disciples were sitting with Jesus by the lake in the shade of a mulberry tree, they asked him, "Lord, would you increase our faith."

"Ah yes! Faith. Well, let's start with a very small faith: faith as small as a mustard seed. That's the size of faith it would take to tear up this mulberry tree and throw it into the lake. A great faith, on the other hand, is an obedience that asks no questions, but simply does what it is told.

"Think of it like this. You have a servant who works hard for you all day on the farm, then comes in and prepares your evening meal. Should that servant expect special thanks? After all, he is only doing what he's told, what's expected of him. Faith obeys like that, expects no thanks, no privileges, but willingly does what it's told.

"So would it take more faith for you to command this mulberry tree to jump into the lake, or for you to obey me if I told you to jump into the lake? You want greater faith, do you? So go on! Jump …"

10

The Funeral

Next day a messenger arrived, urgently looking for Jesus.

"Come quick," he panted when he found him. "Your friend is very sick."

They narrowed it down to identify the friend as Lazarus from Bethany, the brother of Martha and Mary.

"Go back and tell the family not to worry, since this won't be terminal."

Reluctantly, the messenger left, wondering why Jesus didn't come with him immediately. But when he'd gone, Jesus just stayed where he was. Of course, the Disciples were quite relieved. They knew how fond he was of that family, and for one awful moment they had feared he might rush back into that hornets' nest, where the Pharisees were ready to stone him. But there was clearly no need to go, since Lazarus was going to be okay.

Then a couple of days later: "Come on! Let's go back to Bethany."

"That would be suicide! Those guys in Jerusalem will kill you if they hear you're back."

"It's safe enough in daylight hours, but night time can be a little more tricky. But don't forget who it is who turns the darkness to light." They digested that for a little, and then Jesus continued, "Our good friend Lazarus has gone to sleep, so I'm going to wake him."

"That's not a good idea, Lord. Sleep is just what he needs to help him get better."

"It was just a euphemism, guys. Lazarus is dead, and I'm glad I wasn't there to intervene. What happens now will help your faith grow, perhaps more than that mulberry tree. So let's be going."

They hesitated, reluctant to leave the safe place they had enjoyed for the past few weeks, but Thomas, who tended to see the dark side of most things, said, "Come on then! May as well go and get killed with him."

When they arrived a couple of days later, they found the house full of strangers, family, and well-wishers who had gathered to comfort Martha and Mary in their loss. Apparently, Lazarus had died four days previously, probably the very day they had first received the news, so they would have been too late, even if they had left immediately.

Martha came out to meet them. "Thank goodness you are here!" she sobbed. "But if only you had been here sooner, then Lazarus would still be alive." The sounds of wailing filled the air, the professional mourners earning their fee. Through her own tears, Martha choked out, "But Lord, I do know that with God, it's never too late. Even now, he will do whatever you ask him, won't he?"

"No doubt about it, Martha. Lazarus will rise again."

Martha knew this and had been assured of the same by many who had come to breathe pious clichés in a vain attempt to heal her broken heart.

"I know he will rise again, at the last day. But what about the here and now? I want him now!" she sobbed, in terrible grief.

"Look at me, Martha. I am right here, right now, right beside you. It's me, Martha. I am the resurrection, and I am life. Anyone who believes in me will live, and even if he dies like Lazarus has, he will still be alive. Everlasting life never ends. Do you believe, Martha?"

"Yes, Lord. It's you I trust. I do believe that you are the Christ, the Son of God." A peace seemed to replace her tears. She was no longer striving to persuade Jesus to do something, but was simply trusting Jesus, knowing he would do what was best. With a new hope, she hurried back into the house to call Mary.

Martha didn't want the whole congregation to come, so she whispered in Mary's ear, "The Teacher has arrived and wants to see you."

Mary jumped up and went out to meet him. Her sudden departure prompted a general exodus, everyone assuming that Mary was off to the cemetery where she would need their consolation. But Mary was ahead of the crowd and found Jesus just where Martha had left him. She collapsed at his feet, overcome with misery. Choking through her tears, she accused him: "Lord, why didn't you come? If you had only been here sooner, then he wouldn't have died." A moment later, and Jesus was surrounded by weeping people.

His own emotions were fighting a battle. Something in him saw red, blind fury at the fallout of what the devil's lie had brought on this lovely family and on all the human race. "You will not die," the devil had said, but now look at them!

But at the same time, Jesus' heart was breaking with sorrow for the death of Lazarus and the grief of his family and friends. "Where have you laid him?" Jesus asked, fighting to maintain his composure.

"Come and we'll show you." The sisters took an arm each and led him towards the cemetery. As they walked, Jesus' face slowly crumpled, and next moment Martha and Mary were aware that Jesus had lost it. He was weeping like a child.

"He must have loved him a lot," someone commented.

"Well, why didn't he stop him from dying then? After all, he did heal that blind man, didn't he?"

The sad procession eventually came to the cemetery. The grave was a small cave hollowed out of the rock with a slab over the entrance. Jesus, flanked by the sisters, stood there with the crowd gathering behind them.

"Take that slab away!" Jesus ordered some of the men.

"Lord!" exclaimed Martha, disturbed. "He's been dead four days. There'll be a terrible smell by now."

"Didn't I tell you that if you believed, you would see the glory of God?"

The slab was removed, and there it was: the darkness of death, the unavoidable end of every man, the final enemy. And there, facing it, stood the Lord of life. Once again, Jesus was enraged as he confronted his nemesis. For a few moments, he stood there, nostrils flared like a warhorse about to charge into battle. Then he looked up to heaven and prayed in a clear voice so all could hear what he was saying. There was no begging or pleading, just gratitude and confident trust. "Father, I know that you can hear me without my calling out like this. I know that you are always listening, but I am praying out loud for the benefit of these people standing here with me. I want them to believe that it was you who sent me."

Then he stepped forward to the entrance to the cave. "Lazarus," he shouted. "Come out!"

There was a gasp from the crowd, who then fell silent, straining their eyes to see into the darkness. There was movement. Something was shuffling, hopping, shambling in the gloom. It was wrapped from head to toe in linen strips and with a bandage round its head to hold the jaw in place. It stood there swaying, half in the sunlight, half still in the darkness. A woman screamed, and everyone took a few steps back.

"Unwrap him and set him free!" ordered Jesus. To begin with, nobody moved. Finally, it was the ever-practical Martha who responded, closely followed by her sister. Together, they removed the grave clothes that they had so carefully put in place only four days previously. They started at the top, and there was Lazarus' lovely face, smiling at them, blinking in the bright sunlight. Then his arms were free, and there were hugs and kisses and wild cheering from the crowd, high fives and hallelujahs.

"Increase our faith," the Disciples had requested less than a week ago. Now they would never doubt again. And what was more, dozens of others became believers that day also.

But there were some present who did not. Just as in Jesus' story, Lazarus was now the messenger, risen from the dead. And exactly as Abraham had predicted in that same story, those to whom Lazarus was sent did not believe the evidence of their own eyes. It was some of these sceptics who went to report what had happened to the Pharisees, in Jerusalem. Their report precipitated an emergency meeting of the Council.

"So what's going on here?" someone asked.

"Clearly, this man is performing some amazing miracles."

"If we let this continue unchecked, there'll be a popular uprising, and everyone will rally to his side."

"Yes, and before we know it, the Romans will clamp down on us and take away our national identity and our freedom of worship."

Caiaphas, the high priest, rose to his feet. "You really are an ignorant bunch," he said contemptuously. "We simply have to tackle this thing head on, stop pussyfooting around. He has to die. It is far better to sacrifice one man than that the whole nation should be placed in jeopardy." Obscured by his murderous intentions, it's doubtful if he had any idea of the almost prophetic nature of how his words might later come to be understood. The double entendre was also lost on his audience, for, from that day on, their intention was always only to kill Jesus.

11

The Lull

Clearly, Jerusalem would not be a safe place for Jesus; however, he was determined to be there for the coming Passover, which was still a month or so in the future. So they resolved to pass the time by taking a walk about, a loop that would lead them first north through Samaria, then doubling back over the Jordan to Perea. Perea had already proved itself to be a safe haven, and Samaria would be bound to be safe since Jews in general, and Pharisees in particular, tended to avoid the place.

On the border of Samaria, they encountered a group of lepers, Jewish and Samaritan untouchables. When they heard that Jesus was passing through, they approached as close as they dared and then shouted, "Jesus! Please help us."

"Very well," Jesus called back. "So go see the priest." Doing as they were instructed, those lepers set off to find him, and somewhere along the way the miracle happened. Just as soon as the priest had confirmed their health, they all ran off home to rejoice with their families – all except one, that is: a Samaritan who ran back to Jesus and threw himself at his feet, bubbling with thanks for what he had done.

"So what happened to the other guys?" Jesus asked. "I think I saw ten of you in the group. Are you the only one to come back and give thanks to God?"

Some of the Samaritan communities they passed through were less than hospitable and refused to accept a group of travelling Jews. James and John were so incensed that they were ready to call down fire from heaven, as Elijah had done in days of old. But Jesus told them not to be so silly, and they moved on to another town.

Eventually, they crossed the Jordan, relieved to be back in Perea. But no sooner was he recognised than some of the less friendly Pharisees made it their business to make life awkward for him.

"Is it lawful for a man to divorce his wife if he wants to?" Well, what had that got to do with anything? There were shelves of books written on the topic, and it was a subject guaranteed only to cause an argument. But it wasn't simply a debate they were after. King Herod lived just down the road, and his men were everywhere. It was Herod who had beheaded John the Baptist for speaking out against divorce, so divorce was a touchy subject around there. Nevertheless, Jesus addressed their question with the seriousness and grace that this painful subject demanded.

"Your reading of the Scriptures will have told you that it was God's idea to make human beings male and female. The plan was that opposites would attract; they would fall in love, get married, and enjoy sexual union. They would become totally one: one body, in fact. That union has always been God's plan, and making people one is what he does best, so people ought not to seek to pull apart what God has united as one."

"If that's so, how come Moses wrote the commandment that states that all a man needs to do is to give his wife divorce papers, and that's an end of it?"

"That was never a command, but merely a concession to human hard-heartedness, and it certainly was not part of God's original plan. To divorce so that you may marry someone else is to commit adultery, plain and simple. Of course, the adultery may already have been committed by the offending partner."

"Might be better in those circumstances just to stay single. Less complications," somebody suggested.

"Yes, but not everyone can live with that. If God gives you the grace to remain single so you can concentrate on kingdom matters, then go for it."

But happily, not everyone had gone for it, for the very next moment, a joyful group of little children ran up to Jesus. The Disciples tried to shoo them away.

"Don't stop them!" he said indignantly. "They are what the kingdom is all about." Jesus put his arms round them and hugged them close.

The Pharisees looked on disdainfully, with a supercilious, holier-than-thou expression on their faces. "Two men went to pray in the temple," Jesus said, raising his voice so everyone could hear. The children settled down, as they always do when a story is being told, and the Pharisees pretended they weren't listening. "One of the two was a Pharisee ..." (somebody giggled and gave a surreptitious glance in their direction) "... and the other a taxman.

"The Pharisee prayed in a loud, holy sounding voice: 'O God, I thank you that I am not like other people. I'm no thief, criminal, adulterer, and I'm certainly not like that taxman over there. Instead, I fast and I tithe my income.'

"But the taxman stood in a corner with his head hung low, wringing his hands. 'God, I'm so sorry, so sorry. Please forgive me. I'm such a sinner.'

"With which of the two would you imagine God was best pleased?"

Then, addressing his Disciples, he said, "Come on. We'd best be moving." So they set out in the direction of the river and Jericho on the far side.

———————————

They crossed the Jordan and were approaching Jericho. Jesus was striding on ahead, with determination in his step. "It's to Jerusalem we are headed, guys," he called. "You know that, don't you?" They knew the danger full well and so were not wild about the idea. "And in case you are harbouring any false hopes, let me remind you that when we get there, I will be betrayed to the religious authorities, who will condemn me to death and consign me to the Gentiles, who will ridicule, abuse, and finally crucify me. But on the third day, I will be raised to life once again." But they were at a complete loss to grasp what he was talking about.

Sitting beside the road into Jericho was a blind man named Bart. This was a good time of year for a panhandler, for thousands of pilgrims would be passing en route to Jerusalem for the Passover. Bart was no wallflower, sitting there with his hat out, hoping to be noticed. No, as soon as he heard footsteps approaching, he would call out for contributions. On that day, he made out the sound of a whole crowd coming down the road. "Hey! What's going on?" he demanded.

"It's that Jesus from Nazareth that everyone's talking about. He's coming to town."

Now Bart had heard rumours about Jesus, about his ability to heal blind people. The story that had piqued his interest the most was of a young fellow in Jerusalem who had been healed, except this guy, it was said, had been born blind. Bart had only gone blind as a child, so he remembered what it had been like to see. Surely this Jesus had to be the long anticipated Messiah, the one they said would be a descendant of David.

Bart wasted no time wondering if he had it right. This was a once-in-a-lifetime opportunity. So he immediately started yelling at the top of his lungs, "Jesus, Son of David, help me! Jesus, Son of David, help me!"

The people at the front of the crush told him to pipe down. He was spoiling the peace. But that only made him the more determined, and he yelled all the louder.

When Jesus made out what the shouting was about, he came to a halt. "Bring that man over here," he ordered.

Those who had been seeking to repress the irrepressible Bart walked over to him: "Cheer up, mate. This is your lucky day. He wants to meet you."

Bart sprang to his feet, threw aside his precious blanket, and tapped his way forward. Realising that he couldn't see where he was going, others steered him in the right direction.

"So, what do you want me to do for you?" Jesus asked when he reached him. It didn't take omniscience to diagnose the problem. The man was blind. Anyone could see that. So it wasn't Bart's problems Jesus was asking to hear, he wanted to hear Bart telling him of his hopes: what he wanted Jesus to do about his problems. Huge difference.

"Lord, I want to see." Eager expectation was written all over his sightless face.

"Faith! Yes, receive your sight."

To dare to want is the seed of faith. Suddenly, the light came flooding back in, and Bart could see again. If his shouts for help had been loud, his shouts of praise were louder. Soon the whole crowd was clapping and cheering, and it was a noisy throng that marched into town. The tumult threatened to dislodge the few remaining stones in the wall that hadn't come down in the days of Joshua fifteen hundred years previously, and the whole population turned out to see what was happening.

Bart hadn't been the only citizen of Jericho anxious to meet Jesus. On the other side of the tracks lived a wealthy man named Zacchaeus. He suffered from dwarfism, and his diminutive stature had restricted what he could do for a living, so he had pursued a career behind a desk. On graduating, he had signed on as a tax collector for the government, lining his own pockets by extorting from his fellow citizens a few more percentage points than was legally required. He had proved good at his job and had risen in the ranks till he was in a position to employ a gang of lackeys to do his legwork for him.

In Jericho, Zack was almost universally loathed. It was a lonely, empty life, and Zack longed for change. He too had heard reports of the teacher from Nazareth, his miracles, and the revolutionary philosophies he had been preaching. Could this man possibly be his salvation? Yet the chance of an opportunity to seek his counsel was remote to the extreme. Now here he was in town, so it would be nice at least to see what he looked like. But what chance had a little sawn-off runt like him of being able to see over the heads of the crowd?

So Zack used his head, as he had always done. He picked a spot on Main Street where the procession was bound to pass, found a tree with stout overhanging branches, and, with considerable difficulty, pulled himself up. Now he had the proverbial bird's-eye view, and all he had to do was wait. Hidden as he was above eye level, no one would notice his demeaning perch, so he could see without being seen.

The clamour of the approaching throng grew imminent, and soon people were passing right underneath where Zack was sitting. Then there was the man, clearly the centre of attention, with some of the respected members of the community chatting with him as they walked along. For some inexplicable reason, at that very moment, the man looked up, and for a moment, they made eye contact. There was a look of recognition in the man's face, as if he already knew him. He stopped and smiled up at him. "Hi Zack! Come on down from your tree. I'm coming to your place for supper. Okay?"

Hardly knowing what he was about, Zacchaeus scrambled down. The crowd parted, and he found himself embraced by this stranger, who greeted him like an old friend. "Yes, please come to my home. You are most welcome."

Judging by the muttering from the crowd, this was not a popular move on Jesus' part. There were better places to eat in Jericho than chez Zach: "He is going to be the guest of that nasty little man."

His henchmen rallied round as Zack snapped his fingers, and in short order, a meal was prepared in the fine courtyard of that grand house.

When the food was all eaten, Zach rose to his feet. "Stand up!" somebody shouted to a chorus of laughter. But Zack held up his hand for silence.

"Ladies and gentlemen, I have an announcement to make. From this moment onwards, things are going to be very different around here. I propose to give 50 percent of all I own to charity, and what is left I will use to repay all those I have ripped off over the years: with interest, mark you." There was raucous applause and much table thumping.

Then Jesus rose and motioned for silence. "Today salvation has come to this house. Zacchaeus, now I can see the family likeness! You really are a son of Abraham." More applause.

Jesus turned with a big smile and said quietly to his Disciples, "This is what it's all about, don't you think? This is the whole reason I am here: to seek out and to save lost people."

But the speeches weren't over. Everyone knew of Jesus' storytelling acumen, and to have a raconteur in the house without him telling a story would have been unthinkable. Zack tapped his glass for silence and then motioned to Jesus that the floor was his.

"Once upon a time, a man of aristocratic birth – no names mentioned – travelled to Rome to seek from the emperor to be acknowledged as king in his own homeland." (Everyone present knew of whom he spoke: their own King Herod Archelaus.) "Before he left, he summoned his most trusted stewards, giving them each a bag of cash. 'Put this to work,' he instructed them. 'See how much you can make it grow by the time I get back.'

"His bid for the throne was successful, and on his return, the new king summoned his stewards in order to settle accounts with them.

"'Sir, I am pleased to inform you that I have managed to increase your investment by 1000 percent,' announced the first.

"'Good for you,' praised his master. 'You have proved yourself trustworthy in this small matter, so now I will trust you with greater things. I want you to oversee the affairs of the following ten cities.' And off went the newly appointed mayor.

"Next in line was another man, who informed his master that his investment had increased 500 percent. Again the king was understandably pleased and made him mayor of five cities.

"The last man in was defiant. 'Here's you bag of cash, just as you gave it to me. I'm afraid your reputation in business circles didn't make my job very easy. People seem to think that you are always taking advantage of them, always ripping them off. So I hid your money so it wouldn't be stolen, and now here it is intact.'

"'You lazy scoundrel! If that was what you thought of me, why didn't you put my money on deposit at the bank, so I would at the very least get some interest on the investment?' Then turning to his bodyguards he ordered, 'Take the money from this wretch and give it to the man whose investment did the best.'

"The moral of my story is, that if you are faithful in little things, like money, then you will be entrusted with greater things, like people. The more you succeed, the more you will be trusted. But the more you waste, then the little you have will eventually be taken from you.

"And so, Zacchaeus, you are this day entrusted with much: with people from now on, since your money is now invested in others rather than hidden in your own interests."

12

The Storm

Early next morning, they were up with the larks and striding towards the mountains to tackle the rugged winding road up to Jerusalem, some four thousand feet above them. It was a tough slog, made the worse by a growing sense of apprehension as they drew closer to the city. What kind of hostility would be waiting for them? Twice they had narrowly escaped being stoned, and the rumour was that there was now a price on Jesus' head, a reward offered by the Sanhedrin for information that would lead to his arrest.

They arrived in Bethany just before nightfall and headed straight for the house where their friends lived. But the place was in darkness. No one home. Their disappointment was eased by a note pinned to the door. "Come to Simon's house" it read, so off they went. Simon, once an outcast leper, but now thankfully restored by Jesus' loving touch, lived in a large house, presumably a better venue for the dinner party.

The meal was a happy event. There was Simon, their host, happy to be once again in the company of friends. A smiling Lazarus was clearly enjoying his new lease on life. Even Martha seemed relaxed on this occasion and well in control of the catering operation. Mary? Well, she was her usual self: not a lot of help to Martha, but bubbling over with the joy of just being with Jesus.

When the meal was all done, and everyone was relaxing in peaceful contentment, Mary left her place and picked up a bag from the corner of the room. From it she pulled an alabaster jar, clearly very precious. She approached the place where Jesus was reclining and stood for a moment behind him. Then, apparently without a thought for its value, she snapped open the neck of the jar. Kneeling down, she began to pour the contents onto Jesus' feet, and lovingly to apply it with her long black hair. Instantly, the whole house was filled with the fragrance of the nard, a very expensive imported perfume. The loveliness of her worship was a thing of extreme beauty. The conversation died away to an awed silence.

"This is preposterous!" came an outraged protest from further down the table. "That nard has got to be worth a whole year's income! Should have been sold and given to help the poor." Judas! The truth was, he didn't care a fig for the poor, but he was obsessed with the bottom line. That's why they had made him treasurer. But everyone suspected him of helping himself from the kitty, so this outburst was fairly typical.

But the thread was broken, the moment of worship violated.

"Leave her alone!" Jesus said sharply. "What she is doing is simply beautiful. You can address the needs of the poor any time, but you won't have me for much longer. In fact, what she is doing is to begin the process of anointing me for my burial. This act won't be forgotten but will become part of the story to be told all over the world."

A seed of resentment was planted in Judas' heart. How dare Jesus rebuke him, and in front of the whole gang too! He had heard about the reward offered by the authorities for Jesus' arrest. Perhaps …

Next day, being the Sabbath, they took a day off. There's nothing like a day of rest to get your strength back and to sort out your priorities. And if ever a week would require these two benefits, then surely this was to be it.

On Sunday morning, Jesus dispatched a couple of the Disciples to go into the village, where, he confidently assured them, they would find a donkey and her foal tethered outside someone's house. "Bring them to me."

"But what happens if we are caught filching the animals?" they asked.

"Just tell whoever stops you, 'The Lord needs them.'" And so it happened. But when they arrived, it seemed the owners were expecting them, and not only the owners. Word had got out that Jesus was in Bethany. Crowds of eager spectators came flooding into the village, anxious to see Jesus, perhaps some also wanting to see the now famous Lazarus, who everyone knew to have died and come alive again. In fact, Jesus had many new aficionados in Jerusalem precisely because of that event.

Rather than cooling down over the past few weeks, public tension had heated up dramatically, and the authorities were now wondering if they would not have to kill off Lazarus as well as Jesus to put a stop to all this foolishness.

The two Disciples had a hard time getting back to Jesus with the animals because of the crush. The notion of Jesus riding into the city mounted on a donkey, for all the world like a king, seemed to appeal to the fans, for they threw their cloaks over the beast and helped Jesus up into the improvised saddle. And so the procession started up the slope to the summit of the Mount of Olives.

There, with a panorama of the city spread out before them, Jesus halted. To the amazement of those closest to him, they saw tears coursing down his cheeks: "Oh Jerusalem, Jerusalem! You have murdered all the messengers ever sent to warn you. Devastation is all I see for you now. How many times I have longed to gather you to safety, as a hen gathers her chicks under her wings, but you stubbornly refused. Oh Jerusalem, Jerusalem. But one day you will recognise me for who I am and bid me welcome."

But most people in the crowd didn't see his grief. They were in the mood for a party. Someone shouted at the top of his voice, "Hosanna! Long live the king! Hosanna to the son of David!" Immediately, others took up the shout, and before anyone could stop them, the whole crowd was shouting, "Long live the king!" This was not at all to the liking of the Disciples, who would have much preferred a low-key or even secret entry to the city. Was Jesus crazy to have permitted such a high-profile arrival? Didn't he realise that the most powerful men in town were after his blood?

But there was no stopping the crowd now. As Jesus began the descent into the Kidron Valley, people were stripping off their cloaks and laying them in the road before him. Others were breaking off branches from the trees or picking up palm fronds, waving them in salutation.

A sympathetic Pharisee got close to Jesus and shouted to him to keep the noise down. "It's asking for trouble to draw attention to yourself like this," he urged. "Tell them to be quiet!"

"Can't be done," Jesus called back. "If the people were quiet, then the very stones of which the temple is built would take up the shout. And anyway, they are only doing what the prophet Zechariah predicted centuries back: 'Shout and cheer children of Zion. Look! Your king is coming, bringing salvation, gentle and riding on a donkey with its foal.'"

Of course, thought the Disciples. Jesus had thought all this out way ahead of time. He had to do everything in accord with what had been written in the Scriptures.

The most voluble of the crowd were the youngest members, the children, whose boundless energy got them to the head of the procession. They were first through the Golden Gate into the temple.

"Hosanna to the son of David," they shrieked at the top of their excited voices. That got the immediate attention of the chief priests, who came running.

"Stop all this noise!" they shouted. "This is the house of God!" By the time Jesus emerged through the great arch, the message of the children was unmistakable. "Stop them!" demanded the priests. "Do you hear what they are saying?"

"Why, yes," replied Jesus. "Don't you remember the words of the eighth Psalm: 'From the mouth of children you call forth perfect praise.' That's exactly what the house of God is for, isn't it?"

The temple was jammed with pilgrims, there for the Passover. This was the tenth day of Nissan, the day for each family to bring their proposed sacrificial lamb to the authorities for inspection, to ensure it was up to snuff. Soon the two groups became indistinguishable from one another: those presenting their lambs and those presenting Jesus.

So Jesus didn't stay long. When he had taken a good look round, he led his Disciples back the way they had come, to Bethany, where they returned the animals and once again enjoyed the hospitality of their friends.

Next morning, they were up early, even before their hosts, so they set off with no breakfast. On the top of the Mount of Olives, they spied a fig tree. It was covered with spring leaves but, on closer inspection, offered no fruit, since it was way too early in the season. However, it should at least have borne the edible buds that fig trees present as their version of blossoms. That might have taken the edge off their appetites till the markets opened. But no! Nothing but leaves. "No one is ever going to eat fruit from this tree!" Jesus declared sternly. "No buds, no fruit! You can depend on it."

On entering the temple, they saw lots of action. Priests were scurrying in every direction; programmes of all kinds were in session; seminars on every topic were being offered to the inquiring. Blocks of stone and builders' scaffolding were evidence of the reconstruction that had been going on for the better part of the last half-century. But Jesus was looking for something, searching hungrily, just as he had hunted through the leaves on that fruitless fig tree.

"What are you looking for, Lord?"

"Why, for the people who are praying, of course. All this action is nothing more than leaves. But no buds, no fruit. No prayer, no harvest. This is meant to be a house of prayer for the nations, but instead it is nothing but a commercial enterprise."

So saying, he walked up to a nearby table on which a money exchange had been set up and deliberately pushed it over, scattering coins in all directions. The priests had some notion that only the right kind of coinage could be used for donations in the temple. Coins displaying impressions of the emperor were considered idols, since Tiberius Caesar was worshipped by some as a deity. That scruple gave rise to a whole new industry for moneychangers, who made a fortune since they were free to set whatever exchange rate they chose.

From there, Jesus strode over to the livestock enclosures. There were cages full of doves. The lids of these Jesus flung open, releasing scores of startled birds into the morning sky. The most obvious were pens for the sheep, year-old lambs, all ready for the Passover celebration at the end of the week. There were thousands of them, cumbering up the great Court of the Gentiles in the temple. This too was a thriving industry, since all animals sacrificed were required to be without blemish. The inspectors, in cahoots with the vendors, had but to fail the odd animal and thereby obligate the pilgrim to sell it off at a reduced price so they could purchase the perfect specimens on offer round the corner. These perfect beasts, if truth were told, were but the recycled rejects of the previous pilgrims!

Such crooked commercialism made Jesus see red. He flung open the pens and waded in amongst the startled animals, herding them out into the throngs of early-morning pilgrims.

Fighting their way through the fleeing animals came a gaggle of red-faced Pharisees. "What do you think you are doing?" they demanded furiously.

"It is clearly written in the Scriptures: 'My house will be known as a house of prayer for all nations, but you have reduced it to a den of thieves."

Everyone knew the crooked nature of the temple market, and most were tired of being ripped off. So, seeing what was going on, they started to cheer: "Bravo! Good for you! Well said."

There was little the Pharisees could do in the face of Scripture and popular approbation, so they withdrew, leaving the merchants to round up their scattered livestock. Murder was the topic of their conversation when the Pharisees got back to the safety of their cloister.

Jesus had underscored the Scripture that designated the temple a house of prayer for the nations, and it was to the temple that the nations were coming to pray that Passover. The thousands of pilgrims who flooded into the city included some Greeks, Gentiles from beyond Israel's borders. A group of them got into conversation with Philip, whose parents had some Greek connections so had given him a Greek name. Philip understood their language. He lived in Bethsaida, not far from the border with Decapolis, where many Greeks lived. They pumped Philip for information on this Jesus, about whom everyone seemed to be talking. "We would like to meet him," they told him.

Philip wasn't sure what to do, since Greeks, who he took to be intellectuals, always made him nervous. So he asked Andrew.

"Let's go and tell Jesus," Andrew wisely suggested.

But what Jesus said to those foreigners was certainly not designed to impress clever Greeks. Instead, he talked agriculture. He likened sowing a grain of wheat in the ground to gain a harvest, to laying down one's temporal life to gain eternal life. Yet he confessed that he was troubled at the imminent prospect of his own life being laid down, or more precisely, lifted up, as in crucifixion.

"But we thought that the Messiah was meant to live forever, so why this talk of dying?" the Greeks asked.

"I have come to the world as light. Walk in the light. Trust the light. Be sons of the light." So saying, Jesus melted into the crowd and was gone, leaving the Greeks with bewildered expressions on their faces.

Next morning, as they were heading back into the city, there was that fig tree, shrivelled to its roots.

"Would you look at that!" exclaimed Peter. "That's the very tree you cursed only yesterday morning."

"Remember our conversation about faith under the mulberry tree a couple of weeks back? It only takes a little seed of faith, with no doubts, then you could even tell this whole Mount of Olives to be thrown into a lake, never mind a tree!

"Prayer is like blossoms, like the buds on a fig tree. If you have blossoms, then the fruit is almost guaranteed. And if you have the seed of faith, then the answer is as good as yours. But there can't be any breaks in the branches if you want fruit. And there can't be any breaks in your fellowship, any un-forgiveness between you when you pray. If there is, then forgive quickly, so that you may be forgiven by your heavenly Father."

When they reached the temple, it was obvious that they were expected, for the chief priests corralled Jesus before he could do any more damage to their precious market: "Who are you working for? Who authorised you to behave in this outrageous manner?"

"Well, that's an interesting question," Jesus responded. "I'll answer it, but first let me ask you a question, since you are experts in the law. John the Baptist's ministry, his preaching and baptism: was that God ordained or purely a human initiative?"

That shut them up. Everyone had hailed John as a prophet, so to deny him would not win them any points with the crowd, but to admit John was from God was to invite condemnation for their not having believed him.

"We don't know," they admitted, fudging the question.

"Well then, neither will I answer your question. But I'll ask you another question instead."

"Very well," they agreed, glad to change the subject.

"A man had two sons. 'Go work in the vineyard, son,' he said to the first.

"'No, I won't!' he answered, but later he thought better of it and went to do as he had been told.

"To the second son, the man gave the same instruction. 'Yes sir, right away!' was his quick response, but he never actually went.

"So tell me. Which of the two best pleased his father?"

"The first one, of course."

"Quite right. And likewise the tax collectors and prostitutes, who appear to have refused to obey the Father's commands, are now actually obeying and are entering the kingdom of God as taught by John. But not you, who were so quick to say 'yes' to God's commands. No. In the end you refuse to enter.

"And here's another story you might enjoy ..." There was little hope of that, since they hadn't enjoyed much of what he had said previously. But they had to listen, for the crowds were loving it.

"A man established a vineyard, then rented it out to tenants while he went on his travels. The agreement was that by way of payment, he would receive a share of the crop. But at harvest time, when the rent collectors arrived, the tenants refused to pay up. Not only did they not pay, but they actually abused the messengers, going so far as to stone some of them to death. More rent collectors were sent, but they suffered the same fate.

"Finally, the landowner sent his own son. *They are bound to respect my son,* he thought. But he was wrong. As soon as they saw him coming, those tenants conspired to do away with him: 'If we get rid of the heir, then the land will be ours to use as we please.' So they killed him.

"So here's my next question: When the landowner comes back to his vineyard, what will he do with his tenants?"

Knowing full well that they were walking right into a trap, they were forced to respond: "He will give those wretches a sticky end and will find other tenants who will share the crop at harvest time."

"Full marks! So the point is that the kingdom of God will be taken from you also and given to others, who will prayerfully produce fruit."

"Never!" they stubbornly insisted.

"So you say. But haven't you read the reference in Psalm 118 to an odd-shaped stone that the builders of the arch couldn't fit anywhere? So they laid it aside. The grass grew up around it, and people used to trip over it. But finally the builders came to the top of the arch, and that was where the rejected stone fitted perfectly. It proved to be the capstone.

"Sure it was painful to trip over that stone while it remained a snare in the grass, but woe betide anyone on whom that stone might fall, should it ever be dislodged from its proper position at the top of the arch."

If the religious leaders had been angry at the beginning of the week, they were apoplectic by Tuesday. "He's a wordsmith," they agreed. "We have to catch him in his words. If we could get him to say something that would put him outside the law, then perhaps the Romans would deal with him."

So they sent moles to infiltrate the crowd, specially picked Roman sympathisers.

"Hey Teacher," one called out. "Everyone knows you are a man of integrity, that you teach God's truths without bias or prejudice. We have a quandary you might be able to solve for us."

"Ask away," said Jesus, sensing a trap.

"It's about paying tax. [Groans from the audience.] Is it right to pay taxes to Caesar or should we refuse?"

Now they had him, a Catch-22 if ever there was one. Would he please the crowd by encouraging tax evasion, but thereby putting himself outside the law, or would he disappoint the crowd by giving the legitimate answer?

"You bunch of phonies, why are you trying to catch me out? Give me one of those coins that you use for paying tax." Someone spun him a denarius. "Whose face is this?" Jesus asked, holding up the coin.

"Tiberius."

"Right, and whose name is written on the coin? Read it to me, would you please?" Jesus tossed the coin back to the owner.

"'Tiberius Caesar, son of the divine Augustus.'"

"Well, since it has got his name and portrait on it, it must be his. So send it back to him!" The crowd erupted in applause. When they were quiet, Jesus continued, "But whose likeness is stamped on every human being? … You've got it! So give to God what belongs to him." Now there was respectful, prolonged applause. This was wisdom as they had seldom heard it.

In the crowd were some members of the party of the Sadducees, who famously refused to believe in an afterlife. Now it was their turn to come up with a trick question.

"Teacher, in the book of Deuteronomy, Moses wrote that if a man dies childless, his brother must carry on the family name by marrying his widow and siring children for him. Well, we had in our company seven brothers. The first died childless, so his brother married the grieving widow. But sadly he also died with no children. In the end, all seven brothers suffered the same fate. The last to die was the widow herself."

"Probably died of exhaustion!" someone shouted, to the amusement of the crowd.

When there was quiet, the original spokesman continued, "So our question is, if there were to be a resurrection, as our colleagues, the Pharisees, erroneously expect there will be, whose wife will she be?"

Now the whole crowd exploded with laughter.

"You have it all wrong," Jesus responded. "You have misread the Scriptures, which clearly teach the truth of the resurrection, and you underestimate the power of God to accomplish it. But you need to understand that in the resurrection, marriage will be no more, but people will be like angels. And yes, there are indeed angels, whether you believe in them or not.

"But returning to the question of the resurrection of the dead, did you miss the significance of what God said about our forefathers? 'I *am* the God of Abraham. I *am* the God of Isaac. I *am* the God of Jacob.' There is no past tense implied. God never said that he *was* their God, but that he *is* their God: present continuous tense. The living God is God of the living, not the dead."

Even the Pharisees joined in the applause while the Sadducees shuffled uncomfortably.

A scholarly Pharisee stepped forward: "Well said, Teacher. Now I have a question for you. In your opinion, which is the most important commandment of all?"

"Love God and love your neighbour! If you live by those two, all the others will automatically follow."

"Very well said, indeed. You speak wisely and well" – high praise from a Pharisee.

"So let me ask *you* something," Jesus' turn to ask a question. "Tell me about the Christ, his family tree. Whose son is he?"

"Why, he will be the son of David, of course." Everyone knew that.

"Well then, please explain to me how come in Psalm 110, David himself refers to the Christ as 'my Lord'? That's hardly the way a father speaks of his son, is it?"

It was at that point that a blend of grief and fury bubbled up in Jesus. Here before him were the theological teachers of Israel, yet they had missed the whole point of Scripture. They had failed to recognise their Messiah when he stared them in the face.

"Everything you fellows do is for show, isn't it? The way you dress; the special seats reserved just for you; the fancy way you insist on being addressed in public: 'Master!' No! You are all brothers. 'Father!' No! Only God is your Father. 'Teacher!' That designation is reserved for the Christ alone.

"Shame on you, you teachers of the law. You slam heaven's door in people's faces. You neither enter yourselves, nor do you permit others who want to get in to do so.

"Shame on you, you teachers of the law. In your missionary zeal, you travel halfway round the world to win a single convert and then train him to be twice as much a child of hell as you are!

"Shame on you, you blind guides, who confuse people with your teachings about which oaths are binding and which are not. What's wrong with simply telling the truth?

"Shame on you, you teachers of the law, with your nitpicking rules about tithing while you neglect justice, mercy, and faithfulness. You strain a fly out of your soup and then swallow a camel!

"Shame on you, you teachers of the law. You make a good show outwardly, but inside you are a mess of greed, self-indulgence, hypocrisy, and wickedness.

"Shame on you, you teachers of the law. You put flowers on the graves of long dead prophets, yet you are just like your forefathers, who stoned them to death in the first place.

"You bunch of snakes! You progeny of vipers! Do you imagine for one moment that you will escape being condemned to hell? I am sending you a new generation of messengers, but you will surely murder them, just as you have done in past generations. Their blood cries out for justice!"

13

The Valediction

They didn't go into the city on Wednesday, preferring to spend a quiet day amongst friends. They went up to the top of the Mount of Olives. From there, the view of the city was spectacular. Right before them was the temple. They could just make out a huge block of stone being hoisted into position by a crowd of sweating construction workers, hauling on ropes. The previous day, they had passed that section of the wall and had noticed the plaques and wreaths that people had affixed to memorialise their donations, ad perpetuity.

"Impressive, don't you think?" remarked one of the Disciples.

"Yes, and there must be some generous people digging deep to make all this happen," someone else added.

"Well, actually things may not be quite what they seem," said Jesus. "I was watching the people putting their gifts into the treasury the other day. And yes, some of them were contributing large sums. But, by the looks of them, they could well afford it. Then I noticed this little old lady, poor as a temple mouse. She was holding a couple of cents, which she lovingly placed in the box. Do you know, I really think that was all she had in the world. That offering was more valuable than all the others put together."

"But those stones are really something, don't you think? I bet they'll last forever," put in another Disciple.

"Well, there you are wrong. In just a few years, they are all going to be toppled, the whole building razed to the ground."

"You're not serious! When is this going to happen?"

"Okay, I'll tell you." Jesus sat down on a stump, and the Disciples gathered round, eager to hear what he had to say.

"Wars and natural disasters will be only the beginning. Persecution will follow, but be sure to stand firm when that happens and get on with the job. For the gospel must be preached all over the world before the end will come.

"Daniel prophesied something that he described as 'an abomination that causes desolation' that would be set up, right over there," he said, pointing at the temple. "You won't know what that looks like till you see it, but when you do, then run for your lives! Don't look back! Just know that something terrible is about to happen, the worst horror that the world has ever seen. In fact, if it were not stopped, then the whole human race would be annihilated.

"Incidentally, false Christs will present themselves around that time, but don't be fooled. When I come back it will be as obvious to everyone as a brilliant lightning flash from east to west. Remember my warning.

"But, back to the terrible thing I was telling you about … Your attention will next be drawn to the sky above your heads. The sun, moon, and stars will grow dark, and it will be as though the very heavens are being shaken loose. And it will be while men are looking up that they will see the Son of Man coming on the clouds in great splendour. There will be a fanfare of trumpets, and angels will gather God's chosen ones from all over.

"You asked how you will know that this is about to happen? Well, just as soon as spring leaves begin to appear on the trees, then you can be sure that summer is not far away. Likewise, just as soon as these things begin to happen, then you can be sure that the time is close. That will be the very generation who will see it all.

"Exactly when will all this happen? Well, no one knows, not even the angels in heaven, not even me, actually. Just as the flood came in the time of Noah and took everyone by surprise, so will be my second coming. Two people standing side by side: one will be taken, the other left behind.

"So keep watch. Don't be caught out as by an unexpected thief in the night. Be vigilant like a servant watching for his master's return.

"Imagine a wedding party with ten bridesmaids keeping the bride company till the bridegroom should make his dramatic arrival. As you know, the custom is that he'll catch them napping if he can, so the trick is always to be ready. But on this particular occasion, the bridegroom was late, very late. It was midnight before the watchman shouted, "Here comes the bridegroom." The girls all turned up their lamps, but five of them sputtered and went out. No oil!

"'Lend us some oil,' five of the girls pleaded with their more prudent friends.

"'No way! Then we would all run out, and everyone would be in the dark. Go buy some for yourselves.'

"While they were gone, the groom did indeed arrive, and into the banquet hall they all filed. But when the negligent girls got back, the door was locked up tight, and their banging went unheeded. No one would let them in.

"The moral of my story is, Keep watch! You never know when the groom is coming. And that day will be judgement day, the day when the Son of Man comes back in glory, with all the angels. He will sit on a great throne, and all the nations will be gathered before him. A separation will be drawn, as when a shepherd separates his sheep from his goats.

"The king will invite his sheep to come forward: 'Come and inherit the kingdom prepared for you. Why? Because when I was hungry, you fed me; thirsty, you gave me a drink; homeless, you gave me a bed; cold, you gave me a coat; sick, you cared for me; and in prison, you visited me.'

"'We don't remember doing any of that,' the sheep will reply. 'When did we ever help you out?'

"'Whenever you showed a kindness to the most insignificant member of my family, you were doing it for me. Go, live forever.'

"Then he will turn to the goats. 'And as for you …' Off they will go to eternal punishment, for they did nothing to help the needy."

And all the while, on the hill opposite, the city continued in peace, safe behind its protecting walls. Thousands of people scurried like ants about their business, heedless that time was running out. There was something surreal about the things Jesus was telling them. Would the regular pattern of normality ever be changed as radically as Jesus was predicting?

"Come on. Passover won't wait. We'd best be on our way."

They all strolled back into Bethany, all except Judas. Making a vague excuse, he wandered off by himself. As soon as he was out of sight, he hurried back over the hill and into the city. He went straight to the temple and applied at the office for a meeting with the chief priests. When they heard who it was that was waiting to see them in the reception area, they quickly invited him in.

"How much would you be willing to offer me to lead you to Jesus in some quiet place, when no crowds are around?"

It was difficult for them to hide their enthusiasm, but in the interests of wise fiscal negotiations, they did their best to mask their eager smiles. A sum was agreed and the deal was shaken upon.

———————

Over breakfast next morning, Peter asked, "Lord, have you given any thought to where we might celebrate the Passover?" It would be far too late if he hadn't, since every suitable space would be reserved long since.

"Well, since you ask, Peter, why don't you and John head into the city. You will see a man carrying a pitcher of water. Follow him. He will lead you to the place I have booked."

The man stuck out like a sore thumb, since men rarely demean themselves with so domestic a chore! And follow him they did, till he disappeared into a doorway. Without hesitation, they banged on the door. "Excuse us," they explained to the man who answered. "But apparently you have a guest room here, reserved for our master and his friends to celebrate the Passover?"

Clearly they were expected, for they were led upstairs to a large room, all beautifully kitted out with table, chairs, and all the necessaries for the meal. They were thrilled and set about the process of meticulously ensuring that not a crumb of leaven could be found anywhere in the room. Such was the custom established by the law of Moses.

So it was with some excitement that the whole gang gathered at sundown in that upstairs room, theirs for the weekend and particularly for the Passover, next day. They took their places for an evening meal together, which the women folk had prepared and brought with them. Jesus sat in the centre of the table.

Conversation was animated as the guys waited for the women to serve the meal. At one point, the discussion further down the table took a more strident note. There appeared to be some controversy that was being argued back and forth across the table.

The focus of attention being drawn away from them, James and John, who were sitting either side of Jesus, took the opportunity for a confidential chat.

"Master," they began, "we know that this meal is like the hors d'oeuvre to the main event, the feast you will someday host in heaven. We want to ask you a favour."

"What's on your minds?"

"We want to sit next to you in that great feast, just as we are now, one of us either side."

"You have no idea what you are asking," replied Jesus. "Are you prepared to endure what I am about to go through?"

"Certainly are!" they assured him.

"Very well then. So you shall, but the seating plan for that great feast is out of my hands. I can't promise where you will be sitting."

So eager had they been in their request that they didn't notice that the discussion at the far end of the table had died away, and now everyone was listening in to what they were saying. The others were not amused. It came out that the very thing they had all been so passionately debating was which of them would be considered the greatest in the kingdom of heaven. Now it looked like they had been pre-empted by James and John.

Jesus said nothing, but when the conversation started again, he quietly got up from the table and walked over to the water jar in a corner of the room. He stripped to the waist and then ladled some clean water into a bowl. Putting a towel round his neck, he carried the bowl over to the table, knelt down beside the nearest Disciple, and began to wash the dust off his feet, drying them with the towel. Conversation died away, and once again there was an awkward silence. Jesus moved from place to place, washing and drying every foot as he progressed. Finally he came to Peter, but Peter pulled his feet back.

"Do you think you are going to wash my feet?" he demanded incredulously.

"You don't get the significance of this, do you, Pete? Perhaps later."

"Never! I'll never see why it should be you who would wash my feet."

"Peter, if I don't wash you, you have no place at my table."

A look of horror spread over Peter's face. "Well, then, Lord, wash me from head to toe!"

"No Peter," Jesus said, chuckling. "You smell just fine. You had a bath this morning, right?" Now everyone laughed. "It's not *how* you are washed that is important, but it's *who* washes you that matters."

When he had finished, Jesus dressed again and returned to his place. Every eye was on him. "Now tell me about this dispute of yours. Did you figure it out? So which of you really is the greatest?" They all shifted in their seats awkwardly. They hadn't realised that he had known full well what they had been talking about.

"You refer to me as your Lord, am I correct?" There were nods of assent. "So if I, your Lord and teacher, have taken the role of a servant and have washed your feet, ought not you to follow my example? You don't see me demanding to be served, do you? I have come to be a servant, in fact to give my life in the service of others."

The tension was eased by the arrival of the meal, and with some relief, they all tucked in.

Jesus raised his goblet of wine. "Here's something special to drink to. Next time I drink wine will be when I drink it new with you in the kingdom of God." They didn't understand quite what he meant, but assuming it was something to look forward to, they all drank enthusiastically.

There was a bowl of broth in the centre of the table in which they all dunked their bread – unleavened, of course, since it was the eve of the Passover. Jesus took a loaf of bread and held it up for them all to look at. "Listen up, everyone. I want you to remember this. This loaf represents my body – me." There he was, large as life. And there was the loaf, intact and unbroken. Then, with something of a shock, they watched as he ripped the bread into fragments. He held out to them the shattered pieces of the loaf: "This is how my body is being given for you. Eat it! It will remind you of me."

There was a slight pause while the bread was passed round the table. Then he continued, "But I have to tell you that one of you is about to betray me. It would have been better for that man if he had never been born." There was shocked silence.

"You are not serious!" blurted Peter.

"One of you dipping into this bowl, whose hands are resting on this very table, is going to betray me." Several hands were uneasily removed from the tabletop.

"Well, it's not me, I assure you!" asserted Peter.

"Nor me," said the one next to him. And so the protestations of innocence ran right round the table. No one noticed that Judas alone said nothing, but when the talk had resumed, he leant over to Jesus and whispered, "Do you think it's me?"

"I know it's you!" Jesus replied.

No one else heard this aside, and they were still discussing which of them it could possibly be, when Peter, who was sitting on the opposite side of the table from Jesus, caught John's eye. "Ask him who he means!" Peter signed.

John whispered the question everyone was asking in Jesus' ear.

"It's the one to whom I give this piece of bread," Jesus said, dunking the chunk of bread he was still holding into the broth. He shook off the drips and then passed it across the table to Judas.

John, who alone knew what this signified, was watching Judas' face. As Judas put the bread to his mouth, immediately he stiffened. His eyes went dark, and a demonic expression of sheer hatred twisted his face. The room felt chill for a moment, and the darkness around them seemed to close in.

"Do what you have to do, Judas," said Jesus. "Just do it quickly."

Judas rose from the table and left the room, walking out into the night.

As soon as the door had banged shut behind the retreating Judas, Jesus again raised his goblet of wine. Once again he gave thanks to God, then looking round the table: "This wine symbolises my blood, which seals a new covenant. It's for the forgiveness of your sins and those of many others. I want you all to drink it." He passed the goblet round the table, and they all took a draught. "Remember me!" he said. As if they could ever forget! "I won't be with you very much longer, and you can't follow me where I am about to go."

"Why ever not?" Peter blurted, dumbfounded.

"Simon!" (That was his formal name, so Peter knew full well that something heavy was coming.) "Simon, Satan has requested permission to take you out. But I have prayed for you, that your faith won't fail. I want you to use this experience in the future to help others who struggle in their faith."

Peter was shocked. "I am ready to die with you if necessary!"

"The cock won't crow tomorrow morning till three times you have denied that you even know me."

"Never!" yelled Peter, thumping the table, and they all chorused their agreement.

"The prophet Zechariah foretold that the shepherd would be struck down, and all the sheep would be scattered. It is written, Peter. It will happen. But when it does, remember this: I will rise again, and after I have done so, I will meet you back up north in Galilee. But in the meanwhile, I have to leave you. Sure it will be a sad time, especially since everyone else will be rejoicing that I am no more. But hang tough. Your tears will soon give place to joy, just like those of a woman in labour that are quickly forgotten as soon as the baby is born.

"But where are you going?" asked Peter.

"I'm afraid you can't come this time, Pete."

"But why, Lord? Why can't I follow you?"

"Trust me, Peter. I am going to my Father's house to get things ready for you to join me later."

"What, all of us?" someone asked, imagining the crush of a dozen guys crammed into one house.

"Don't worry!" Jesus replied, laughing. "There are lots of spare rooms! And anyway, you already know how to get there."

"Well actually, no," said Thomas, the realist. "We have no idea how to get there."

"You know me, don't you, Thomas?"

"Well, yes."

"So it's me, Thomas. I'll get you there. In fact, I am the only way. I am the truth – all you need to know is me. I *am* life itself – everlasting life. To know me is to know the Father."

Philip chimed in, "We'd love to see the Father. Can't you introduce us?"

"But you've already met him, Phil. Don't you recognise me? To see me is to see the Father. To hear me is to hear the Father. The Father is in me, and I am in the Father.

"Now I am going to ask the Father to give you a companion to take my place, someone who won't just live with you, as I have done, but will live right inside you. Just as I am in the Father, and the Father is in me, so we will be in you and you will be in us. I am talking about the Holy Spirit. The Father and I, represented by the Holy Spirit, will come and take up residence inside each of you. Then the Holy Spirit will be your teacher. He will remind you of all I have ever taught you and all I have yet to teach you. He will help you to understand me better. And he will enable you to give fearless testimony about me to others while convincing them of the truth of what you are saying.

"And now I have a new command to give you: 'Love each other, just like I have loved you.' That's how people will know if you are genuine or not. Love will be your hallmark. And the ultimate expression of love is to give your life for another. But don't expect the world to love you. They hate both my Father and me, so you will be in the very best company. I have warned you about this so that when I leave, my peace will be in your hearts and my joy will shine through you. Don't let your hearts be shaken. Don't be afraid. You are on the winning side."

"But why didn't you warn us sooner that all this was going to happen?" someone complained.

"Because you didn't need to know then, did you? I was still with you. Come on! Let's be going."

So saying, he got up from the table, and they all followed him out of the door, down the stairs, and into the night. The moon shone bright that evening, so they had no trouble finding their way out of town and into the countryside. They passed through the vineyards that covered the slopes around the city. Jesus paused for a moment so they could all catch up. When they were all there, he spoke to them, his words clear in the stillness.

"I am like one of these vines, and you are like the branches. My Father is like the vinedresser. He prunes you so you can be more fruitful." Then picking up a dead branch from the ground: "You can no more produce fruit without my help than can this branch. So, whatever you do, stay connected. Let my words ooze through you like sap. Ask with open hands, held out like blossoms drawing up life to produce fruit. Remember that fig tree? All you have to do is to ask; ask whatever you want in my name and the Father will give it to you. You don't have to wait for me to ask him on your behalf. No, the Father really loves you, so go right ahead and ask him direct. Then he will make you fruitful, and you will produce a bumper crop that will last forever."

There was silence for a moment, and then Jesus continued, "And now I am going to pray for you."

Right there in the corner of a vineyard, Jesus knelt, and they all knelt with him in a circle, arms over each other's shoulders. Raising his face to heaven, Jesus poured out his heart to the Father: "So it's time, Father. I have completed the task you assigned to me. I have brought glory to you on earth, and now you will bring eternal glory to me in heaven. I have shared life with these fellows, and now they will live forever, knowing both you and me. I am coming back to you now, but they have to stay here. Please Father, look after them when I have gone. I am sending them back into the world, just as you sent me. But the world is a hostile place. I'm not asking you to rescue them *from* the world, but to protect them *in* it.

"So here is my prayer, Father. I want you to make them one. Just as you and I are one, may they also be one, one with each other and one with us, completely unified in love. Let that be the evidence that will make their message believable to others. And I further ask that those in subsequent generations, who hear and believe their message, will also share this unity of love."

When he had finished, they gave each other a squeeze and slowly got to their feet, glad of the darkness to hide their tears.

Jesus led them down to the bottom of the valley, where they jumped over a creek and moved into an olive grove known as Gethsemane Gardens.

It was late, well past bedtime, so they collapsed, exhausted, onto the ground. "Okay. You guys stay here. I am going to pray for a while. Peter, James, and John, why don't you keep me company."

They left the others and moved off with him a little way. Then he sat down. There was silence for a while, and then they heard a sob.

"What's the matter, Lord?" they asked. "Don't be sad!"

"I am sad enough to die! Stay with me, would you, and keep watch. Pray!"

Jesus got up and moved away a few steps, then fell on his face, apparently in anguish.

"Father, my dear Daddy. Please help me. You can do anything. If there is any other way, please don't let me have to go through with this ..." There was a long silence, broken only by his sobs. Then … "Very well, Father. What I want is not important. It's up to you. Your will is best."

To their acute embarrassment, the Disciples were fast asleep when Jesus next spoke to them: "Sleeping on the watch? Was it too much to ask for you to pray with me for just one hour? Now pray!"

They kept awake just long enough to hear him pray once again for his Father to rescue him. In his extreme anguish, Jesus appeared to be sweating blood. Through their sleepy haze, they discerned a stranger standing beside Jesus, an angel perhaps? But they didn't stay awake long enough to see.

"Get up and pray!" he said as he shook them back into consciousness. "Evil is near and you are in grave danger." They didn't know what to say to that, but as soon as his back was turned, they were out for the count once again.

As they struggled back into consciousness for the third time, they were immediately aware of shadows moving amongst the trees, menacing figures carrying lanterns and flaming torches, and armed with clubs and blades. And there was Judas, right in the front, clearly having led the arresting party to this spot that he knew well to be a place where Jesus loved to come for quiet prayer.

"Hi friend," Jesus greeted Judas. "What's up?" Judas stepped forward and embraced him. "Are you really going to betray me with a kiss?" Then, addressing the soldiers, he called out, "Who are you looking for?"

"Jesus of Nazareth!" came the gruff response.

"Well, that would be me," Jesus said, stepping forward.

The soldiers retreated a few steps, stumbling in the darkness.

"No need to be afraid," Jesus reassured them. "It's just me you want, right?"

A group of soldiers grabbed Jesus by the arms before he could make a run for it.

"So why the weapons?" Jesus asked. "I have been with you every day in the temple, and you could have taken me any time you wanted. But now, suddenly, you are treating me like a violent criminal."

It was at that moment that Peter launched himself into the fray, yelling like a banshee. He made a botched attempt to attack the leader of the group but only managed to give him a bloody ear. Instantly, a bristle of swords was at his throat.

"Stop this at once," Jesus yelled, pulling free from his captives and stepping between Peter and those about to kill him. "Put your swords away! Those who draw the sword generally wind up being killed by the sword."

Then reaching out to the wounded man: "Here, let me fix your ear."

The moment of crisis passed. "It's just me you want, right? So let these men go in peace.

"And Peter, I don't need your protection. There are legions of angels standing by at this very moment, but if they intervened, how would the Scriptures ever be fulfilled?"

Fearing reprisals for Peter's precipitous action, all the Disciples took the opportunity to make a run for it. A soldier made a grab at one fleeing figure and got a hold on his sleeve. Whoever it was got away but must have left buck-naked since the amused soldier was left with nothing but a torn cloak in his hand.

14

The Trial

Once safe from the flickering light of the torches, the fleeing Disciples stopped running and watched from the anonymity of the darkness to see what would happen next. They were panting hard and badly shaken. Jesus' arms had been bound, and he was being taken back towards the city, stumbling along the way they had come, jostled by the soldiers. Peter and John followed together at a discreet distance. In through the city gate the procession went and straight to the high priest's residence. The soldiers passed through an arch, and Jesus was lost to view.

"I'm going in," John hissed, running forward.

"Wait for me!" said Peter. As Peter panted to catch up, he saw John speaking to a girl who was holding the gate. She must have known him, for she opened the gate and let him in. Just waiting long enough to turn and beckon to Peter, John went on inside.

"So you are a friend of the prisoner, eh?" asked the girl.

"Who, me? No! Don't know him from a hole in the ground."

Peter felt ashamed, but at least he was in, unscathed. There was a fire burning, and several of the arresting party were holding their hands to its warmth. Nights were chilly up there in Jerusalem at that time of year, and Peter was shaking with cold or delayed shock. It had been dark in the garden, and it was unlikely that he would be recognised as the ear-slasher, so he moved into the circle to catch a little heat. He could now clearly see Jesus on the far side of the courtyard.

John, who apparently knew his way round the place, was close enough to Jesus to hear what was going on. Annas, the godfather of the high priest's household, was at the centre of the ring, with Jesus, still bound, standing before him. Annas had been high priest years ago, but now his son-in-law Caiaphas occupied that exalted position, yet the old man was still hovering in the background, unwilling to completely relinquish the reins of power.

"Firstly, I want to know about the people who are with you, those you call your 'Disciples,'" Annas rasped. John's blood ran chill. So they were all for it. But the old man continued, without waiting for an immediate answer, "Then I want to hear first-hand what is this nonsense you have been teaching."

"I have always spoken openly and publicly with no clandestine subversion. I'm sure your colleagues have reported to you all I have been saying, so why do you ask me now? Ask them if you want to hear it again."

Someone stepped up to Jesus and slapped his face. "How dare you address the high priest so disrespectfully!" he shouted.

On the far side of the yard, Peter, who by then was seated on a log by the fireside, winced when he heard the slap. Someone noticed his discomfort. "You have to be one of that man's followers then."

"Not me!" said Peter.

"But you have a northern accent, so you must be a Galilean."

"There are lots of Galileans. That doesn't make me his Disciple, does it?" Peter said, adding some colourful language to emphasise the point.

Jesus' cross-examination continued for some time through that long night. After a while, Annas retired, and Jesus was left for the entertainment of the soldiers. They wanted to see if they could get a rise out of him. It started with insults and names. Then someone suggested a game of blind-man's-buff. "Let's see if he'll do a miracle! Do you think he can see in the dark?" They blindfolded him, and then someone punched him in the stomach. "So give us the name of the man who just hit you!" And they all fell about laughing.

Just then someone really did recognise Peter, who was unmistakably shaken by what was happening to Jesus. He had jumped to his feet and was gaping across the yard, fists clenched.

"Hey you! I saw you in Gethsemane this evening. You *are* one of them." Peter recognised his accuser as a relative of the arresting officer whose ear he had slashed.

"No, I am not!" Peter insisted, once again embellishing his prose with expletives. The words were still on his lips when the sound of a rooster announced the approach of dawn.

Remembering Jesus' prediction, Peter whirled around and looked across the courtyard to where Jesus was being taunted. His blindfold had just been removed, and he turned to catch Peter's eye. For one moment they stood, looking at each other: Peter's face distorted with horror and shame, Jesus' with indescribable love and compassion. They held each other's gaze for what seemed a lifetime, then Peter turned and fled from that place and into the night. There in the darkness, he sobbed as only a broken man knows how.

———————————————

It was getting towards dawn when members of the Council started to arrive, one by one, groggy from their beds. Finally Caiaphas himself entered and called the Council meeting to order. A hush replaced the hubbub of conversation. He told them that during the night, Jesus of Nazareth had been arrested, and it behoved them to decide what should be done with him before the crowds would be around to confuse things. In any case, they had a busy day ahead, since it was Passover and the priests among them would be busy with the thousands of lambs to be sacrificed that afternoon.

Jesus was brought in between two soldiers. When he had formally identified himself, the high priest asked what charges they had in mind to bring against him. They didn't really have anything specific that could be described as a formal charge. A couple of witnesses were called. What they shared with the court was not exactly true, but there were shreds of truth in the mix.

"We heard the defendant threaten to destroy the temple."

"And did you believe him?"

The other blew the credibility of a terrorist threat out of the water by adding, "Yes, and he promised to rebuild it in three days." The court dissolved in derisive laughter, and the witnesses were dismissed.

No other witnesses were called, so the high priest called Jesus himself to the stand.

"Have you nothing to say in your defence?" he asked of Jesus. Up to this point, he had not been accused of anything credible, so Jesus said nothing.

"So what's this we hear about your claim to be the Messiah?"

"If I answer your question, you won't believe me. And if I were to ask you a question, you would not give me an answer. So there's nothing to be said."

The high priest made an expression of annoyance, and then he left his seat and walked to face Jesus in the stand.

"You, sir, are under oath before the judges and rulers of this land, and before God himself. I charge you then, by the living God, to tell us the whole truth. Are you the Christ, the Son of God?"

"Yes, I am. What you say is the truth." There was a gasp from all round the room. But Jesus wasn't finished: "The day will come when you will see me sitting at God's right hand, then coming in judgement, on the clouds of glory."

"That's blasphemy!" the outraged high priest roared, tearing his cloak. Then he turned to the Council: "What do you say, gentlemen?"

"Blasphemy!" they all screamed, jumping to their feet and shaking their fists. "We don't need any more witnesses. We have heard it from his own lips."

"So what's to be done?" the high priest put to them.

"Kill him!" they shouted as one. Some of them ran up and spat in his face. Then Jesus was led away.

There was, of course, a technicality that still had to be addressed. That court did not have the power to impose capital punishment. Only a Roman court could do that. They would have to take him to the Roman governor, Pontius Pilate, for their sentence to be ratified. They hated Pilate, and the feeling was mutual. There was no way that some religious misdemeanour would warrant death in Pilate's eyes. "So we'll leave it to you legal guys to come up with a political angle to this," Caiaphas said, turning to the lawyers.

Judas, who had accompanied the arresting party back to the high priest's house, had followed Jesus' cross-examination with interest. No one ever knew quite what Judas had been expecting the outcome to be, for he didn't live long enough to explain. But when the death sentence was handed down, Judas was very shaken. Perhaps he had been imagining that Jesus would work his accustomed magic and talk his way out of it, maybe even work a miracle. But condemned to death?

He jumped forward before the priests could leave the room and called out, "He is innocent, you know. You can't kill an innocent man." They just looked at him with contempt. Judas was sobbing by now. "I have betrayed innocent blood!" he howled.

"Why don't you tell that to someone who cares? That's your problem!" They all left to get on with the business of the day.

Judas just stood there for a moment, uncertain quite what to do. In the end, he ran after them, following them right into the temple. Still they ignored him, so he took the handful of silver they had paid him for his treachery and flung it at them. Then he turned and ran like a mad thing.

What happened next is not clear. Apparently, for some time Judas had had his eye on a parcel of real estate, a field that had formerly been used as a pottery, but was now worked out. It was situated over in the Hinnom Valley but still conveniently close to the city. Judas had signed an agreement to purchase, contingent upon the funds becoming available. In all likelihood, it had been the desire to facilitate this purchase that had motivated Judas' money-grubbing betrayal. To all intents and purposes, that field was already his, perhaps the nearest thing that he had to call home.

But for whatever the reason, it was to that field that the distraught man fled. It must have seemed a very poor trade, as Judas surveyed his intended acquisition that terrible morning. "What will it profit a man if he trades his soul for the whole world?" he had heard Jesus say. But for an acre of dirt?

In an agony of remorse, Judas made a clumsy attempt at hanging himself, but forensic evidence later suggested that the rope must have broken, causing him to fall to his death, disembowelling himself in the process.

The priests must have been aware of Judas half-completed real estate transaction, for when they heard what had happened, they later used the scattered silver to complete the purchase. They all agreed that those thirty silver pieces were blood money and so couldn't be used for any holy purpose in the temple. But to purchase a field that could be put to the ignoble use of providing a cemetery for foreigners? Well, that seemed appropriate.

Happily for the prosecuting Jews, Pilate was in town. Normally based in Caesarea on the Mediterranean coast, he was in Jerusalem just in case of trouble during the Passover feast.

Few men are at their best first thing in the morning, and Pilate was no exception. His mood was not improved by the irritating piety that prevented the Jewish leaders from entering his office lest they should thereby be defiled. So he went out to see what they wanted. They pushed before them a prisoner, already looking somewhat the worse for wear.

"What's the accusation?" he demanded in a bored tone.

"Well, if he weren't a criminal, we wouldn't have brought him, would we?" That didn't do a lot to improve Pilate's temper. He said nothing for fear of saying something he might regret. So they continued, "We have found this man guilty of corrupting our nation."

"Well then, take care of the matter yourselves. Don't waste my time!"

"Roman law forbids us from imposing the death penalty, and this is a matter that is relevant under Roman law."

"Oh yes, and how's that?"

"He discourages people from paying taxes to Caesar."

"Doesn't everybody?"

"Perhaps, but he's also setting himself up to be some kind of a king."

At this, Pilate motioned for his own soldiers to take charge of Jesus and had him brought inside.

"So is this true? Are you a king, the king of the Jews, perhaps?"

"I am not king of any earthly kingdom that could marshal military support."

"So it's true that you are a king, then?"

"If that's how you want to put it. But truth is what counts, and to affirm the truth is why I am here."

"Truth? What *is* truth?" Pilate spat, irritated, and went out to talk to Jesus' accusers. "Gentlemen, I can find no basis for a charge against this man."

"Sir, he causes trouble wherever he goes. It started up north in Galilee and has now spread here, to Jerusalem."

"He started in Galilee, did you say? So is he a Galilean then?"

When they assured him that he was from Nazareth in Galilee, a look of relief crossed Pilate's face: "Galilee is under King Herod's jurisdiction. So take him to Herod!" Problem solved.

As luck would have it, Herod was also in town for Passover, just a couple of blocks away. Herod had heard many reports about Jesus; in fact, he had known of him since childhood. He had vague recollections of his father being furious when some foreign dignitaries had come calling at the palace, asking for the one who had been born "king of the Jews." Now here he was, a grown man, still making the same ridiculous claim. Yes, there was much Herod wanted to know about Jesus. Besides, it would be interesting to see a real-life miracle first-hand.

However, the encounter was a disappointment. Jesus replied not a word to any of his questions and never rose to the bait of the vehement accusations thrown at him by the priests. In the end, Herod made sport of him and sent him back to Pilate, dressed up as something between a clown and a king: "'King of the Jews?' I don't think so!" Relations between Herod and Pilate, which had previously been strained, took a turn for the better from that day on.

Pilate went back to the accusing Council members: "Neither King Herod nor I myself can find anything about your prisoner that warrants more than a flogging."

"Sir, that may be true under Roman law, but we Jews have a law that says he ought to die."

"And what might that be?"

"Blasphemy. He claims to be the Son of God."

Pilate may have had little time for the nit-picking legalism of the Jewish faith, but superstition wasn't beneath him. This new revelation disquieted him. The last thing he wanted was to incur the displeasure of the gods.

So leaving the priests, he went back inside. "Tell me about your origins," he demanded. "Where exactly *are* you from?"

Jesus said nothing.

"Answer the question!" Pilate shouted. "Don't you realise that I hold your very life in my hand? I could release you or have you killed!"

"You only have that power because it was delegated to you from above." Pilate was uncertain whether his prisoner was implying that his authority was derived from Caesar or from God. "But the one who handed me over to you must carry the final responsibility for sin." Again, the man before him was being ambiguous. Was he blaming the high priest for his predicament, or was he going right to the top, pinning the blame on God? After all, who was finally liable for human suffering and injustice: the priests or the Creator?

Time was ticking, and a crowd was gathering outside in the street. When Pilate went out once again, determined now to release Jesus, he was greeted by shouts. Quite what they wanted was not immediately clear, but after a moment, it became obvious that they were demanding a prisoner be released. It was a custom that every Passover the governor would free one convicted criminal as chosen by the people. Three terrorists were due to be executed that very morning, and it appeared that the favourite was their leader, a violent man named Barabbas, responsible for all manner of murder and mayhem.

A sudden inspiration occurred to Pilate. He knew that Jesus had been popular with the people. After all, only a week ago he had been reportedly riding into town on a wave of popular adulation. And in any case, Pilate guessed it was sheer jealousy that was motivating the priests in their denunciation of this harmless if misguided man. Perhaps the popular vote would solve the problem.

Pilate motioned to the crowd to quiet down and then addressed them: "Ladies and gentlemen, it is my custom to release to you one prisoner at this time of year. I propose this man," he said, pushing Jesus forward, "Jesus of Nazareth, who says he is your king."

"Not this man!" someone in the crowd shouted. "Give us Barabbas."

Pilate was frankly amazed that they would prefer an antisocial terrorist over Jesus, but before he could ask why, the whole crowd was chanting, "Barabbas! Barabbas!"

"So what should be done with Jesus?" Perhaps they might still demand his release as well.

"Kill him!" someone shouted, and a moment later, the whole mob was yelling for his blood.

He turned to the Council members: "I really see no reason to have him executed, so I will have him flogged, and that's an end of it." Accepting no arguments, Pilate flicked his fingers, indicating that his soldiers should take him away.

Pilate went and snatched a bite of breakfast. His wife joined him, clearly not having slept well. "I had terrible dreams last night," she offered by way of explanation. "I dreamt about that man Jesus, who I understand you have in custody. You are to have nothing to do with him, do you hear? He is innocent, I tell you. Have nothing to do with him!"

By the time breakfast was finished, the soldiers had done their worst. Jesus was barely recognisable as the same man. Blood was matting his hair and beard. His face was cut and bruised, one eye swollen shut. Following his flogging, someone had covered his lacerated back with the gaudy cloak that Herod had supplied, and a ring of spiky thorns had been twisted round his head like some kind of royal crown. He was a pathetic sight, no threat to anyone. Surely if the crowd were to see him now, they would be bound to show some pity.

Pilate went out and called for silence. "I present to you Jesus and declare to you all that I find no basis for a charge against him. Here is your king!" Jesus stumbled through the open door. There was a gasp from the crowd, and then one of the priests shouted, "Crucify him! Crucify him!" and before long, the howl had been taken up by the whole pack. How easily people can be manipulated!

One of the lawyers representing the Council stepped up to Pilate and spoke quietly into his ear: "With all due respect, sir, to let this man go free would be disloyal to Caesar. Surely anyone who sets himself up to be a king is guilty of treason against Caesar." Pilate, who was already out of Caesar's best books, could ill afford an unfavourable report being sent about him to Rome. So this stroke of legal genius delivered by the clever lawyer was the final nail in Jesus' coffin. For Pilate, there was no way round this. Jesus had to go.

Pilate took his place on his judge's seat and had Jesus brought before him. "So this is your king," he said, scornfully disparaging the Jewish people in general. "Would you really have me crucify your king?"

"We acknowledge no king, but Caesar!" the lawyer shouted so that all could hear. And the priests chorused their agreement. Now there could be no turning back.

Pilate called for a bowl of water and a towel to be brought. He stood up before the assembly and washed his hands, drying them on the towel. "I wash my hands of this matter. I am innocent of this man's blood."

"Then let his blood be on us and on our children!" the priests readily agreed.

Pilate motioned to his soldiers to take him down then turned and walked away.

15

The Execution

Jesus was still dressed up in Herod's gaudy outfit, so they gave him back his own clothes for his final walk. Then they marched him off to be executed, together with the two remaining terrorists. Each man was forced to shoulder an eight-foot timber that would soon become his gibbet. Around the neck of each man hung a placard spelling out his crime, so no one could be in any doubt. "Jesus of Nazareth – king of the Jews" read Jesus' sign.

The narrow streets of the city were already packed with throngs of pilgrims, even though it was barely nine o'clock. But many of Jesus' supporters, who had heard the shocking news of his arrest, now surged forward to see what would happen next. The soldiers had a tough time clearing a passage for their condemned prisoners to pass. Jesus was close to collapse from the ordeal that he had already been put through since the early hours of the morning, but he staggered resolutely forward. Inevitably his knees buckled before he had gone but a few hundred yards, and he collapsed to the ground, his burden crashing down on his lacerated back. Despite the kicks and threats of his captors, there was no way he could regain his feet under that load.

To carry the crossbeam was below the dignity of the soldiers, so they waylaid a passerby, demanding that he carry the wretched beam. Judging by his swarthy complexion, the man they picked was clearly a foreigner, so he would be unlikely to cause a fuss. They pulled Jesus to his feet, and he staggered forward, with his burden-bearer walking behind him.

When he had caught his breath, Jesus thanked the man for his help.

"I'm Simon," the voice behind him said. "I live in North Africa. In town for the festival."

"Do you have a family back home?" enquired Jesus.

"Yes, a couple of lads: Alexander and Rufus."

Most of the crowd that surged along behind them were men, but a number of women had somehow pushed their way to the front. Their presence was unmistakable because of the wailing lament they kept up.

Progress was slowed to a halt for a moment as the soldiers fought to make way for their prisoners. Jesus took the opportunity to speak to the grieving women. "Don't weep for me, ladies, but rather weep for yourselves and for your children. Tough days are ahead, when you will wish you had no children to worry about. In fact, everyone will be wishing the mountains would fall and bury them. If they can kindle such a flame with a green plank of wood," he said, indicating Simon's load, "imagine the inferno that will rage when it's bone dry?"

Out through the city gate they passed, till they came to a hillock whose cranial shape caused it to be known as "Skull Hill." It was a public place, close to the city gate, beside a main thoroughfare, so ideal for an execution. A number of permanently set poles crowned the top of the hill, and at the foot of three of these, the condemned men threw down their burdens. Someone thoughtfully offered Jesus a drink that might have done something to take the edge off the pain of what was about to happen, but he refused, determined to have his wits about him.

The soldiers stripped Jesus and then pushed him to the ground, his back over the beam. Three men held him down while a fourth took a hammer and nailed each wrist to the wood. Then the beam was hoisted high on the pole and slotted into position. Finally, his feet were nailed to the upright. The finishing touch was his placard – "King of the Jews" – nailed over his head. It was thoughtfully written in several languages so that the multi-cultural crowd could all understand.

"With all due respect, sir," objected the Council's lawyer to Pilate, when he saw the notice, "it would be more accurate to say that he *claimed* to be king of the Jews."

"I have written what I have written," snapped Pilate dismissively. So the sign stayed.

It was a pitiful sight: three criminals condemned to die a terrible death, hanging up for all to stare at. As the prophet had long ago foretold – "He will be numbered amongst criminals" – and there was Jesus, nailed between two of them.

Blinking away the blood and tears, Jesus could now look down on those who had just crucified him. "Father, please forgive them. They have no idea of the significance of what they are doing," he choked. John, standing in the front row, remembered how Jesus had talked about loving your enemies. So this is what he had meant.

With their grisly duty completed and nothing more to be done till all their charges were dead, the soldiers settled down to their vigil. One of them had brought a couple of dice so they could gamble the boredom away. Jesus' clothes were shared out between them, but the coat was a fine piece of work, presumably woven by a loved one. Perhaps she was in the crowd somewhere? But what did they care? They rolled the dice to decide which of them would take the prize.

And standing close by were three Marys: Jesus' mother, his aunt Mary, and Mary from Magdala. John was there too, doing his best to comfort the womenfolk.

As soon as Jesus became aware of their presence: "John!" he rasped. "Hey John. Look after my mother. Take her home, John. Take her now." John put his arm round the broken old lady. "It's okay, Mother," Jesus said. "Go with him now."

John led the weeping figure through the crowd and took her away. "A sword will one day pierce your own soul also," old Simeon had told the young mother thirty-some years earlier, when Jesus had been a newborn baby. Today, that sword had pierced deep.

There were crowds of passersby on their way into the city who stopped for a look-see. Some were surprised to recognise, if not the disfigured face, then the name on the sign above his head: "Isn't this the man who claimed that he could demolish the temple and rebuild it in three days?"

"Hey, you!" someone shouted at Jesus. "Come down off that cross and we'll believe you."

"He may have claimed to be able to save others, but look at him now! He can't even save himself!" someone else jeered.

Members of the Council were there to gloat over their erstwhile tormentor: "So if you really are the Christ, come down off that cross, and we'll believe you."

Even the soldiers looked up from their game for a moment. There was the prisoner to whom they had paid mock homage earlier that morning, now here he was, their helpless victim. They couldn't resist adding to the taunts of the crowd. "Hey you! If you really are a king, then behave like one! Come down off the cross."

Finally, a spectator, a few skins of wine the worse for wear, staggered up to take his turn. "Hey, God," he prayed in mock reverence, waving his drink towards the cross. "This man claims to be your son. Even tells us that you love him!" Roars of derisive laughter rose from the spectators. "So if that's true, you won't want to disappoint him, will you? He trusts you. Come on, God! He's waiting. Rescue him; just about now would be a really good time!" The laughter knew no limit. But clearly, God so loved that he gave and gave and went on giving, refusing to withdraw his gift, no matter how unworthy the recipients.

Sensing the hostility of the people to their fellow sufferer, one of the condemned terrorists joined the taunts, perhaps hoping to garner some sympathy for his own plight. "Hey, Jesus!" he croaked. "Save yourself, for heaven's sake, and while you are at it, save me and my mate in the bargain!"

When the laughter subsided, the man on Jesus' other side called back, "Shut your stupid face! Don't you have any respect for God when you and I are hanging here, condemned to death along with him? The pair of us are only getting what we deserve for our crimes, but this man is innocent. He hasn't put a foot wrong." The crowd fell silent at this exchange, and for a while the only sound was the rasping of laboured breathing from the three men. Then: "Jesus! Don't forget me! Keep me in mind when you get to your kingdom."

"There's a beautiful garden waiting for us, and this very day you and I will be strolling there together." Sobs of relief and gratitude came from the dying man.

A strange thing happened after that. The sun refused to shine. It was midday, but the light faded, and darkness descended on the scene like a shroud. At first, there were exclamations of astonishment, then there were screams. But as it persisted, the people simply sat where they were. They couldn't see to go home, so they stayed put.

There was confusion all over the city. Not far away in the temple, thousands of lambs were due to be slaughtered for the Passover, but in the velvety darkness, everything was put on hold till lamps could be lit. "Just like the original Passover," somebody suggested. "Better get ready! Something's about to happen."

For three long hours, the darkness persisted. "People who do evil prefer darkness to light," Jesus had told Nicodemus three years earlier, so perhaps his colleagues were glad that they could not be seen.

At about three o'clock, the silent darkness was shattered by a cry of appalling desolation: deep anguish twisted from a soul in torment. It carried a sense of loss and aloneness in an infinite void of emptiness, a bottomless pit of despair: "My God, my God, why have you deserted me?"

Jesus had spoken in Aramaic, and those present who did not understand that tongue misunderstood his meaning. "I think he's calling for Elijah," someone suggested.

A moment later, Jesus spoke again, more quietly this time. Through cracked lips he rasped, "I'm thirsty!" Someone ran forward to give him a drink from a sponge on a pole.

"Leave him alone!" someone called. "I want to see if Elijah will come to rescue him."

Jesus took a suck on the sponge, just enough to moisten his mouth for his final words. He heaved himself up to take a deep breath, and then, with a shout of triumph, he called out for all the world to hear: "It is finished!"

Then he slumped down to hang once again from his wrists: "Father, I now entrust my spirit into your hands." So saying, he ceased to struggle and hung limp, still as death.

Two things happened almost immediately. Firstly, the afternoon sun stole back to illuminate the scene. There hung Jesus, eyes open and staring, heedless of the flies that buzzed and settled. His jaw was slack, and his mouth hung open. Blood still dripped from his toes and fingertips. But he was quite dead.

Next, the ground beneath their feet started to heave. The cross shook in its socket, and the body on it was jerked this way and that, still secured by the nails. The crowd screamed and scattered.

Then everything returned to normal, and there was a shocked stillness.

Even the soldiers, who had seen it all before, were unnerved. The centurion in charge of the execution was heard to mutter, "This must have been a righteous man, perhaps even the Son of God."

Meanwhile, pandemonium had broken out all over the city. The great stones of the temple shifted and threatened collapse and the huge curtain that guarded the holy presence of God from the prying eyes of the general public simply tore like a rag, top to bottom. Someone who had been walking through the cemetery at the moment of the quake reported seeing tombs split open and swore they had seen dead people emerging from the darkness.

Those who had been on Skull Hill hurried home, some to join their families for the Passover celebration that evening, but everyone anxious to put space between themselves and that terrible scene. Only the women who loved Jesus still stood watching at a distance, waiting to see what would happen next.

First, they saw a couple of priests approaching the soldiers who remained at their post. There was some shouting and gesticulating, then the soldiers seemed to concede. One picked up a two-by-four, approached the first victim, and without a moment's hesitation, smashed first one shin then the other. The terrible scream was cut off by merciful unconsciousness for a moment. Then the other terrorist got the same treatment. But when the soldier came to Jesus, it was obvious that he was already dead, so they spared him this final cruelty.

"Better make certain he's dead, though," the centurion said, and one of his men jammed his spear up into Jesus' side, under his ribs, and then twisted it so there could be no doubt. Unusual though it was coming from a man already dead, blood and water gushed out of the wound when the spear was withdrawn. John, who had by then returned from taking Jesus' mother home, witnessed this phenomenon. He had no doubt whatsoever what he had seen and of its significance. Blood and water flowed from Jesus' side.

Next, the attention of the watching women was attracted by the sight of two finely dressed men. They recognised them both as members of the Council, and their hearts sank. Would they never leave him alone?

They approached the centurion and showed him an official-looking paper. The centurion barked an order to his men, who pulled the spike from Jesus' ankles and then together lowered the cross beam with Jesus' corpse still limply hanging from its wrists. When the body was laid out on the ground, they pried out the nails and then motioned to the two Council members that they were free to proceed.

To the utter amazement of the women, the two men, heedless of their fine clothes, manhandled the bloody corpse down the hill and into a nearby garden. The women followed and watched as they laid him out on the grass. They had with them linen sheets and what appeared to be spices, a considerable quantity by the look of it. Darkness was fast approaching, and the Sabbath was just minutes away, so they did a rudimentary job of cleaning up the body and then wrapped him up to the shoulders in the sheets, folding in the spices as they went. Finally, they wound a bandage round his precious head, like an extended turban. When all was done to their satisfaction, they carried the bundle into the darkness of a cave, a tomb that appeared to have been hollowed out of the solid rock face. A moment later, they emerged once again into the dying light of the evening. There was the sound of a chock being knocked out of the way, and a grating noise told the women that a heavy rock had rolled into position, sealing off the entrance to the tomb.

Only then did the women hurry home. They later discovered that the two men had been Joseph of Arimathea, an important Council member, and Nicodemus, one of Israel's most respected teachers, also a member of the Council.

The next day was the Sabbath, so nothing much moved. The chief priests and Pharisees, however, were uneasy. They remembered what a Sabbath-breaker Jesus had been, so on this day of all days, they didn't trust him to stay put, even though they knew full well he was dead. To further heighten their fears, they recalled some wild claims Jesus had made to the effect that after three days, he would rise again. So off they went to further irritate Pilate. They explained their misgivings and asked that a guard be posted to keep the tomb secure. "It's not that we expect him to rise again, but we fear the likelihood that his followers will come and steal the body, then circulate the lie that he is risen. The consequences of that would be unthinkable."

"You have your own security men in the temple. Use them to guard your own fantasies. Be sure to seal that tomb up tight, mind," Pilate called after them. "Sure would be a terrible thing if a dead man were to escape!" He who laughs last ...

But they left nothing to chance, even going so far as to affix a wax seal to the closed entrance, lest there be any jiggery-pokery when no one was looking. But jiggery-pokery there was, just not the kind anyone had anticipated.

---------------------------- 16 ----------------------------

The Renaissance

Life is at its lowest ebb at four o'clock in the morning, and the temple security men outside the tomb were dozing. To them the whole assignment was something of a farce, so after a few cemetery jokes had been exchanged, they had taken it in turns for one of their number to stay alert, leaving the others free to sleep. Suddenly, an aftershock from the quake two days previously had them all wide awake and on their feet.

Their terror multiplied when a flash of lightning illuminated the scene. The massive rock that blocked the entrance to the tomb was moving. Was it the quaking of the ground that was making this happen? The lightning was no mere flash but continued to shed a dazzling light. Gradually, as their eyes adjusted to what was happening, they made out the figure of a man, if indeed he was a man, for he himself was the source of the light: intense, incandescent light. And he was pushing the rock, rolling it up the incline to reveal the darkness of the tomb. His task completed, the shining figure jumped up and sat down triumphantly on the top of the rock, looking defiantly down at them. So appalling was the spectre that they all dropped to the ground, out cold in sheer terror.

Moments later, when their wits returned, they found themselves once again in total darkness. There was no question of it having been a dream, for they had all seen the same phenomenon. As reason returned, one of them took a faggot from their fire and, showing remarkable courage, took a look inside the tomb. Sure enough, it was empty. The body they had been guarding was gone. Those big tough men simply took to their heels and ran for their lives in a blind panic.

Never had a Sabbath rest been so irksome a discipline to observe. Never had the practical women in Jesus' entourage so longed to have it over so they could get to the task they needed to accomplish but dreaded to tackle. Jesus' body lay on a cold slab, untouched by the loving hands of those who adored him most. As soon as the end of the Sabbath had been announced by the setting sun, the women had got together and began the task of preparing the spices for embalming. There was no sense in starting the process before daylight next morning, so they had contented themselves with mixing the spices and perfumes.

A half-empty bottle of very expensive nard had been contributed to the mix by Mary of Bethany. Tears flowed free as the women recalled the dinner party just over a week previously, when Mary had first opened the jar to anoint Jesus' feet. Jesus' mother also had contributed an ancient bottle of eastern myrrh that she had been keeping for this very purpose for the past thirty years.

So now in the cold light or dawn, the ladies were up before the sun, and sharing out their precious load, they set off towards the cemetery.

"One very practical thought, girls," said Salome, the mother of James and John. She had followed Jesus south from Galilee, helping with the domestic side of maintaining a dozen helpless men in their nomadic lifestyle. "My recollection is that the rock that seals the tomb is rather large. How are we going to shift it?"

"I'm sure we'll think of something," Mary Magdalene replied, ever the optimist.

The sun had just crested the horizon when they reached the cemetery. They knew nothing of guards having been posted to watch the tomb, so they were not surprised by their absence. But what did surprise them was the rock. Instead of blocking the cave, as it had been when they had left on Friday evening, it was rolled back. The tomb was open.

Cautiously they approached, uncertain what to expect. They put down their burdens by the entrance and peeped inside, but it was too dark to see much.

"What's happened here?" Salome asked.

"Why are you looking for the living in a place of the dead?" came an unexpected voice behind them. They swung round to find themselves face to face with a couple of strangers, whose cloaks appeared to be reflecting the rising sun with an unearthly radiance. Terror gripped the ladies, and they bowed their heads in respect.

"Don't be frightened," one of the angels reassured them. "We know you are looking for Jesus. But he's not here any longer. He is risen, just as he has been telling you he would be ever since you left Galilee. 'After three days I will rise again' – remember? Take a look for yourselves at the place where you saw him laid the other day." Obediently, the ladies stepped inside the tomb, which was indeed empty.

When they returned to the morning light outside, there was nobody there. The women stood looking at each other in astonishment. Then they turned and fled, abandoning their unused spices where they lay.

Mary Magdalene ran straight to the house where she knew Peter and John were staying. Breathlessly, she blurted out her news: "Someone has taken the Lord's body from the tomb, and we have no idea where they have put him." Somehow she missed the part about the angels telling them that he was risen.

Not waiting to ask further questions, the two men ran out of the house and sprinted to the cemetery. John got there first and stood panting at the entrance to the tomb till Peter arrived. Mary, who had already run the distance in the opposite direction, was a little slower in getting there. Peter never paused but bent down and ran straight into the cave, like a terrier after a rabbit. He stood in the gloom, gasping for breath and trying to make sense of what was before him. The tomb had obviously been very recently hollowed out of the solid rock. The mason had fashioned a stone shelf on which Jesus must have been placed by the two Council members, but there was no body there now. The linen sheets in which his body had been wrapped were still lying there, but it somehow didn't look right.

A moment later, John stood next to him. What amazed them both was that the linen sheets didn't appear to have been ripped off or even thrown aside. It was as though the body had simply evaporated, allowing the linen to sink down where it was. And there lay the bandage that must have been wound round his head, right where it should have been, but again, just empty space.

An inexpressible peace was born in John's heart at that moment. He believed and knew for certain that God really had raised Jesus from the dead. Everything from that moment on would be different. This was the dawn of a new day, the birth of a new world. Jesus really was Lord of all.

Peter, however, didn't know what to make of the evidence before his eyes. Three days ago, he had denied his Lord, and that still tore at his conscience. Now, mysteriously, Jesus' body was gone. Peter turned and walked back into the sunlight, confused and uncertain.

The two friends walked away, leaving Mary alone outside the cave. When they had gone, Mary gave in to her grief and let it all out. She cried till she thought her heart would break. When eventually her sobs began to subside, she noticed through her tears a light coming from inside the tomb. She bent down to look in, and there again were the two angels she had seen earlier, sitting at either end of the slab on which the grave clothes lay.

"Why are you so sad, lady?" they asked.

Well, that was a lame question, even from an angel. Wasn't it obvious? "Because someone has taken away my Lord, and I have no idea where they have put him." Unimpressed by this heavenly apparition, Mary turned away. All she longed to see, but never would again, was Jesus.

Then she realised that she was not the only one up early in the garden that morning. The gardener was there already, standing with his back to the rising sun, so it was hard to see his face: "Why are you weeping, lady? Who are you looking for?"

"Sir, if it's you who have removed his body, please tell me where you put him."

"Mary!"

"Teacher!" she gasped and threw herself into Jesus' arms.

For a long time, he hugged her as her tears turned from grief to inexpressible joy. And she would never have let him go had not Jesus gently pushed her away: "No need to hang on to me, Mary. I am around for a while yet, before I finally ascend back to my Father. Now he's your Father as well, you know: my Father is your Father, my God is your God. Go tell that to my brothers."

Reluctantly Mary left Jesus in the garden and ran to share the news with the Disciples – "brothers," as Jesus was now calling them. The room they had been using for the weekend was where she expected to find them, so it was to there that she hurried. Just before she arrived, she ran into Salome, the other Mary, and Joanna, coming in the opposite direction. They were laughing and all talking at once. "We have seen Jesus, alive!" they all told her as they united in happy hugs.

"I know," said Mary. "I saw him too." They shared their similar experiences. "I must tell the boys," Mary said, turning to go.

"We already told them, but they didn't believe us."

"Well, I'll tell them!" Mary announced, marching off determinedly. "They had better believe me!" But they didn't.

The leading priests over in the temple did, however, believe the security men when they finally plucked up their courage to report to HQ what had happened in the early hours of that morning. Messengers were immediately dispatched, and a few available Council members were hastily gathered to decide how best to address this new crisis.

"Word of this never leaves this room. Agreed?"

"Yes, but what about the guards? How will we keep them quiet?"

"Money talks, and money can stop people talking. We will pay them to circulate the story that the wretched man's followers came during the night and stole his body."

When the proposition was put to the guards, "All very well, sirs, but what happens if word of this gets to the governor? He'll have our heads for sure."

"We'll have a word with him. You'll be okay. Trust us." Whether or not they did is questionable, but the men left with fat purses, and the lie began to circulate. However, the fact that no body snatchers were ever arrested did much to undermine the credibility of their tale.

The holiday week being now over, the tide of pilgrims was in full ebb, everyone keen to get home and back to work. Amongst those who had spent the week in Jerusalem were many followers of Jesus. They had cheered his arrival, worried as the tension had heightened almost every day, booed at the injustice of his trial, and finally mourned at his execution and burial. Now there was nothing for it but to head back to normality, disappointed and disillusioned. There were conflicting rumours circulating amongst the crowds thronging the roads that led away from the city. There was the resurrection version of the story, contradicted by the official alternative: "his friends came during the night and stole the body." But everyone was talking of nothing else.

So when a couple of Jesus' erstwhile devotees were accosted by a stranger who appeared to know nothing of all this, they were understandably surprised at his ignorance.

"What are you guys looking so long-faced about?" he asked as they walked along, heads hung.

They stopped as the traffic flowed round them. "Same thing everyone else is talking about."

"And what might that be?" he enquired, innocently.

"Where have you been all weekend? You must be the only one here who is out of the loop."

"So tell me."

"Okay, so we were talking about Jesus, the man from up north in Nazareth."

"What about him?"

"You really don't know? Well, he was widely recognised as a prophet – except by the Council, that is. They disowned him and had him crucified just before the weekend."

"So how do you feel about that?"

"Devastated, of course. We were so sure he was the Messiah."

The stranger said nothing but nodded sympathetically. They resumed their walk, hustled along by the crowds. "But something really strange happened before we left this morning, and we are not sure what to make of it."

"What was that?"

"Well, some of the girls from our group went to the cemetery at dawn, only to find his tomb empty and the body gone. The icing on the cake was that they reported seeing angels at the tomb who told them that Jesus was alive. Fancy that, eh? Angels! A couple of the guys went to check it out, but they didn't see any angels. But, right enough, the tomb was empty."

"Excuse my saying it, but you guys really are such a bunch of dimwits. What's so difficult about believing that what the prophets foretold would surely take place? Ever since the days of Moses, the prophets have been saying that the Christ would suffer unjustly before being raised." The way he said it was so disarming that they couldn't take offence. And there was something familiar about the voice. They had heard it before somewhere but couldn't quite place it.

As they walked towards home, the stranger gave them a Scripture lesson like they had never heard before. He was an encyclopaedia of knowledge and could quote the prophets liberally. He made all the old familiar passages come alive, but through them all, they could see for the first time that it was all about Jesus. Their hearts thrilled to what they were hearing. Why had they never seen this before?

The village where they lived was some three hours' walk from Jerusalem, and the afternoon was wearing thin by the time they neared home. The stranger was making like he was going further. "No," they insisted. "You must stay with us. It'll be dark soon."

As they sat round the table for the evening meal, the two were amazed when the stranger assumed the role of host. He reached to the centre of the table and took the loaf of bread and broke it into pieces, which he held out to them. There was something very familiar about that action. "Remember me whenever you break bread," Jesus had said only three days previously, when they had eaten that last meal with him. And there was something familiar about the stranger's hands: scarred hands, like those of a crucified man, like Jesus' hands!

There was a big smile on the face that glowed back at them in the candlelight as they looked up at him for the first time. One moment he was there with them at table, and the next his chair was empty. Vanished!

Not waiting to clear the plates, the two of them jumped up, grabbed their coats, and headed out of the door. They literally ran all the way back the way they had come and didn't stop till they reached that rented upstairs room where lights and a hubbub of voices assured them that the gang was there. They ran up the stairs and burst into the room, but before they could come out with their news, they were trumped by a chorus of shouts from the excited throng: "It's all true, guys!"

"The Lord really is risen!"

"Yes, just like the girls told us this morning."

"Simon has seen him too."

Peter was sitting at the table, beaming from ear to ear.

"Quiet, everybody!" someone hissed. "For goodness sake, keep the noise down or we'll all be arrested." While their joy was bubbling over, their fears of arrest, and what other horrors might well follow, were ever present. The shock of what they had witnessed on Friday was all too fresh in their minds, and they had no idea how far the authorities were planning to take their clamp-down on the Jesus movement. "Did you guys lock the door behind you?"

The two new arrivals were ravenous, having left their supper sitting untouched on the table at home. So they tucked into the generous plate of broiled fish that was on the table.

No one was quite sure what happened next, but they swore later that none of them had opened the door. In fact, they remembered that someone had just checked that the door was securely locked. One moment, they were quietly chatting, enjoying their meal. The next, everyone froze. There was silence.

"Good evening, friends. Don't be frightened. Be at peace." Jesus!

Being at peace was easier said than done. Here they were, face to face with what could only be a ghost.

"Why are you so scared? You knew I was alive – the women told you this morning. And, by the way, you are a bunch of doubters. You should have believed them straight away. How do you expect others to believe your message if you yourselves are so slow to cotton on? But anyway, be assured that I am no ghost. Touch me if you like." He held out his hands to them, but they were scarred with the fresh injuries of his crucifixion. Their eyes dropped to his feet. Same story.

"Hey, give me some of that fish. I'm starving. It's been a long weekend."

The sight of him tucking into a fish sandwich reassured them all that this indeed was no disembodied spirit. The fear ebbed away to be replaced by jubilation. There were hugs and high fives.

"Don't say I didn't warn you, guys. I told you again and again that everything written about me from Moses on – all the prophets and David in the psalms – it all had to be fulfilled." Forever after that, they would read the Scriptures with new understanding.

Jesus was by now sitting at the table, munching his supper and drinking his wine. The Disciples and the women, together with a couple of dozen others, were all crammed into that room, crowded round the table, looking intently into the face that smiled round at them all. They were determined not to miss a single word he had to say.

"It's in a troubled world that you all live, but I am going to give you a precious gift to pass on. Peace! It was for this that the Father sent me into the world, and it's to pass on that gift that I am now sending you into the world. Forgiveness! Forgiveness makes peace, but un-forgiveness maintains conflict.

"Now come close." Those sitting round the table leant forward, and those standing round the outside leaned into the circle. Jesus took a deep breath and then breathed out over them all. "Receive my spirit, the Holy Spirit." It was to them all like an act of re-creation, like the day must have been when God first took the dust of the ground and breathed into it, giving life to Adam. "Remember what I told you in this very room last week about the Spirit? Well, very soon now I am going to send you what the Father has promised. Remember John the Baptist's predictions as he baptised in water, about one day being baptised in fire? In the next few days, you will be baptised in the Holy Spirit. So don't go far. Just stay in the city till you find yourselves equipped with power from above. Then you are to be my witnesses, starting right here in Jerusalem, then all over Judea and Samaria and finally throughout the world."

Not everyone was there that evening. Of the twelve Disciples, Judas was dead, so obviously not present. But Thomas was also absent. Next day, they excitedly told him what he had missed.

"I don't believe you! I'm sorry, but I don't believe a word of it. Unless I see him for myself, the scars on his hands of those terrible nails and feel that gash in his side, I simply won't be able to bring myself to believe what you are telling me."

The Disciples retained the use of that upstairs room, using it as an unofficial headquarters, a convenient place for them all to meet. Every evening, they gathered, hoping Jesus would show, but a whole week passed before they saw him again. This time, they were all there, even Thomas.

"Peace to you all," Jesus greeted them as he suddenly appeared at the head of the table. "Hello, Thomas. Good to see you again." Jesus reached out to grip his hand. Tom looked at the hand stretched out to him in welcome. "That's right, Tom. Scars. You can touch them if you like. And here," he said, pulling his cloak aside. "Feel my side! Thomas, it's time to stop doubting. Time to believe."

Thomas fell to his knees at Jesus' feet. "My Lord and my God!" he gasped.

"'Seeing is believing': that's the world's proverb, but seeing is not the key that unlocks genuine faith. There are generations to come that will never see me but will be blessed by believing what they hear – what you tell them."

But as word of Jesus' appearance spread to his many other admirers, so grew the numbers of expectant people who gathered, hoping to catch a glimpse of him. After the first week, they had to move their meeting place to one more commodious so no one would be excluded. There were over five hundred present when next Jesus showed his face.

Confrontation with the authorities was bound to happen sooner or later. So since Jesus had told them that he wanted to meet with them in Galilee, or perhaps because half of those fellows were addicted fishermen who just wanted to get back on the water, they left town and travelled north to Galilee.

"I don't know about you guys," Peter announced when they got there, "but I'm going fishing tonight."

"Now that's a plan," someone agreed. "We're coming too."

In the end, half a dozen of the others joined Peter in his boat, and they headed out into the fading light of the evening. The expedition turned out to be a disappointment: not a bite all night. There was nothing for it but to head for home: breakfast and some shut-eye.

As they approached the shore near Capernaum, they noticed that someone was up early and had a fire going on the beach. The smoke was lazily drifting over the glassy surface of the water.

"Good morning," the guy on the beach hailed them when they were about a hundred yards from shore. "Did you catch anything, anything we could eat?"

"Not a minnow. Got skunked, I'm afraid."

"Well, have another try. Drop your net right now off the starboard side of the boat, and you'll catch some."

A memory stirred. Jesus had given them exactly that same advice three years previously. It had worked then, so why not give it another go?

It worked! In fact, it worked so well that it was beyond them to pull up the net, so heavy was it with fish.

John tapped Peter on the shoulder. He was straining to pull in the catch. Peter paused to look round: "You know who that is on the beach, don't you, Pete?" From his blank expression, it was clear that Peter had no idea. "It's the Lord, dummy!"

Peter released his hold on the rope he was hauling and dived into the water to swim for the beach. The other guys were left to tow the bulging net to shore, since there was no way they would be able to get it on board. When they reached the shallows, Peter waded in to give them a hand hauling it up the beach.

And there was Jesus. He had a good fire going and was roasting some fish over the glowing embers. "We are going to need some more fish. You guys must be hungry."

Peter ran to fetch some. What a catch! When they counted them later, there were 153. And they were no tiddlers either. Any one of them could have stretched the credibility of a fisherman's tale! But there was not so much as a frayed rope to lend credence to the story.

"Breakfast's ready," Jesus called and served them all with fish and fresh baked bread.

"Come walk with me, Peter," Jesus said when the meal was nearly done. Together, they walked up the beach. It was on that same shore that Peter had first placed his feet in the footsteps of his Lord, three years previously. "Follow me!" Jesus had said, and Peter had done so ever since. Well, *almost* ever since. There had been that terrible time in the high priest's courtyard … Three terrible times he had denied he even knew Jesus. He would live with that failure till his dying day.

"Simon, son of John." Peter blanched. His formal name! This was the big lecture he had been dreading for the past couple of weeks.

"Yes Lord?" he mumbled.

"Do you love me more than these?" Jesus asked, nodding over his shoulder at the other Disciples still fussing round the fire.

Peter was embarrassed. He well remembered his bragging assertion that even if all of them deserted Jesus, he, Peter, never would. Most of the others had stood with Jesus, but Peter had hidden in his humiliation.

But Jesus was wanting an answer to how Peter was feeling now, on that particular morning: "Yes, Lord. You know I love you."

"So, feed my lambs." Well, that was an odd response. Peter was expecting a heavy rebuke, not a commission to be a shepherd. "I will make you a fisher of men," Jesus had promised him on that very spot three years ago. Now he wanted him to be a shepherd, presumably a shepherd of men.

They crunched on farther up the beach in silence. After a while: "Simon, son of John. Do you love me?"

This time, there was no competition implied, no comparison between his devotion and that of the others. It was just him and Jesus.

"Yes, Lord. You know very well that I love you."

"Look after my sheep." Again, the reference to shepherding.

There was a prolonged silence between them as they walked yet farther along the sand. Finally, Jesus stopped, turned to face Peter, and placed his hands on his shoulders. He looked deep into Peter's eyes: "Simon, son of John. Do you really love me?"

Well, that upset Peter. Three times he had denied Jesus; now, for the third time, Jesus was inviting Peter to confess him.

Choking back the tears, Peter responded, "Lord, you know everything about me. You already know that I love you."

"Yes, but I love to hear you say it! Feed my sheep."

For a while, Peter was blinded by his tears. Then Jesus put his arm round his shoulders and led him farther along the uneven beach.

"When you were a kid, Pete, you used to run where you would, free as the wind." Peter remembered those halcyon days when, as a child, he played on that very beach. "Even as a man three years back, you were free to follow me or to stay in your boat. But the day will come when you will no longer be free to go where you will. Others will take your outstretched arms and drag you to a place you would never choose to go. Follow me, Peter. That's what I called you to do three years ago, and to follow me is all you will ever need to do. And you will still be following me right at the end." So now Peter knew what his end would look like. That was something to swallow.

He heard a sound behind them and turned to look over his shoulder. John had left the other Disciples and was following them: "So what about John, Lord? What's going to happen to him?"

"That's none of your business, Peter. If I want him to stay around till I come back, that's between him and me. All you have to do is to follow me."

After breakfast, Jesus once again took his leave, but not before making a plan to meet with them again, this time when all eleven of the Disciples would be present. And not by the lake, but on a mountaintop. So there they all met him. For Peter, James, and John, this was reminiscent of the previous time they had been with him on a mountaintop, along with Moses and Elijah. On that occasion, he had sworn them to silence about the experience till after his resurrection. Then they had had little notion of what he was talking about. Now all was clear.

But not clear to everyone. There were some present, some of the more fringe members of the group, who were still sceptical. Jesus' own brothers had once been among the sceptics, back in the early days. But Jesus had a very special commission for his little brother James, so he held a private meeting with him, about which James never said a word to anyone. However, after that meeting, James was a changed man, soon to become a leader of Jesus' followers.

These occasional appearances of Jesus continued for some six weeks, and then finally one day they all met up back in Jerusalem in that same upstairs room. When Jesus joined them, they were all excited. They had been dying to ask him what would happen next: "Lord, is it time yet? Are you finally going to restore the kingdom to Israel?"

"I have told you before that knowing times and dates is in the Father's domain only. That's all under his control. Meanwhile, all authority in heaven and earth has been entrusted to me. So now I am giving you authority to go throughout the whole world to preach good news everywhere you go. Those who believe what you say, you are to baptise in the name of the Father, the Son, and the Holy Spirit. You are to make them into Disciples, just like you are. Teach them all I have taught you. And – never forget this – I am right there with you, always will be, even to the very end of time."

Then he led them down the stairs and out of town, just as he had on the night of his arrest. He didn't pause in Gethsemane Gardens but kept on going, right up to the top of the Mount of Olives. There was the withered fig tree and the stump he had sat on to tell them about the days to come.

When they were all assembled, he climbed onto the stump and smiled round at them all. He lifted up his hands and silently blessed them. Then before their startled eyes, he began to rise from the ground. Up and up he went, higher and higher, till he was little more than a speck in the sky. Finally he disappeared into a cloud and was gone. For a long time, they just stood there, gazing up into the sky, speechless.

Then a voice drew their attention back to earth. Standing beside them were two men whose cloaks shone like the sun. "Men of Galilee," they addressed them, "there's no point in gazing up into the sky any longer. Remember he told you that the day would come when you would see him coming back on the clouds of glory." Yes, they remembered all right. On that very stump, he had sat and told them all about it, barely six weeks ago. "This same Jesus will come back much as you have seen him leave today."

They fell to their knees in worship, and then, with a fresh spring in their step, they joyfully headed back into the city to commence the next phase of the adventure.

The Assembly

Waiting is rarely easy. Waiting for the Holy Spirit to come was difficult. What would he be like? Would they recognise him? "He's no stranger to you," Jesus had assured them. "He's been living with you for the past three years!" So he would be like Jesus' alter ego, they assumed.

But what were they to do while they waited for his arrival?

"Well, what would Jesus do?" someone asked.

"Pray, of course," was the unanimous answer.

So they prayed. But even that felt a little awkward. Who were they praying to? Jesus always had prayed to the Father and had taught them to do the same. But he had also told them that he and the Father were one. To see him was to see the Father. To talk to him was to talk to the Father. But did the equation work the other way round? Was it also true that to talk to the Father was to talk to Jesus? Every day, they met in that same upstairs room. And there was Jesus' empty chair, at the head of the table. Did they address their prayers to the chair, or were they still bowing before the throne in heaven?

"So what are we to do to fill Judas' boots?" Peter asked one day. "There ought to be twelve of us." Actually, there were regularly ten times that number who crammed themselves into that upstairs room, including Jesus' mother and siblings. But Peter's question was about the number of the Disciples, or "Apostles," as they would gradually become known, since they were no longer so much Jesus' followers as they were his emissaries.

"We'll have to pick someone else to take his place."

"Jesus did the picking when we all were chosen."

"So we had better ask him who he wants."

Someone spoke up: "Lord, you know us all inside out. Please let us know who you choose to take Judas' place."

But there was no reply. If only Jesus was really there to tell them. Maybe it would be easier when the Holy Spirit arrived?

Meanwhile, they settled the matter by the time-honoured fashion. They rolled the dice and picked Matthias.

About a week had gone by since Jesus had left. The streets of Jerusalem were once again jammed with pilgrims, there for the Pentecost festival, this time. A hundred and twenty people were keeping their vigil in the upstairs room when they became conscious of a strange sound. It was like the rushing of a mighty waterfall, or was it the roar of a furnace? "Twister!" someone cried out in alarm. It was wind, right enough, somewhere above the roof over their heads. Then the whole building was vibrating with its intensity, and right into the room it came. They could see the eye of the storm, like a glowing fire, right there over the table. Then suddenly it divided into individual tongues of flames that leapt to alight on each of them individually. For a moment, they glowed with the heat of it, and then the flames seemed to be absorbed right into the core of their being. Then all was still.

They just sat there in stunned silence, looking at each other. Then the sound of singing started from somewhere, quietly at first, but such sweet melody. They became conscious that it was they themselves who were doing the singing, and the room swelled with the harmony. The words of their song were foreign to their ears, but not their meaning. They were praising God with an eloquence that their own normal words could never have expressed.

They found themselves on their feet, hearts fair bursting with love for

God that just bubbled out of them, cascading from their lips in ecstatic praise. They just had to let this out, had to share it with the whole world. Out into the street they spilled, still singing, sometimes shouting at the top of their voices. They surged towards the temple, and as they went, others fell in behind them, drawn by the sound, thrilled by the vibrant, contagious joy. The people around them strained to make out the words of the song. What at first appeared to be a confused jumble of sound gradually resolved itself into intelligible words, not just any words, but words they knew, words of their own native languages. No matter what their tongue or where they were from, everyone understood perfectly.

"How could this be?" someone asked. "These folk are locals, country people most of them, from up north in Galilee. They speak their own language with such a thick accent that it's hard to understand them at the best of times. But multi-lingual?"

"If you ask me, they've had a few too many," some joker cracked.

Seizing the opportunity, Peter jumped up onto an upturned crate: "Ladies and gents, if I might have your attention ..." The clamour died away, and people turned to listen to what the man had to say. "We are not drunk, as someone just suggested. Hey! It's only nine in the morning!"

Laughter rippled through the crowd.

"What you are witnessing today is the fulfilment of what God promised long ago through the prophet Joel. He promised God would one day pour out his Spirit on all people, young and old, men and women. He said they would see visions, dream dreams, even prophesy. And he promised that anyone who would call on the name of the Lord would be saved. But the important question is: to what name was he referring?

"You are all well familiar with the reputation of Jesus from Nazareth. It was no accident that he found himself at your mercy and that you had him crucified. It was all part of God's great plan. But that was not the end of the story, for God has raised him back to life, just as David foretold he would in Psalm 16: 'You won't abandon me to rot in the grave, but will lead me into the path of life.' David died, and you can still go and visit his tomb to this day, so he can't have been talking about himself. But he knew that one day one of his descendants would assume his throne – the Messiah – and he would be the one God would raise to life. That promise became reality less than a couple of months back. My friends here and I myself were witnesses to the whole thing. We saw Jesus raised to life. So where is he now? God has promoted him to assume his proper place at God's own right hand. And that's why he has now sent his Holy Spirit, hence all that you see and hear going on around you.

"Therefore, make no mistake about it: God has declared this same Jesus, whom you crucified, to be both Lord and Christ."

The effect of Peter's words was dramatic. People were weeping and falling to their knees. "What have we done?" they wailed. "Whatever can we do to put this right?"

"Repent," Peter called. "Make a complete turnaround, each and every one of you. Express your repentance by being baptised, calling on the name of Jesus Christ. He will forgive you for all you have done wrong. Be baptised in water, and let him baptise you in the Holy Spirit. The promise is for you too, and for your kids and to people everywhere."

The response was overwhelming and immediate. People simply surged forward, begging to be included. Finding water in which to baptise that many people was a challenge, so they led the crowd down the hill to the pool of Siloam, and there some three thousand were baptised.

Together, these new followers of Jesus became known as "the church." In the days that followed, others kept a respectful distance, but one by one, more people crossed the floor to join them. People didn't just wander in by mistake. They were either in or they were out, and the rite of passage was baptism. It was rather as it had been when the Hebrews had left their slavery in Egypt: Moses led them through the sea to safety on the far shore. After that, they knew they were on their way – no turning back.

What to do with this growing throng of new believers was a practical question that had to find a solution. Clearly, the upstairs room was now totally inadequate to house their meetings. So, confident in the conviction that there was safety in numbers, they boldly held their meetings right in the temple. The Council could never arrest that many people!

Gradually, a schedule developed that would be the pattern for the church thereafter. The essential truths that Jesus had taught them, the Apostles now passed on to others. These teachings, which became known as "the Apostles' Teaching," gradually became recognised as core material to be passed on from generation to generation.

But it wasn't just for lectures that the people gathered. They loved each other and wanted nothing more than to enjoy each other's company. They even ate meals together, and no one ever went hungry, for they shared everything they had with unstinting generosity. They broke bread, ever reminding themselves of Jesus' brokenness so they could all be made one. Their meetings always included time spent in prayer. They may have started with the traditional prayers they had learned in the synagogue, but that soon morphed into spontaneous conversations with their Lord, despite the fact that they could no longer see him. And when they were done with the big meetings, they would carry on with more of the same, but in smaller groups back in their own homes. Every day, more and more people joined, and their numbers just kept on growing.

One afternoon, Peter and John mounted the steps that would take them through the Beautiful Gate and into the temple for the three o'clock meeting. There was the usual clutter of panhandlers, anxious to relieve worshippers of their loose change.

"Spare a coin for a lame man," called a voice. Peter looked down at the pathetic figure at his feet.

If only Jesus was still here, he thought. But then he remembered that he was now Jesus' representative, required and empowered to carry on his business. It was just that he had never tried it since Jesus left. What if it didn't work? What if nothing happened? The church would be dead in the water. So wouldn't he be smart just to offer a silent prayer and then walk on by?

"Hi guys." Never make eye contact if you don't want to get involved, but it was too late. The man was looking right at them.

"I don't have any cash, but I do have something better. In the name of Jesus Christ of Nazareth ..." The man knew that name all right and had seen him chasing the market operators out of the temple. Several times, Jesus of Nazareth had walked up those very steps, right past him. Stories of his miraculous healing powers were well known, but it only ever happened to other people. Anyway, he was dead and gone now. Too late!

"In the name of Jesus Christ of Nazareth, I tell you: get up and start walking!" Not taking "no" for an answer, Peter reached down, grabbed the man's hand, and hauled him to his feet. Suddenly, for the first time in his life, the man was standing upright, on his own two legs. A look of amazement spread over his face, and then he let out a yell and took a step forward, then another and another: walking! Soon he was jumping up and down, dancing a jig and running in ecstatic circles, shouting, laughing, and crying all at once.

Peter and John made to move on into the temple to be in time for the meeting, but there was no way the man was going to let them get away. He grabbed onto Peter's arm. Everyone recognised the familiar face of the man who had sat begging at the Beautiful Gate every day for as long as they could remember, only now that face was at eye level, smiling at them. A curious crowd hemmed them in, craning their necks to get a look at the now-upright cripple and the men standing with him.

"Well, don't stare at us as though we were something special. All credit is due to Jesus, the same Jesus you disowned before Pilate, asking for the release of Barabbas, a murderer, instead of Jesus, the author of life. But God raised him back to life, and it is by faith in the name of Jesus that this man is now completely healed. Okay, you acted in ignorance when you killed him, but now it's time to repent and turn back to God so that your sins can be forgiven. All the prophets from Moses onwards have been telling us of the coming Messiah, saying that he would have to suffer. But even before that, God promised Abraham that through one of his descendants, everyone on the face of the earth would be blessed. Well, Jesus is that descendant. He is that suffering Messiah, and now God has raised him back to life. The blessing of the whole earth starts right here and now with you, as you are among the first to receive forgiveness as you turn from sin."

It was with a sense of déjà vu that Peter and John saw a group of priests and Sadducees pushing indignantly through the crowd, but on this occasion, they were accompanied by the temple security guards. It was Peter's reference to the resurrection of Jesus that had been the last straw. The Sadducees' whole theology was based on there being no resurrection, and those same security men had been the ones bribed to say that Jesus' resurrection had never happened: "His Disciples stole the body during the night." Yet now here were two of these Jesus people, openly bragging about the resurrection, and no one was arresting them for bodysnatching. To save face, they had to do something, so they arrested all three of them:

Peter, John, and the healed man. But the damage was done, and another couple of thousand joined the church as a result.

Peter and John, together with their new friend, were kept in jail till the next morning, when they were brought into the council chamber to face the music. The big guns were all present, and amongst them, no fewer than four of the leading men of the high priest's family. When the defendants had been sworn in, the questions began.

"What strange power did you employ yesterday, and in whose name were you acting?"

Prompted by the Holy Spirit, Peter assumed the role of spokesman: "Presumably, you are referring to the kindness that was shown to this formerly disabled gentleman yesterday afternoon? Very well then, here is the straight goods. It is by the name of Jesus Christ of Nazareth that this man stands before you healed. It was you who crucified him, but it was God who raised him back to life. No one else can give salvation, and Jesus is the only name under heaven by which we must all be saved."

Against their better judgement, the Council members were impressed by Peter and John's courage: just a couple of uneducated men, by the looks of them. They remembered seeing them in Jesus' company on several occasions. Now here they were, alongside a man who was clear evidence of Jesus' posthumous healing ability. What could they say in the face of that?

"You are hereby ordered and required to refrain from saying anything further in this name or talking about him any more." That was the best they could come up with.

"You will have to judge for yourselves what you think is right: to obey you or to obey God. For our part, we have no choice but to pass on what we have seen and heard."

"You say one more word about this man, and you'll rue the day you were born!" Threats were the only weapons in their arsenal, for only a fool would deny that a spectacular miracle had been accomplished before their very eyes.

As soon as they were released, Peter and John headed straight back to HQ on the upper floor. There they found a worried group of people, whose relief to see them safe home was palpable. They all joined in prayer when they heard what had happened. In God's presence, they reminded themselves of how great God was and how pathetic, by contrast, were man's attempts to challenge him. "So, Lord, they are at it again, threatening to silence us. Please give us boldness to keep speaking the message you entrusted to us and to continue to perform miracles in Jesus' name."

Scarce had they said "Amen" when the whole building started to shake, and they each felt a surge of fresh courage as the Holy Spirit filled them again.

In those early days, the members of the church were a very close-knit group. They would not countenance any of their number going short, so they shared everything they had. It was not so much a requirement for membership as a spontaneous expression of generosity. Some even went so far as to sell their homes and entrust the proceeds of the sales to the Apostles to share out with any they knew to be in need. One such was a Cypriot named Barnabas, who lived up to his name as a great encourager of others. But not everyone was so open handed.

A couple named Ananias and Sapphira, impressed by what Barnabas had done, also sold some land and donated what they claimed were the proceeds of the sale to the kitty. However, they secretly kept some cash for themselves, just in case...

"Was that really what you got for your property?" Peter asked when they handed over the money. They both assured him that it was. "You were both free to give as much or as little as you wished, but you are never free to lie about it. It was God's Holy Spirit that you were seeking to deceive when you withheld some of the proceeds of the sale for yourselves." Both husband and wife dropped dead on the spot, one after the other.

News of this tragedy struck the fear of God into the membership. Non-church members kept a respectful distance. Yet, in the main, the church was highly regarded by their fellow citizens, and more and more people kept joining every day. Soon people from out of town were coming, bringing their sick or demented for a healing touch by the Apostles. And, it seemed, they didn't even need to be touched. Just Peter's passing shadow was enough.

But inevitably, trouble happened. It was those anti-resurrection Sadducees who stirred it up: "We can't let them get away with it. They are deliberately flouting the court order to keep quiet about this man and his purported resurrection." They took their complaint to the high priest, who ordered his security men to arrest the offenders. Doubtless, these officers were only too glad to oblige, since the Apostles' daily insistence on the resurrection of Jesus must have been a constant embarrassment to their body-snatchers story.

The Apostles were thrown into the town jail. Just before dawn, they were woken by the doors of their cells mysteriously opening. Blearily, they perceived an angel beckoning them to come out. When they were all assembled outside the jail, the angel gave them their instructions: "Go back to the temple and keep preaching."

So as the sun rose, there they were. Business as usual.

However, for the Council, it was hardly business as usual. A full meeting had been called to discuss this growing threat. On arriving at the jail, the temple security men found the jailers at their posts, with the doors firmly locked. But when they opened up, an all-too-familiar sight met their eyes: The cell was as empty as had been the tomb on that embarrassing night in the cemetery. Now how were they to explain this to their lords and masters? But to look on the bright side, perhaps more hush money might be extorted?

As it happened, no explanations were called for. Word had already reached the Council that the Apostles were at it again: "The men you put in jail are out there in the temple, preaching like they always do. Now go get them!"

The security men might gladly have done the Apostles a mischief, but the mood of the crowd that surrounded them dictated that they use kid gloves. Church members this crowd might be, but it would not be beyond them to throw rocks at any who might threaten their precious leaders.

"What is the meaning of this?" the high priest demanded when the twelve men were marched into the Council meeting, under heavy police escort. "Did we not clearly order you to refrain from so much as mentioning this man's name? Instead, you have infested the whole city with your pernicious teachings, and now you are accusing us of murdering this man. You have shown contempt for this court!"

"Our first responsibility is to obey God," Peter responded on behalf of the others. "That is why we continue to speak openly about Jesus, the one you did indeed murder. But God raised him from the dead and has seated him at his right hand in heaven, honouring him as Prince and Saviour. From that elevated position, he now readily offers you the gifts of repentance and forgiveness of your sins. We stand here before you today as first-hand witnesses to these things, inspired as we are by the Holy Spirit, whom God readily gives to all who fall in step with him."

So incensed were they that the Council might well have executed the whole lot of them right there and then, had not a wise old voice intervened: "Gentlemen, gentlemen! Be careful what you do to these men." The voice came from the side of the house occupied by the Pharisees: Gamaliel, venerated teacher of the law and descendant of the great theologian, Hillel. His was a voice to be reckoned with. "Recent history has revealed the folly of others who have claimed to be somebodies, but whose movements quickly came to nothing. My advice is to let time do its work. If this Jesus movement is a purely human initiative, it is doomed to failure, but if it is God ordained, then you'll never stop it, and perish the thought, you might even find yourselves at war with God."

The Council finally resolved to have the prisoners flogged and then let go with a restraining order on them to prohibit any further teaching about Jesus.

Bruised and bleeding, the Apostles hobbled back up the stairs to HQ, but the joy of having been privileged to suffer disgrace for the name of Jesus soon bubbled to the surface. Next day, they were back at it, proclaiming the good news about Jesus, right there in the temple and wherever else they could find an audience.

Growing numbers inevitably breed administrative headaches, and such was the case for the church. With a membership now running to several thousand, and everyone dependant on the common purse for daily food, sooner or later someone would be bound to grumble: "It's not fair!"

The single women, widows mostly, were bottom of the food chain, and bottommost of all were the Greek-speaking women.

The Apostles found themselves increasingly distracted from teaching and preaching by these administrative headaches. Finally, they convened a meeting to address the problem: "We Apostles are not called to be in the catering business! Our first responsibility is to teach the word of God."

There was no argument about that. "So here's what we should do. Identify from amongst the membership wise and Spirit-filled men who are gifted in the areas of administration and catering. Let them take care of this matter."

Seven candidates were proposed, most of them Greek-speaking, and all were elected and then prayerfully commissioned by the Apostles. Problem solved. Of the seven elected "deacons," as they would later be dubbed, two names were to stand out: Philip, who turned out to be better at preaching than cooking, and Stephen, who was a gifted storyteller and debater.

Greek-speaking Jews were initially attracted by Stephen's ability to speak their language, but when they cottoned on to what he was actually saying about Jesus, they became argumentative. "If your argument is weak, shout louder" was the technique to which they resorted in the face of Stephen's skill as a debater. They employed some ne'er-do-wells to publicly accuse Stephen of blasphemy. The ploy worked, and Stephen was arrested and dragged before the Council, where the same hired "witnesses" testified against him. There was a familiar ring to their accusations. They said that they had heard Stephen threaten that Jesus would come back to destroy the temple, though they failed to add the part about his promise to rebuild it in three days.

"Is this true?" the high priest demanded.

Stephen's response can hardly be called a "defence." He just retold the story of God's dealings with Israel, starting with the days of Abraham, Isaac, and Jacob, then tracing God's continuing grace to Israel through the years in Egypt and into the promised land, under the leadership of first Moses and then Joshua.

"Moses," he reminded the court, "was himself rejected by his own people." Stephen stressed the persistent rebellion of Israel against the determined grace of God. He led them through the glory days of King David and Solomon, the building of the temple on the very spot on which they now were standing, the temple Stephen was accused of threatening to destroy. "But God doesn't live in buildings constructed by human beings," Stephen reminded them, quoting the words of Isaiah the prophet. "No, the very heavens are not great enough to provide a dwelling for the Creator of all things. So why would you feel obliged on his behalf to spring to the defence of this little temple?"

If the Council had imagined that Stephen would use his closing remarks as an attempt to win their support, they would have been disappointed. "You stubborn and obstinate people!" he accused. "Like father, like son. You have always resisted the Holy Spirit. Your forefathers murdered the very prophets who foretold the coming of the Man of Righteousness, and now you have murdered him. You claim to be defenders of the law of God, but will you obey it? Never!"

At this point, Stephen's words were cut short by a furious outburst of hatred from all sides of the Council chamber. But somehow, Stephen didn't seem to be listening. He was looking up, transfixed. And there was something strange about his face. It was glowing with the reflected glory of heaven.

"Don't you see him?" Stephen called out, pointing to the sky above their heads. "Look, there he is: Jesus, standing next to the throne of God in heaven."

They didn't see a thing, but the whole Council jumped to their feet, howling like a pack of wolves. They rushed at him and dragged him bodily out of the temple. And there they vented their hatred for Jesus and everything he represented. They stoned Stephen. The church members who were at the back of the mob confidently expected that at any moment, God would do something, but no such intervention came. Stephen staggered under the onslaught of rocks that rained down on him.

"Lord Jesus!" he cried out, still seeing the one to whom he prayed. "Forgive them! Please don't hold this sin against them!" Then he was down, crawling on his hands and knees. Those closest to him heard his mumbled prayer: "Lord Jesus, receive my spirit." With that, he lay down and was still, but for the rocks that still smashed into his lifeless body. Such was their hatred and frustration that they removed their coats and kept stoning till the bundle on the ground was a bloody pulp, barely recognisable as a human being.

Standing there, guarding the pile of discarded coats, was a young Pharisee named Saul. No one saw him actually throwing any rocks, but if looks could kill, then there was no doubt that he was in part responsible for the murder that took place that terrible day.

18

The Scattering

His youthful energy and pharisaic zeal caused Saul to ride the crest of the wave of anti-church sentiment that swept through Jerusalem from that day forward. The establishment had had just about enough of this Jesus stuff, and popular opinion, fickle as the weather, turned against the church.

With the Council's blessing, Saul led a posse of men who moved from street to street, house to house, bursting in on suspected Jesus sympathisers, dragging them off to jail. It was the Greek-speaking Jews who bore the brunt of the persecution. They were viewed as immigrants who had no right to be cluttering up the city in the first place: "First they take our jobs, now they are messing with our religion."

While the Apostles stood their ground, this wave of hostility caused an immediate exodus of many of their followers from Jerusalem. They scattered in all directions, fleeing from Saul's inquisition, yet inspired with the passion to share the good news about Jesus everywhere they went. Amongst these refugees was Philip, one of the recently elected deacons and a close colleague of Stephen. Like his dead friend, Philip was a powerful preacher of the gospel. He travelled north into the district of Samaria. Jesus had himself spent some time in Sychar, where his encounter with a local lady by a well had caused the whole city to pay close attention to what he had told them. Inspired by the example of his Master, Philip proclaimed the good news of the kingdom of God. It was as though Jesus himself had come to town, for demons fled in terror, and paraplegics got up and walked. Joy erupted in the city, as many believed and were baptised.

Amongst the crowd was a well-known face, that of Simon Magnus, the wizard, a performer of dazzling magic, allegedly exhibiting the "Great Power," whatever that might be. He had long enjoyed the respect of his fellow citizens, so for him to step forward to submit to the humbling rite of baptism was quite something. It was probably Philip's superior ability to perform miracles that did the trick for Simon.

There was, however, one mystifying feature in this overwhelming response to the gospel: The Holy Spirit appeared to be absent at the baptisms. Back in Jerusalem, he had made his presence felt by causing miraculous manifestations of his power, enabling the newly baptised believers to worship in words beyond human language. But in Samaria, nothing happened. Philip carried on undaunted, simply trusting that to preach the gospel and baptise those who believed was obedience to his commission. What God might or might not do next was up to him.

Word that a significant awakening was taking place in Samaria was greeted back in Jerusalem with mixed feelings. The long-held prejudice of Jews against Samaritans tainted the reception of this news with suspicion, but since Jesus had commissioned them to preach good news beyond their native Judea, specifically in Samaria, they felt obligated to look on the bright side.

Peter and John were delegated by their fellow Apostles to go and investigate. They shared Philip's concern that the newly baptised converts did not appear to have been baptised by the Holy Spirit. Peter and John talked to God about the problem and then placed their hands on the new believers; the evidence of the presence of the Holy Spirit was immediately obvious. The church in Samaria, which might have been born into a family divided by prejudice, was at once united with her sister in Jerusalem in joyful celebration. Peter had again used his God-given key to unlock Samaria's door into the kingdom of God.

Yet it was clear that outward expressions of faith and baptism were no guarantee of a genuine work of God. Simon Magnus had ticked all the boxes and now was impressed by the Apostles' magical power to confer the Holy Spirit by touch. "I would like that ability," he said, pulling out his wallet. "How much to enable me to lay my hands on people so they can receive the Holy Spirit?"

"The gift of God is not for sale!" Peter barked. "May your money rot with you in hell for even thinking it might be. Clearly, your heart is not right before God. You are twisted with bitterness and enslaved by sin."

Simon was terrified. "What should I do?" he wailed.

"Repent and pray that God will forgive you!"

"But would you please pray for me?" the badly frightened Simon begged, imagining that Peter's prayers might carry more clout than his own.

Peter and John didn't stay long but headed back to the troubled church in Jerusalem.

Philip might well have stayed longer to nurture the newly formed church had not his marching orders been delivered to him personally by an angelic messenger: "Take the desert road that leads south from Jerusalem to Gaza." Philip, happy to operate on a "need to know" basis, set off immediately on his mystery mission. He was well south of Jerusalem when he became conscious of the crunch of chariot wheels and horses' hooves coming up behind him. He stopped to watch this obviously important entourage pass by.

It was while he waited by the roadside that the next instalment of his orders was revealed to Philip. "Stick close to that chariot!" nudged the Spirit. With no hesitation, Philip sprang forward and jogged along beside the carriage.

Judging from both his dress and his entourage, the sole occupant was a personage of some importance. From his dark complexion, it was a reasonable guess that he was from a long way south. The man was sitting behind his driver, reading out loud. The words were immediately familiar to Philip. He was reading from a copy of the writings of Isaiah the prophet. Well, there was a surprise!

"Excuse me!" called Philip. "Do you understand what you are reading?"

"However could I, without some help?" There was a moment's hesitation and then: "I don't suppose you could help me, could you?"

Philip jumped up and sat next to the man.

Turned out Philip's host was a long way from his home in the land of

Cush, part of Ethiopia, south of Egypt, where he was minister of finance, responsible to Queen Candace herself. He was on his way home from a pilgrimage he had made to the holy city of Jerusalem.

Something had caught his attention as he scrolled through Isaiah's beautiful prose: "Let no eunuch feel that he is only a withered tree.' He was a eunuch, a common precaution required of those in the service of queens and princesses. A family of his own was therefore a joy he would never know. "Let no foreigner think himself excluded from God's family. God promises to give him a name that will be better than family, a welcome to his holy mountain and joy in his house of prayer."

He had scrolled back a few paragraphs and was just rereading the strange passage that preceded the words that had caught his attention: "He was led like a lamb to the slaughter. He was humiliated and suffered injustice, his life cut short before he could have children of his own.'

"Tell me, please, sir, if you can. Of whom was Isaiah writing: of himself or of somebody else?"

Philip told him all about Jesus, starting from the early days in Galilee, right up to the coming of the Holy Spirit and the thousands who had recently been baptised.

"So why shouldn't I be baptised?" the Ethiopian asked eagerly. For the past few hours, there had been a very practical answer to his question, since there was no water in the desert. But by this point in their conversation, they were not far short of Gaza City, close to the western sea. As the road rounded a sand dune, there before them was a lake known to the locals as Wadi el-Hesi: "Here's some water. What's to stop me?"

Philip and the minister of finance climbed down from the carriage and waded into the water. There, the Ethiopian confessed Jesus as his Lord, and Philip baptised him. But when the Ethiopian came up from the water, he found he was quite alone. The man with whom he had shared his carriage all afternoon had simply vanished.

Yet his joy knew no limit as he resumed his long journey south to start a whole new life as the first missionary to Africa.

Philip was surprised to find himself twenty miles north in Azotus (or Ashdod, as the Philistines had previously called it). Unfazed, he resumed his preaching of the gospel, gradually working his way up the coast till he reached Caesarea, where he settled down and raised a family: four daughters, at the final count, who following in their father's footsteps, became gifted preachers.

While Philip was extending the outer limits of the church, back in Jerusalem trouble was still bubbling. Saul, the young Pharisee appointed by the Council to harass the church, was proving himself to be just the man for the job. His murderous hatred of the church, or "the Way," as it was now becoming known, was like a dragon's fire. He travelled from synagogue to synagogue, arresting Jesus' followers and then dragging them off to prison. There he did his best to torture them into blaspheming the name of Jesus, some even succumbing to death rather than renounce the name they held so dear. "Love your enemies," Jesus had taught them. "Pray for those who abuse you." So the church did just that.

When Saul heard that the seeds of this sect of the Nazarene had blown up into Syria and were germinating in Damascus, he resolved to root them out before they spread further. Armed with extradition papers authorising him to arrest and bring back to Jerusalem followers of the Way, he led his posse a hundred and fifty miles northeast.

Not long before reaching his destination, everything changed. A bolt of lightning struck the ground just ahead of the company, stopping them dead in their tracks. Saul, who had been leading the way, fell to the ground, completely dazzled. The rest of the company heard what they took to be thunder, but to Saul there was no mistaking the voice that addressed him:

"Saul, Saul, why are you persecuting me?"

"Who's there?" he stammered.

"I am Jesus, the one you are persecuting."

There was a horrified silence as the realisation of his terrible mistake hit him like a physical blow. "So what shall I do now, Lord?"

"Get up and stand on your feet when I speak to you!" Saul did so, swaying uncertainly, for he was still blinded by the light before him. "You are now my servant, and I am sending you to witness to what you see this day and to what I will yet show you. I am sending you back to your own people and then to the Gentiles, worldwide. Your job will be to open the eyes of the blind, to lead them out of darkness into the light, releasing them from the oppression of Satan into the freedom that God will give them by forgiving their sins and making them holy, as they place their faith in me." Saul stood there, stunned. "Now get going! Continue your journey into Damascus, and there your assignment will be confirmed."

Saul felt hands gripping his arms and found himself surrounded by his companions, but unable to see them. He was gravel blind.

Eventually, they resumed their journey till they arrived in Damascus. They found their way to Straight Street, to the address where they were expected. Saul was in no mood for idle chitchat but retired to his room, declining all offers of refreshment.

For three days, he remained in seclusion, and it was during those days of darkness that an amazing transition took place. He found himself desperate to pray. It was not that he had never previously prayed, for he had long been a devout man. But now how was he to pray? The last thing he had seen was the dazzling brightness of the unexpected presence of Jesus before him. He had heard his voice; in fact, he had held a conversation with him. So now to whom should he address himself when he prayed? Tentatively, he spoke the name of Jesus into the darkness. To his amazement, there came an immediate reply:

"Stay right where you are, Saul, and wait for a man named Ananias to come to you. He will lay his hands on you to restore your sight."

So Saul was the only member of that household who was not surprised when a prominent follower of the Way came knocking, asking for the man from Tarsus known as Saul, who he fully expected to find at prayer.

"Ananias, I presume," Saul said when they came to tell him he had a visitor. "That's his name … right?"

"Brother Saul!" Ananias said, embracing the stranger, of whom he had previously been terrified. "The Lord Jesus, who I understand appeared to you on your way here, has sent me to help you to see again and to be filled with the Holy Spirit." It was as though the blinkers were removed from his eyes, for the light of day flooded back into his being, and he rose to meet it.

"Now what?" he asked, eagerly.

"First, you must be baptised, then you had better have something to eat, since I am told you have had nothing for three days." And so it happened. Saul was a changed man, filled with the Holy Spirit. "You are God's chosen instrument to take the name of Jesus to Gentiles, to kings, and to your own people, Israel," Ananias told him.

Saul's arrival in the local Damascus synagogue, in company with a gang of followers of the Way, was, to say the very least, a surprise to the regulars. There was much whispering: "Isn't that the guy who came up from Jerusalem to arrest followers of the Way? So what's he doing here, and with all these people? Doesn't he realise who they are?"

But if his presence was a surprise, then his message was a real shock. When the opportunity presented itself, Saul took the podium and gave testimony to what had taken place in his life during the previous week. His conclusion was a definite statement that Jesus really is the Christ, the Son of God. The following week, he was back again, only this time it was no simple testimony but a well-argued case for the deity of Jesus.

And then, he just disappeared off the map. No one was quite sure where he had gone. All he would tell them when eventually he re-emerged three years later was that he had been somewhere in Arabia, taking time out to think things through. Apparently, he didn't want to rush into his new commission before processing this paradigm shift in his understanding of God. And since this truth had been delivered to him by divine revelation, rather than taught by human instructors, he wanted it to be God alone who would further explain to him his message and mandate.

So when Saul came back to civilisation, it was to Damascus that he returned, the only place where he could expect to find a friendly welcome from those who alone would appreciate what had happened to him. Though he may have enjoyed a welcome from the followers of the Way, the reception from the wider Jewish community in Damascus was frosty. Word had evidently reached them from the big guns in Jerusalem that, should he ever show his face back in Damascus, Saul should be treated as persona non grata. To further exacerbate Saul's situation, the Roman governor, encouraged by the Arabian King Aretas, collaborated with the Jewish leaders to issue a warrant for Saul's arrest. The city gates were watched night and day so that he wouldn't get away again. Mercifully, one of the church members had access to a house built into the city wall, with a convenient window that opened out. Saul blanched at the prospect of climbing down a rope, since certain inherited physical disabilities had always restricted his athletic abilities. So they attached a basket to the rope and thereby lowered Saul to the ground during the night.

Finally, after three years, Saul came back to Jerusalem. He was not sure of whom he ought to be the most wary: his former colleagues, the Pharisees, or his former enemies, the church. As it turned out, the Pharisees left him alone. He was, after all, an embarrassment to them. But the church also shunned him. They were sceptical of his so-called conversion, still afraid of his ruthless cruelty. They had merely heard rumours that their former tormentor was now preaching the gospel.

It was Barnabas who eventually broke the stalemate: Barnabas, whose generosity had started the cascade of giving soon after the church was first established, Barnabas the encourager. He sought out Saul, took time with him, listened to his story, and sensed the genuineness of his change of heart. So it was Barnabas who introduced Saul to Peter. Realising the significant role that Saul was to play in the future of the church, Peter spent much time with him over a two-week period. But all the other Apostles kept their distance, and only James, Jesus' brother, ever dared cross the divide to meet him.

But Saul didn't seem to mind. He was understandably shy in the company of these followers of the Way, whom he had so brutally abused. He spent his time in the city in dialogue with his former friends, the Greek-speaking Jews with whom he had hounded the hapless Stephen to his death. But it wasn't long before they recognised and resented his change of heart. They turned on him with such venom that he was forced to leave town to save his skin. Saul headed to the coast, where he boarded a ship in Caesarea and travelled north, back to the city of Tarsus, where he had been born. Where better to start his life all over again?

Saul stayed in Tarsus for fourteen years. There was no doubt in his mind that his God-given ministry was to share the gospel with the Gentiles, so he preached it with all the zeal of a young man on a mission. His own family did not approve of the new Saul, who soon found himself disinherited. In fact, he quickly suffered the loss of just about everything he had previously called his own but still counted that a small price to pay for the privilege of gaining Jesus.

The Jewish community in Tarsus was also quick to identify him as one to be discouraged, subjecting him during those turbulent years to no fewer than five beatings of thirty-nine lashes a time. Hunger, cold, danger, betrayal, and plain hard work all were part and parcel of Saul's new inheritance.

But one incident sparkled like a star on a dark night and was to have a profound influence on the rest of his life. Saul never spoke in specifics of what happened that day, always insisting that it was beyond the power of human language to adequately describe. All he would say is that somehow he had been caught up to heaven – to paradise. "No human eyes could ever have seen such beauty, no human ears ever heard such harmony, no mind ever imagined such wonder," was his testimony.

Doubtless the contrast of this experience, against the background of such hardship, left him utterly fearless of whatever might come his way in the future. He always said that he felt torn between continuing his work on earth and departing to be with Christ. But, given the choice, he would have opted for the latter.

Back in Jerusalem, things had returned to normal. Several years had passed since the death of Stephen and the troubles that had followed. Now things were settled into a steady rhythm, as the new believers grew in their faith, and the overall number continued to grow at a manageable pace.

So Peter was able to leave town from time to time to check up on the scattered members of his flock. He took a tour in the west country, the plains close to the Mediterranean coast. Lydda, situated at an intersection in trade routes, was fast expanding from a village to become a city. There was a small contingent of followers of the Way who were known to meet there. Amongst them was a paraplegic who had been bedridden for the previous eight years. "Jesus Christ heals you," Peter said when he saw him, and instantly the man was up on his feet. Word of this spread like a brush fire, reaching as far as the coast, where the church in Joppa had just suffered a terrible bereavement.

Everyone had loved Dorcas, a dear lady who was forever helping needy people. Dorcas had unexpectedly fallen sick and died. With not a moment's hesitation, her friends dispatched a couple of fellows to run the ten miles to Lydda to fetch Peter.

When he arrived at the house of death, the grief was overwhelming, as people showed Peter examples of the things Dorcas had made for them. They led him upstairs to the room where the body was laid out. Now what was he to do? Raising the dead was something he had seen Jesus do, but never before had he or any of his fellow Apostles been faced with so daunting a challenge as a dead body. "You are going to do greater things than you have seen me doing," Jesus had promised them. Raising the dead might not be greater, but it sure would be a stretch! The whole scene was reminiscent of one in Capernaum, where in the home of Jairus, a cacophony of noisy mourners and a child lying dead in her bedroom had greeted them. What had Jesus done? For a start, he had got rid of the mourners.

"Give me some space," Peter said, shooing them all out of the room. Alone with the corpse, Peter knelt down by the bed and prayed for a while, still wondering what to do next. Then he recalled Jesus taking the little girl's hand and telling her to wake up. Peter got to his feet, and taking the lifeless hand, he said, "Dorcas, time to get up." And she did. She was understandably a little taken aback to find a strange man standing in her bedroom. "How do you do?" Peter said, who was still awkwardly holding her hand. "I'm Peter." The joy when the two walked down the stairs together was overwhelming. Possibly the most stunned was Peter himself!

Consequently, the church in Joppa exploded, and Peter stayed in town to help them find their feet. He took lodgings on the waterfront, near the harbour, in the home of Simon, a tanner by trade, a choice of billet that raised some eyebrows, since tanning was considered by some to be unclean. But for a fisherman to be by the water was an opportunity Peter simply could not pass up. The place had a terrace on its flat roof with a spectacular view of the sea. To Peter, this proved both a refuge, where he could relax, and a place where he could be alone to pray.

It was there one day about noon that something unexpected happened. Peter may have gone up there to pray, but the smell of lunch being prepared and the warmth of the sun conspired to make him drowsy, and before he could shake himself back to alertness, he was dreaming. It was one of those particularly vivid dreams that stay with you after you wake. He saw a huge tarpaulin attached at the four corners to a rope, being lowered from above. The whole canvas was bulging with something that was wriggling, clearly alive. When it reached the ground, out spilled all manner of creatures: snakes, birds, and animals. "Quick!" a voice he recognised ordered. "Get up, Peter. Kill and eat!"

Hungry though he was, Peter was horrified. "You can't be serious, Lord. You know me. I have never eaten anything non-kosher or unclean in my whole life!"

"Don't you dare call anything that God has purified 'unclean'!"

Three times the dream came to him, till eventually consciousness began to lure him back to reality. In that hazy twilight zone between sleep and cognizance, Peter wondered if his dream meant anything. Food! He was hungry, and the smell of cooking was assailing his senses. Uncleanness! He was staying with a tanner, the smell of which process was far from pleasant when the wind was in the wrong direction.

"Someone's looking for you, Peter," said the Spirit. "Get up and go with them."

Then he heard someone calling his name, so he went downstairs to find three strangers at the gate. "Are you Simon Peter?" they asked.

"Certainly am," Peter assured them.

They explained that they had travelled down from Caesarea, farther up the coast, on the instructions of their boss, a Roman centurion by the name of Cornelius. "He's a well-respected, God-fearing man," they assured him. "An angel told him to send to this address for a Simon Peter, who would tell him how he and all he holds dear can be saved."

These were Gentiles at his gate. To invite them in, let alone eat with them, would be to contaminate the whole Jewish household. But on the tail of so vivid a dream, how could he send them away?

"Then you had better come in," said Peter, and they spent the rest of the day together.

First thing in the morning, they hit the road towards Caesarea, some thirty-five miles north. Conscious that he was about to take a controversial step across a hitherto uncrossed gulf, Peter wisely invited half a dozen of the local believers to accompany him. They would be able to act as witnesses should criticism be forthcoming later on from some of his more conservative colleagues. They arrived the following day to find a fine Roman residence crowded with people. Cornelius, who had been looking out for them, was first out the door. Before Peter could stop him, Cornelius fell to his knees before him. "Stand up, for goodness sake," Peter said, flummoxed. "I'm just an ordinary guy."

Cornelius' guests turned out to be his close friends and relatives. "You do realise, don't you, that what I am doing, coming in here, is against our Jewish laws? But God told me to come, so here I am. Now, how can I help you?"

Cornelius explained that some four days previously, he had seen an angel who told him to send to Joppa for a man named Simon Peter, who he would find at the tannery on the waterfront. "So I did and here you are," he concluded in his formal military style. "Now, what have you got to tell us?" What an introduction for a preacher!

"Well, this is an eye-opener for me!" Peter confessed, when they had all settled down to listen. "God has no favourites, after all, but welcomes people from every nation, not just Jews." Then Peter told them everything: all about Jesus, from the Galilee days till his crucifixion in Jerusalem. He stressed Jesus' resurrection and pointed out that he and his fellow Apostles were eyewitnesses to the whole amazing saga. "And everyone who believes in Jesus will receive forgiveness of their sins." Before the words were out of Peter's lips, the Holy Spirit came on the whole assembly, and they started to praise God in other tongues, much as they had done on that day of Pentecost back in Jerusalem, when it all began. It was a good thing that Peter had had the foresight to invite along with him some of the Joppa believers, for they all saw exactly what happened and were glad to bear witness later to the fact that there was no manipulation on Peter's part. The whole thing was God's initiative, from beginning to end.

"Can you guys see any reason why we should not baptise these Gentiles with water, since the Lord has seen fit to baptise them with the Holy Spirit?" And they did.

At Cornelius' request, Peter and his companions stayed there for a few days, explaining the basics of following Jesus.

The news of this significant expansion of the church beat Peter back to Jerusalem, and his critics were waiting for him when he got in. "We hear that you have been mixing with uncircumcised Gentiles," they accused. So Peter explained exactly what had happened. By the time he had finished his account, everyone was as thrilled as he. "So the door is open to Gentiles as well to find life through repentance," they all rejoiced. Peter's key had now unlocked the third door to the advance of the kingdom.

Of the seven men chosen as deacons to administer fair distribution of the daily food rations, Stephen was dead, Philip was serving as an evangelist based in Caesarea, and now Nicanor left the kitchen to carry the flag back to his native Antioch.

Antioch was a thriving city of half a million inhabitants some three hundred and fifty miles north of Jerusalem. It was a cosmopolitan community, a mixture of cultures and morals, with a dubious reputation to match. Nicanor and his fellow delegates from Jerusalem started by concentrating their efforts on the Jewish community alone, but since Nicanor and his buddies were mainly Greek speaking, they soon found themselves in dialogue with the Gentile Grecian sector of Antioch. The response was immediate, and great numbers poured into the church.

When news of this reached the ears of the Apostles in Jerusalem, there was consternation. It had been a stretch for them to accept Samaritans, more so when Peter had included a contingent of Gentiles in Caesarea. But a mixed congregation of Jews and Gentiles? This had to be checked out. So they sent Barnabas, a man of integrity they could trust, a good man, full of the Holy Spirit, who would be able to appreciate exactly what was going on.

It was with some trepidation that the church in Antioch welcomed the man from HQ, but their fears proved ungrounded, for he was soon as overjoyed as were they all with what God was doing in their city. Numbers grew, and Barnabas soon realised that he would need reinforcements. It was well known that Saul, the man he had introduced to Peter years earlier, was doing stalwart work in Tarsus, which was but a hundred miles round the coast, a day's trip by boat. When eventually he found Saul, Barnabas was amazed at his altered appearance. The hardships of the past dozen years had left their mark. But he readily agreed to accompany Barnabas back to help with the work in Antioch.

The year that followed would live in both their memories as special. The church grew and went from strength to strength. The locals dubbed the followers of the Way "Christians." At first they may have shrugged the title off as a nickname, but it stuck and soon spread to the wider community of the church.

It may have been due to the exodus from Jerusalem of several prominent members of the catering corps, or it may have just been because of the famine that had been predicted by one of their prophets, but for whatever reason, food supplies for the church in Jerusalem ran short. Word reached Antioch that there were hungry Christians back home.

They had an immediate whip round and dispatched their best men to accompany their contributions to Jerusalem. Barnabas was the obvious choice, since it had been from Jerusalem that he had come to them. But Saul was anxious to go too. He explained that he felt constrained to bounce off the Apostles his message. He had never met any of them, except Peter. So he had just gone ahead with ploughing his own furrow. Now he wanted to ensure that the gospel he was preaching was in harmony with that which the Apostles themselves preached. Saul feared that certain issues he had encountered on the Gentile front might not yet have been addressed by the church fathers. So they took along with them a young Greek named Titus, ostensibly to lend his muscle to the task. But Saul had an ulterior motive. Titus was a Gentile Christian. So would the Jewish Christians in Jerusalem insist on his being circumcised?

Circumcision had always been a heavy burden for Jews to carry, ever since the days of Abraham, when first it had been instituted. But would this rite now have to burden Gentile converts? This issue had been a bone of contention in Antioch ever since spies had infiltrated their membership to check out what they vilified as their "liberal practices," but what the church welcomed as "freedom in Christ." So Saul was determined to guard the integrity of the gospel that offered being made right with God simply by trusting in his grace and kindness, rather than through the performance of certain religious rites. And Titus went along as a test case.

So fourteen years after he had last left town, Saul came back to Jerusalem, in company with Barnabas and Titus. A private meeting was arranged with the Apostles. Saul set out before them, in his characteristically precise language, the message he had been preaching to Gentiles in Antioch and Tarsus, and shared how people had responded to his message. When he had finished, there was applause and unanimous acclamation of his work and his message. Formal handshakes were received from those who were now acknowledged as the big three: James (Jesus' brother), Peter, and John. Recognition was given to Saul as their missionary to the Gentiles, while

Peter, it was acknowledged, would continue to pioneer the work with the Jews. Saul had got the message right. Salvation was given entirely by the grace of God alone, in no way dependant on a person being circumcised. No one insisted that Titus be circumcised, so he returned to Antioch unscathed as a living example that salvation was by faith in God's grace alone, and the circumcision promoters could get lost.

But they didn't get lost, and trouble resurfaced when Peter himself came for a visit to Antioch. At first, things were fine. Peter joined the mixed Jew-Gentile church, eating and drinking with them all in united fellowship. "Don't you dare call anything that God has purified 'unclean,'" Jesus had told Peter, and he didn't. But a few days later, when reinforcements arrived from Jerusalem, Peter became self-conscious. Such mixing of Jews and Gentiles didn't happen back home, and Peter was thereafter careful to sit at a different table from his Gentile brothers. Soon other Jews followed Peter's example, even Barnabas among them.

Saul, who had been out of town when this split had been gathering momentum, was outraged when he got home and saw what was going on. Right there in the refectory, he stood up and called for silence. "Peter," he said, fearlessly calling out the big man in public, "you can't live like a Gentile one moment and then revert to living like a legalistic Jew the next. Or are you forgetting that we are all made right with God, not by obeying the law, but by trusting Jesus only?"

There was a terrible silence when he had finished. No one knew where to look. The whole unity of the church that Jesus had stressed would be the hallmark of genuine discipleship was up for grabs. Should Saul have submitted to this pillar of the church? But then the freedom of the gospel would be forever compromised.

Slowly, Peter got to his feet and walked across to where Saul was still standing and, with tears on his cheeks, gave him a hug. To admit he was in the wrong was the sign of a truly great man. Everyone rose to their feet and cheered. Gradually, both factions came together across the room and gave each other a family hug.

Inspired by the memory of Peter's courage, Saul would later write to encourage others: "Make every effort to keep the unity of the Spirit, the bond that keeps us all together in peace." But he never would give an inch to any who sought to compromise the gospel. "If we or even an angel from heaven should ever preach any variation of the gospel of God's grace, then let him burn in hell," he would say.

While it is true to say that things in Jerusalem had been relatively peaceful for the church once Saul had turned from foe to friend, it would be wrong to imagine that the religious authorities relaxed their antagonism to the Jesus movement. An unexpected ally against the church emerged on the political front.

King Herod Agrippa inherited the whole united kingdom of his grandfather, Herod the Great, when his uncle, Herod Antipas, was deposed by Rome. Something of a playboy in his youth, this new king was determined to make a success of his royal job, and to do that would necessitate his making friends with the religious set. This objective got off to a flying start when he successfully challenged Emperor Caligula's blasphemous proposal to erect a statue of himself in the Jerusalem temple. The subversive activities of the Christian church next caught his attention as a likely object for his religious fervour. He imprisoned some of the ringleaders, including the Apostle James, John's brother. From past experiences, everyone anticipated a miraculous release. But none was forthcoming: rather the opposite, in fact. James was beheaded.

This so boosted Herod's popularity with the Council that he had Peter imprisoned, intending to give him the same treatment as soon as the Passover festivities were done. While the Council rubbed their hands in gleeful anticipation, the church joined their hands in earnest prayer. But Peter's hands were shackled and chained in a deep dark cell in Herod's palace.

Gloomy memories of a previous Passover, when he had denied Jesus, were doubtless haunting his thoughts, as he lay there chained between the two guards. "The day will come when you will no longer be free to go where you will. Others will take your outstretched arms and drag you to a place you would never choose to go," Jesus had warned him on the beach near home. This might be it. Eventually, he dozed off to sleep.

But almost immediately, he found himself awake again, woken by a kick in the ribs. The cell was flooded with light, and there beside him stood an angel. "On your feet! And be quick about it," he ordered. As Peter scrambled to the vertical, the chains fell from his wrists. "Get dressed, and don't forget your shoes," prompted the practical angel to the bleary man. "Grab your cloak and follow me."

"This must be a dream," Peter concluded in his befuddled state. Certainly it had that dreamlike quality as the door of the cell swung open and the guards just stood at their posts, never even glancing in their direction. They reached the main prison gates, which opened before them like magic. They were out in the street with not so much as a "Who goes there?" to start the adrenalin pumping. They had walked the length of the street before Peter realised that he was now alone.

"So I'm not dreaming," he muttered to himself. "This is for real."

So where was he to go in the middle of the night? Mary's house was but a few blocks away: Mary, John Mark's mother and Barnabas' aunt. *There's bound to be people there praying for me,* Peter thought as he set off in that direction. Just as he had anticipated, there were lights on inside and a murmur of voices could be heard, even out on the street. Peter knocked on the door, not loud enough to attract unwanted attention from the law, but enough to alert those inside that someone wanted in.

It's not clear why Rhoda was so quick to respond. Perhaps she had been anticipating an answer to the prayers that were so urgently being offered in the room upstairs, or maybe she was just doing her job as a house servant by watching the entrance. But a moment after Peter knocked, the peephole in the door flashed open. "Who's there?" she enquired.

"It's me, Peter," he hissed.

The peephole slammed shut, and Peter heard the sound of retreating footsteps running up the stairs.

Bubbling with joy, she burst in on the subdued tones of the earnest prayer meeting.

"You'll never guess who is at the door," she announced breathlessly.

"Quiet! Can't you see we are praying?"

"But it's Peter!"

"You're nuts!"

"No. It really is Peter."

"Can't possibly be. Don't you know he's in prison?"

"Perhaps he's already dead, and it's his ghost come to say good-bye," someone else suggested unhelpfully.

But then they all heard it: the sound of knocking coming from the front door. And there stood Peter, smiling at them. The joy of their greeting was enough to disturb the entire city, so Peter held up his hand to quiet them down. Back inside they all went, and Peter told them the whole story.

"Someone had better go and tell the others," Peter said, mindful of the unnecessary worry that was likely being expressed on his behalf.

There was consternation in the jail when the cell was found to be empty the following morning. "Heads will roll for this!" asserted the captain of the guard, and they did. Herod was furious, but so was God, for Herod had dared to lay a hand on his church.

Soon after, Herod travelled to Caesarea. There was a festival he needed to attend, and also some of the city fathers of Tyre and Sidon were requesting an audience. "Something to do with the food supply," Blastus, his trusted PA, informed him.

So on the appointed day, Herod entered the great amphitheatre. He was wearing his shimmering silver cloak, and the morning rays of the rising sun reflected back around the arena, lending him an almost divine aura. Herod took his stance on the dais and addressed the crowd.

"It's the voice of a god!" someone shouted, and almost immediately Herod clutched his chest and collapsed to the ground. A few days later, he died in agony, and the worms took him. "He who touches you, touches the apple of my eye!" God had said.

---- 19 ----

The Mission

The world was a big place with undefined edges over the horizon, only hinted at by travellers and explorers who had been there and lived to make the return journey. Jesus had commissioned his Apostles to preach the gospel in Jerusalem, Judea, Samaria – and thus far, they had made a commendable start on covering those territories. But what of "the ends of the earth"? Saul's commission to take the gospel to the Gentiles inspired in him an insatiable urge to travel to those far-flung places and the lost shreds of humanity who lived there. "It is my ambition to preach the gospel to people who know nothing of Christ. I am not the man to build on someone else's foundation," he would say. So it's not surprising that his days in Antioch were limited.

It was while the church there was meeting to worship that one of the members, who was recognised to have a prophetic bent, called out, "The Holy Spirit is telling us to release Barnabas and Saul for the work to which they have been called." When they had taken a few minutes to digest this, it was agreed that they would all fast and take time to pray on it. The following week, when they met again, everyone gathered round the pair to lay their hands on them and officially commission them to whatever the Spirit might be calling them to do.

They had little idea of where they should go but were determined to follow the Holy Spirit's lead. Saul had recently spent a dozen years preaching in Cilicia from his home base in Tarsus, so they decided to bypass that territory and instead travelled down to the port of Seleucia, with the vague idea of taking a boat to somewhere. Barnabas was a native of Cyprus, and when a boat bound for that destination presented itself, they took passage. John Mark, Mary's son from Jerusalem, was with them. He was Barnabas' cousin and shared his enthusiasm to explore their family roots. Mark was a great writer and loved to record the story as it unfolded; he had already got the outline for a book on the life of Jesus. Most of his information he had gleaned from Peter who, of course, had seen it all first-hand. Mark was by now a man, having matured from the youth who had fled naked from the garden when Jesus was arrested.

The ship docked in the port of Salamis, the threshold of their new adventure. Now where were they to start their mission? Following the pattern prescribed by Jesus – to begin in Jerusalem – they went first to the local synagogue. To start by taking their message to the Jewish community became their modus operandi from then on, and only when they were rejected would they address the non-Jewish community.

They travelled the length of the island, talking about Jesus everywhere they went, till they came to the capital, Paphos. There in the synagogue, they encountered a man with the delightful name of Bar-Jesus: son of Jesus. His friendly response seemed promising, and he undertook to introduce them to his boss, no less a person than the proconsul himself. But the more they got to know Bar-Jesus, the more uncomfortable they became. Nevertheless, they were introduced to the great man, Sergius Paulus, an intelligent man who graciously invited them to explain to him their message. So here it began. Now Saul was preaching to men of influence.

He introduced himself, not as "Saul," a name that served him well in the Jewish community, since it evoked connections with the first king of Israel, but now as "Paul," the Greek version of his name, that mirrored that of his host, Sergius Paulus. They later agreed that it would be smart to continue to use that name, since their mission was primarily to the Gentiles.

Paul was barely halfway through his discourse when Bar-Jesus began to fidget and then jumped to his feet and interrupted, "Your Excellency,

I must protest. This is complete and utter nonsense, and you shouldn't believe a word of it."

Illuminated by the Holy Spirit, Paul suddenly recognised the man for who he was: "You child of the devil! You enemy of righteousness! You deceiver!" he shouted. "How dare you seek to distort the Lord's truth." Paul remembered his own past and what God had used to stop him in his tracks, en route to Damascus. "You are going to be struck blind for a while till you come to your senses." Bar-Jesus blinked and then reached out to steady himself, feeling for something or someone to hang on to.

Sergius Paulus was, to say the least, impressed at this display, especially since he was already amazed at what he had heard about Jesus. To say that he became a Christian would, perhaps, be an exaggeration, but he certainly was inclined to believe Paul's message.

With some reluctance, they sailed away north from Cyprus for Perga on the mainland. Paul had the bit between his teeth and was determined to keep moving on. Mark was irritated. How come Paul was suddenly taking over the leadership of the mission from Barnabas? It might have been nice to have been able to spend more time with their family on the island. And there was something else that troubled the young man. Was Paul not in danger of getting off track by sharing the gospel with Gentiles, with no regard for drawing them back into the tradition of Jewish practices? Maybe he could better serve God by concentrating on writing his biography of Jesus than by trailing around after this overbearing and risqué ex-Pharisee. So he took ship back home, leaving Barnabas disappointed and Paul's feathers ruffled.

Paul and Barnabas travelled inland a hundred miles, high up into the mountains to the north, till they came to the Roman-built road that crossed Asia Minor, east west. "*Pisidian* Antioch," as the city they entered was called to distinguish it from all the other cities with the same name, was another of those multi-cultural communities that thrived along the trade routes. They sought out the synagogue and took their places for the service the following Sabbath. After the Scripture reading, someone tapped Paul on the shoulder: "If you have a message of encouragement for us, we would love to hear it." It was perhaps the fact that Paul was a Pharisee that had elicited this invitation, but he gladly accepted the opportunity.

"I certainly do have something significant to say," Paul said, rising to his feet. And he told them all about Jesus. He was careful to base all his comments on Scripture, quoting extensively from the Psalms and noting that David's words about immortality found fulfilment in Jesus' resurrection alone. "The bottom line," Paul concluded, "is that through Jesus, forgiveness of sins is now available to you and to anyone who believes."

"We'd love to hear more about this," several people assured Paul and Barnabas as they shook hands after the service. "Could you come back next week?" And so they did, as did almost the entire population. The place was packed and overflowing with people of all religious persuasions and ethnic stripes, all of them eager to hear this extraordinary new teaching. Jealous for their exclusivity, however, some of the leading Jews bad-mouthed Paul and refused to let him speak.

"Very well," Paul said, speaking loud enough so the crowds both within and outside could clearly hear what he was saying. "We gave you Jews first opportunity to hear our message, but since you obviously don't consider yourselves worthy of eternal life, we will talk instead to the Gentiles, for that is the commission the Lord has given us."

There was jubilation amongst the Gentile visitors, who withdrew from the synagogue to a safe distance and then respectfully listened to all that Paul and Barnabas had to tell them. Many became believers and enthusiastically passed on what they had heard, till before long, there was a new church established in the city that drew in people from all over the region.

The Jews were not at all happy about this and persuaded the town council to have them expelled. Paul and Barnabas headed out of town, shaking the dust from their feet in contempt for the Jews, yet leaving behind them a church full of friends, brimming with a newfound joy in the Holy Spirit.

They travelled west down the Roman road. Praise God for Roman engineering, which made travel so much easier and was now paving the way for the spread of the gospel. The Via Sebaste led them over the hills and past snow-capped mountains, eventually bringing them to Iconium, a predominantly Greek city.

The response was at first positive, their message being confirmed by miracles, but some of the more conservative Jews stirred up trouble, and before they knew it, the city was divided, and they were forced to move on, but not before they had carefully laid the foundations of the new church.

Paul was always very careful to ensure that any new church started out on a right footing. He saw his mission similar to that of a master builder, who would start by laying a proper foundation, in this case, that of Jesus Christ himself. After he was gone, others would be able to build, hopefully using only materials that would stand up to the test of fire, as would gold, silver, and precious stones, since the more temporary approach would be bound to burn up like wood, hay, or stubble in the inevitable flames of persecution.

The Roman road forked at Iconium, so they headed south down a newly constructed extension of the road to Lystra, which they found to be a much less sophisticated community than Iconium. For a start, the common language was not Greek, so communication was more difficult. But more of a challenge was the absence of a synagogue. So they shared their message in the marketplace. Paul watched the expressions of the crowd, and as preachers often do, he spotted a particularly attentive face. Something about the way the man leant forward in his eagerness to catch every word, particularly when he spoke of Jesus' ability to heal, suggested to Paul that this man wanted to be healed. They discovered later that he had been lame from birth and was well known in the community.

"You, sir," Paul called, pointing at him from his improvised pulpit. It was not clear how well the man understood Greek, so Paul motioned with his hands as he called to him to stand up. One way or another, the man must have understood, for he instantly sprang to his feet, took a few tentative steps for the first time in his life, and then was fully mobile. The market square erupted with cheering and applause. As it continued, a discernible chant emerged from the enthusiastic shouts, but it was in the language of the peasants, so Paul and Barnabas failed to catch on to what it was about.

Then they saw a procession of pagan priests with bulls for sacrifice heading their way. They had garlands that they would have hung round their necks had not somebody interpreted to them the meaning of the chants: "Welcome to the gods! Welcome to the gods!" Apparently, there was a local legend about a surprise visit from Zeus and Hermes, and the people took Paul and Barnabas to be them. Anxious to avoid the recent fate of King Herod, Paul and Barnabas quickly denied deity, rushing into the crowd and tearing their clothes in horror.

When eventually the crowd quieted down long enough to listen, Paul did his best to explain the truth. "We are just human beings, like any of you," he started. "We are here simply to tell you good news. The time is come when you can be free of these worthless traditions and worship instead the living God, who made heaven and earth, the sea, and everything in them." Paul didn't bother to quote Scripture, since these people had never read it, so instead he used the natural world around them to give a context to what he was saying. "He is the one whose endless kindness is responsible for giving you plentiful harvests, full bellies, and hearts full of joy." They could relate to that all right, but even so, they were barely restrained from going ahead with the sacrifice.

In the end, they did get a hearing from a group of serious listeners, some of whom became committed believers. Amongst them was a timid young man named Timothy, the product of a mixed marriage. His father was a Greek, but both his mother and grandmother were God-fearing Jews. The whole family became the core of the new church in Lystra.

But trouble was snapping at their heels. Some Jews from Iconium and Antioch happened to be visiting town, and when they recognised Paul and Barnabas, they immediately spread a bad report about them. Coupled with this, the people of Lystra did not appreciate the repudiation of their plan to honour Paul as a god, so their adulation quickly turned to resentment, and they dragged him out of the city gates and stoned him till their fury was spent. The new believers then gathered in sorrow round their fallen hero, assuming he was dead. But to their amazement, he stirred, got to his feet, and walked with them back into the city. They cleaned him up as best they could, though the scars would linger.

Paul always wore his scars as badges of honour: "the marks of Jesus," he called them. When anyone commented on them, he would shrug it off by saying that it was a privilege to share Christ's afflictions and to suffer for the sake of his body, the church.

Next day, they limped out of town, heading farther south till they reached the hilltop town of Derbe. Their visit there was brief yet fruitful. And it wasn't trouble that moved them on from there, but just their consciousness that time was ticking, and they ought to be thinking of getting home. However, they weren't in so much of a hurry as to have taken the short cut south through Cilicia. They wanted to check up on the new believers in the towns they had recently visited, so it was back up the Roman road, the way they had come.

Knowing that the local authorities in each town would be unlikely to roll out the welcome mat for their return visits, Paul and Barnabas made no attempt at public proclamations of the gospel but concentrated rather on establishing the new believers into proper church structures. Their friends were shocked when they saw Paul's new scars. "Trouble is all part of the package," Paul assured them nonchalantly. "If we are to share Christ's glory, it is reasonable that we should expect to share his suffering as well."

In each town, it was apparent that the gifts of the Holy Spirit were already at work, preparing the people for active service, building up what had once been a random collection of diverse people into one coherent body: "Christ's body," as Paul called it. "As everyone does their part, you will find yourselves becoming increasingly united in your faith and knowledge of Jesus, changed to be more and more like Jesus himself." The gifts of the Spirit were expressed through the individuals that made up the whole. Some were like Apostles, always pioneers of new things, like Paul and Barnabas. Others were prophets, bringing to the attention of the church the heart of God. Then there were the evangelists, forever goading their fellow church members to share the good news with others. There were those whose gifts of instructing others in the truths of the faith identified them as teachers. And then there were the shepherds, the pastors who just wanted everyone to be together, safe in the fold. "Like body parts, you all have your own unique functions and abilities: eyes for seeing, ears for hearing, noses for smelling, and so on," Paul explained.

Leadership was vital in each of these local churches: God-ordained elders. So before they left, Paul and Barnabas took time to pray and fast with each congregation to identify who these people were. The kind of people who emerged were good family men who loved their wives and whose children were a credit to them. These people were not overbearing or quick-tempered and never alcohol abusers or dishonest, but were patient, self-controlled, and disciplined. They loved to entertain, loved goodness, loved the fundamental truths on which the church was founded, and encouraged others in that direction also.

And so Paul and Barnabas returned to the coast, only pausing for a few days to preach the gospel in Perga, which they had somewhat bypassed earlier, possibly because of their disgruntlement over Mark's departure.

Back in Antioch, the church was thrilled to see them safe home and listened with amazement to all their adventures. They were overjoyed to hear how God had opened the way for so many Gentiles to have faith in Jesus.

20

The Message

Both Paul and Barnabas stayed for a long time in Antioch, content for a while to sleep in their own beds each night.

When Paul wasn't preaching, he loved to set his words down on paper, sending his thoughts to the leaders of the churches he had helped to establish. It was disturbing news from the churches in Galatia that prompted Paul to send them a carefully worded letter. Apparently, someone had been following their footsteps from town to town, demanding that new Gentile believers must be circumcised. The worst of it was that many had been sucked in to this false teaching.

Paul never dated his letters, but at some point following his and Barnabas' visit there, he wrote:

> "Dear foolish Galatians,
>
> "I am horrified to hear that you are so quickly turning from the true gospel I preached to you, and instead submitting to the yoke of religious slavery. You remember the testimony I shared with you of how God freed me from all that, to find life in Jesus. And you knew that I didn't invent my own message or attempt to copy ideas from others. No, it was God's message and his alone I shared with you.

"It was never because you kept the requirements of the law that you received the Holy Spirit. I told you the truth about Jesus; you believed; the Holy Spirit came on you – simple as that. And that process is nothing new. It was always that way right from the start. God promised great blessings to Abraham; Abraham believed; God declared him righteous. Yes, the law was introduced in the days of Moses, the intention being to keep us in line till Jesus would come. But no one has ever managed to keep all the law, and as you know, it is all or nothing. Break one and you are guilty of all. That's the curse of it. But Jesus took that curse when he was crucified on our behalf. It's all a gift. You don't pay for a gift, it is just given to you. And God's gift is for everyone, not just for a few favourites. God has no favourites. We are all one in Jesus: Jews and Gentiles, men and women. No favourites! No exceptions! All God's children.

"So why turn back to legalism, for goodness sake? Why this nonsense about everyone must be circumcised and observe religious festivals? Smarten up!"

Paul concluded the letter with his own squiggly writing so they would be sure it was him writing, not some imposter.

And it wasn't just in Galatia that this pernicious teaching was being peddled, but right in their own back yard, in Antioch. "Unless you are circumcised, you will not be saved," these false teachers were saying.

Paul and Barnabas confronted them publicly, and there was no small dispute. It was the truth of the gospel that was at stake and not some minor detail of procedure, over which they could seek a compromise. In the end, Paul and Barnabas were appointed to lead a delegation to take this matter up at HQ in Jerusalem.

The assembly that welcomed them was quite impressive: Apostles, elders, and many other leading members of the church. The first item on the agenda was a report from the missionaries on their adventures in Galatia. This was received very positively. But then a spokesman for the section of the church made up of former Pharisees delivered his written speech, insisting that "in order to be accepted into the church, Gentiles must be circumcised and then taught to obey the whole law of Moses."

Paul, a former Pharisee himself, bit his tongue. He wanted to bide his time to see which way this was headed. It was with mixed feelings that he saw Peter rising to his feet, Peter with whom he had had words on that famous visit to Antioch some years previously, when Peter had distanced himself from the Gentile section of the church for fear of offending the more conservative visitors from Jerusalem. But to his enormous relief, it quickly became clear that Peter was on the right side: "Brothers, you will recall that God sent me to a group of Gentiles in Caesarea to share the gospel, and when they believed, it was God who welcomed them by giving his Holy Spirit, just as he did to us. If God made no distinction between Jews and Gentiles, why should we? We are all saved by grace alone."

Sensing the advantage, Paul rose to his feet and built on Peter's point by re-emphasising how God had confirmed his approval of what they had been doing in Galatia by miraculous signs and wonders.

James, Jesus' own brother, who was chairing the meeting, stood up and cleared his throat. Once again, Paul held his breath. James was known to be a disciplined, austere man who held to a traditional, conservative view of things. Which way would he lean on this vital issue?

He started out with a quote from the prophet Amos, referring to a time when the Gentiles would seek the Lord: "In my opinion we should not make their seeking the Lord any more difficult than it need be." A sigh of relief escaped Paul's lips. But then James continued, "However, in the interests of preserving good relations between Jews and Gentiles, we should recommend that Gentile believers avoid offending their Jewish counterparts by refraining from eating food that would be contrary to Jewish traditions and sensitivities, and from sexual practices that might be judged by the conservative element to be immoral." Well, Paul could accept that compromise, for it excluded nobody.

James' proposal was unanimously agreed, and minutes of the meeting were written up to be sent first to Antioch and then circulated to branches of the church all over the world, with a covering letter from the Apostles. They even sent a couple of elders, Silas and Judas, along with Paul and Barnabas to confirm first-hand the authenticity of the letter. And someone else tagged along: Mark. His young mind had been set at ease by the decision of the council, so he need no longer be concerned that Paul might be getting off track.

Once the letter had been delivered to Antioch, Paul was anxious to take it also to the Galatian churches. "It would be good to see how they are doing," Paul told Barnabas enthusiastically.

"Good plan," agreed Barnabas. "Let's take Mark with us."

Paul was not at all sure that was a good idea. After all, had Mark not deserted them on the last trip? And had not Mark proved a little wobbly in his conviction of full acceptance of the Gentiles, with no strings? The last thing Paul needed on this next trip was a half-hearted team member.

But Barnabas was determined to take him: "Give him another chance!" For the first time in their long walk together, sparks flew. Blood being thicker than water, Barnabas stuck with his cousin and resolved to take him along, Paul or no Paul.

"Fine! I will take Silas," said Paul. So Paul and Barnabas, two strong-minded men, went in different directions. Barnabas and Mark sailed back to Cyprus to renew contact with their long-lost cousins, while Paul and Silas headed towards Galatia. They chose to travel over land this time, so they could visit some of the places where Paul had planted the seeds of the church in Cilicia during his years in Tarsus. Eventually, they reached Derbe and then travelled on to Lystra. Paul was overjoyed to find the two churches thriving and anxious to talk about the letter he had sent them.

Young Timothy was particularly pleased to see Paul again. He badly wanted to join him in his missionary endeavours, but there was one great stumbling block. All his life, his Greek father had held out against his being circumcised, despite the protests of his Jewish mother and grandmother. But now that his father was dead, what should he do? Paul's letter assured him that as a Gentile, he would not need to be circumcised, but his fellow Jewish Christians in the local church in Lystra were continually on his case to get done.

"He's a good man," everyone assured Paul, "but he has not shown proper respect for Jewish traditions. Okay, we take your point about Gentile believers not needing to be circumcised, but Timothy is a Jew. You are not suggesting now that even Jews should throw out the traditions of our forefathers when they become Christians, are you?"

No, Paul was certainly not doing that. So he himself circumcised

Timothy, and everyone was happy – even Timothy, when the discomfort wore off. Timothy joined Paul and Silas in their travels as a living example of Paul's respect for Jewish traditions, while he still championed Gentile freedom.

So the threesome travelled west along the Via Sebaste. Paul's plan was to head for Ephesus, the capital of Asia. But when the road offered the turn-off to Ephesus, the Holy Spirit wouldn't let them take it. And neither would he permit them to swing north into Bithynia. Silas was something of a prophet and just didn't feel at peace in his spirit to progress in any direction other than northwest. Paul was more the scholar and teacher, and he recalled the words of Isaiah the prophet: "Whether you turn right or left, you will hear a voice behind you prompting, 'This is the way you should take. Follow it!'"

"So it's to Troas that we are headed," they all agreed.

But even Troas turned out to be but a temporary staging post, for that night, Paul had a vivid dream. He saw a man standing on the seashore, calling to him over the waters. "Come over here, to Macedonia. We need your help." There was desperation and urgency in the man's appeal. Surely this was the voice that Isaiah had spoken of: "This is the way you should take. Follow it!"

"We are going to take a ferry," Paul informed them all over breakfast. "We are going to Europe!"

So they headed for the waterfront to buy tickets. It was while they were killing time, waiting for the boat, that they encountered a fellow traveller, a doctor whose company Paul found most beneficial, since he rarely enjoyed the best of health. The doctor, they discovered, kept a meticulous journal, recording the most precise details of his daily adventures. He turned out to be a devoted researcher, who ferreted out details that others missed and then checked them and cross-checked till he was sure he had written an orderly account for all to read. Luke was his name, and to everyone's joy, he was booked on the same boat to Neapolis as were they, en route back to his native Philippi.

After anchoring for the night off the island of Samothrace, they reached Neapolis and, from there, travelled inland to Philippi. This was indeed a fine city, a Roman colony and proud of it. While Luke's company was a great encouragement to the three travellers so far from their homes, the doctor had no suggestions to offer as to where they might find local God-fearing Jews. But Jews were adept at finding each other in strange cities. The "when" part of the "when and where" rendezvous was a given: the Sabbath. But the "where" was more difficult, particularly so when, as in the case of Philippi, there was no synagogue. Some natural gathering place, preferably by the sea or by a river, was the rule of thumb. There in a park on the riverbank just outside of town, they were rewarded by the sight of a group of women who were reading the Scriptures and praying.

Naturally, the ladies gave their attention to three Jewish men who appeared to be teachers of the law. But what these men shared with them was amazing, like nothing they had ever heard before. Their hearts warmed to the good news that the Pharisee of the group, plainly the leader, was sharing with them. One of the ladies was called Lydia. The locals had called her that ever since she had settled in Philippi from her former home in the province of Lydia, over the water in Asia. She didn't mind the nickname, since her business was selling purple cloth, and the province of Lydia was famous for exactly that.

As Paul spoke, Lydia found her heart opening like a flower to the sunshine. She had long worshipped God, but what she was hearing now was like the fulfilment of all she had been reaching towards all her life. So when Paul told the group that the way to show their faith in the Jesus of whom he was talking was to be baptised, she was first into the water, closely followed by all the other members of her family and several of her employees.

"Where are you folks staying?" Lydia asked, still dripping wet from her baptism. "You are welcome to stay at my house, that is if you consider me now to be a true believer." They did, and that is where the first church on European soil was established. Nevertheless, they continued their weekly meetings by the river, and soon many others were joining them to hear the gospel.

There was a young slave woman who had an annoying habit of following them around, shouting, "These men are servants of the most high God, and they can tell you how to be saved." All publicity is not always good publicity, and this certainly was not the right variety. A demonic spirit, they discerned, was clearly the girl's inspiration and enabled her to tell fortunes, earning her master a tidy income by the exercising of her "gift." After several days of this, Paul had had enough. He rounded on her and addressed the troublesome spirit: "In the name of Jesus Christ, come out of her at once." And it did.

Fortunes were no longer told for her clients, and fortunes were no longer made for her master, who decided to sue Paul for damages. He had his men seize Paul and Silas, and drag them into the market square, where the injured man pled his case before the magistrates. "These Jews are upsetting the proper balance of things for us Romans in this city." Nobody bothered to ask the nature of exactly how they were upsetting things. They were Jews, and since everyone despised Jews, they had to be in the wrong, no matter what they were alleged to have done.

So without so much as a "How do you plead?" they were stripped, flogged, and thrown into jail. With a howling mob threatening to cause further disruption, the magistrates ordered the jailer to make them doubly secure, so he picked the deepest, darkest cell, clamped their feet into the stocks, double locked the door, and went to bed, confident that they could never escape. But he didn't get the sleep he had expected, for the sound of singing kept him awake. It was coming from the cells, not at all the usual sound to hear emanating from that quarter. He took a torch to investigate and found it was the Jews, who were singing religious songs. The whole cellblock was wide awake and listening, enthralled. But there were no rules that prohibited singing, so he left them all in darkness and returned to bed.

He was just dozing off when he was thrown out of bed by a powerful earthquake. When the shaking subsided, he grabbed his torch once again and ran for the cells, terrified of what he would find. If the prisoners were gone, then he would pay for it with his own life. His worst fears were realised: the whole structure of the building had shifted in the quake. The doors were off their hinges and standing open. The chains had all come loose from where they had been secured between the heavy blocks of stone from which the prison was constructed. He was a dead man. He was just about to make a quick end of it by throwing himself on his own sword when a voice called out of the darkness of the cell, "Hey, don't do that! We are all still here."

By now, some of his fellow wardens were rushing in to survey the damage. "Bring some light," he shouted. And there were all the prisoners, chains dangling from their wrists and ankles, but no longer attached to anything, not a single prisoner AWOL. What kind of magic did these men possess that would enable them to sing when others would curse and stay put when others would run?

He had been informed that the charges were simply that they had silenced a girl who announced to the city that "these men can tell you how to be saved." Shaking with fear, the jailer fell to the ground in front of Paul and Silas: "So can you really tell people how to be saved? What must I do to be saved?"

"Actually, there is nothing you can do to be saved. But I'll tell you who can save you: Jesus. Believe on him, and he'll save you: you and all your family."

The whole prison listened as Paul shared the good news: prisoners, wardens, and the jailer's family.

As the shock of the quake began to recede and the wonder of the gospel began to bring peace, good manners asserted themselves. The jailer led Paul and Silas into his own living quarters, where he washed the blood from their lacerated backs and dressed them. But he wouldn't wait a moment longer before requesting that he and his whole family be baptised, right there and then. The same tank that had just served for Paul's and Silas' ablutions now served as a baptismal. Then they all shared a joyful breakfast.

Scarcely was that done when there was a pounding on the door, and in came the local police officers. No doubt surprised to witness so happy a gathering round the breakfast table, they nevertheless delivered their message to the jailer at the head of the table: "These vagrant Jews, the prisoners Paul and Silas, are to be released, effective immediately."

"Excuse me," Paul said, rising from the table and surprising everybody. "We, upstanding Roman citizens, receive an arbitrary flogging in the public square, then are thrown in jail for the night, and now they want to get rid of us quietly? I don't think so! Tell the magistrates to come and give us an official escort out of the prison gates."

The police officers' faces drained of colour, and they turned to leave immediately.

"You are free men," their host urged them. "Go in peace. Don't make a fuss."

"Yes, I know we're free to go," said Paul. "But you and the church in Lydia's home have to go on living here. We have to make the point that you are not part of some crazy illegal sect but members of a legitimate society."

The apology that the magistrates later delivered was somewhat perfunctory and stopped well short of inviting them to stay in Philippi as honoured guests. "It might be best if you were to leave town," they concluded.

Taking along with them their erstwhile jailer, Paul and Silas headed to Lydia's house, where the whole church was gathered. Luke and Timothy were greatly relieved to see them, bloodied, but breathing. Introductions were made, and the jailor and his family found themselves enveloped by welcoming brothers and sisters.

"So you see, we have to leave you," explained Paul. Realising that this was likely his last opportunity to encourage this fledgling church, Paul added a few words beyond the standard farewells: "Don't worry about us or be anxious about anything, come to that. And remember, whatever may come your way, face it prayerfully, asking for God's intervention, but always confident and grateful that you already have it. That way, prayer won't be like your worry beads, but instead God's peace will be the guardian of your hearts and minds.

"Never be obsessed with your troubles, but concentrate rather on the positive: the true, noble, right, pure, lovely, admirable things of life. And always think of others as better than you are, giving them preferential treatment, just as Jesus did. He didn't hang onto his elevated position as God, but instead, for the sake of others, he made himself the lowest of the low, dead on a cross. That's why God has raised him up to the highest of the high, where one day soon everyone will honour the name of Jesus.

"I am quite confident that he who has started to do such wonderful things in your life will finish the job. He is by no means finished yet. So keep on keeping on, ever reaching for the reason Jesus Christ took hold of you. Ignore the failures of yesterday and strain forward to the hopes of tomorrow, conscious that it was God himself who called you to the highest prize of all."

And so Paul, Silas, and Timothy bade their new friends farewell and headed south on yet another marvel of Roman engineering: the Via Egnatia. They passed through a couple of sizeable towns without stopping, and some one hundred miles southwest came to the thriving seaport of Thessalonica. The couple of hundred thousand inhabitants included a fair complement of Jews who had established a synagogue, and it was there that the three travellers found themselves for the following three Sabbaths.

Being a long way from their home base in Antioch, their supply lines were stretched thin. The kind people of Philippi followed them with a love gift and a care package, but even so, they were forced to go back to work to earn an honest crust. Like every Jewish man, Paul had been apprenticed in a trade, along with his studies in theological school, and so was a skilled tentmaker. He showed his two companions how it was done. "If a man won't work, then he shouldn't eat," Paul would fume. They worked together on weekdays, but it was back to the synagogue every Saturday, where they did their best to convince the congregation from the Scriptures that Jesus really was the Messiah and that his suffering and resurrection were the final proof. And their efforts were rewarded by a good number of Jews and God-fearing Greeks believing what they had to say.

But, as was so often the case, there were others who didn't believe, and not content to remain passively unconvinced, they stirred up trouble. A disgruntled mob formed, and since the three visitors had made themselves scarce, the mob instead vented their ire on Jason, one of the new Christians. They dragged him before the magistrates and accused him of harbouring "these men who were responsible for causing trouble all over the world. They defy the emperor's decrees and have some notion of setting up a new king whom they call 'Jesus.'"

News from Rome had recently reached the magistrates that Emperor Claudius had expelled all Jews from the city. Apparently he was tired of stories of riots at the instigation of someone named "Crestus." Could Crestus perhaps mean Christians, the magistrates wondered? Well, whatever! They wanted none of that nonsense in Thessalonica, thank you very much. So they required of Jason that he deposit cash with the city, to be forfeited should these visiting Jews ever set foot there again. The three offenders slipped out of the city under cover of darkness.

In the months that followed, they heard that the persecutions had grown in Thessalonica. Some had even paid for their new faith with their lives. Paul and his companions longed to go back to encourage them but realised that such a visit might cost poor Jason his life savings or even their own lives. "But," they surmised, "perhaps young Timothy might be able to sneak under the radar undetected." So they sent the lad back for a visit and then followed it up with a letter from Paul. They might be banned from showing their faces, but there was nothing to say that they couldn't write.

In his letter, Paul shared his concern that they were suffering and expressed his deepest sympathy over the loss of their friends who had given their lives in the struggle. He underscored the truth of the resurrection of Jesus, which guaranteed the future hope of those who had fallen. "Very soon Jesus will return, and we will all be reunited as one," he reassured them. "So keep up the good work, and help those who are lagging." Then he added some thoughts that he wished he had taken the time to say while he was in Thessalonica, stressing the importance of working for a living. "If a man won't work, then he shouldn't eat!" was his latest mantra. He also added words on the topic of sexual purity, just as the edict from the council in Jerusalem had stressed. As was his habit, Paul signed the letter and wrote the final words in his own illegible hand.

Fifty miles across the fertile plain to the east, the Via Egnatia brought the three fugitives to Berea. Once again, there was a synagogue, and once again, that was their first stop. But the Jews in Berea were of a very different stripe than those in Thessalonica. They were immediately captivated by the message and met again next day to hear more. In fact, for a while they met every day with open Scriptures, carefully studying the relevant passages. Many became believers.

But trouble was snapping at their heels. The Thessalonians had heard what was happening and had sent agitators. So, confident that the seeds of the church were planted in fertile soil, Paul left town, leaving Silas and Timothy, now returned from his clandestine visit to Thessalonica, to finish up. Paul headed back to the coast and took a ship south to Athens, sending a message to Silas and Timothy to join him there.

So Paul found himself alone in a city famous for culture, art, and philosophy. The first thing that struck Paul was that there were more idols per square mile than there were people. The throbbing heart of Athens was the market square, under the shadow of the Parthenon. In that crowded place, Paul stood up to declare the truth about Jesus and the resurrection. He must have been daunted at the thought that the likes of Socrates, Aristotle, and Plato had stood on that very spot. But, fired by his anger at the ignorance of a people who, with that kind of intellectual heritage, still allowed themselves to be seduced by dumb idols, he spoke out passionately. How those people loved controversy and new ideas! Debate was their favourite pastime, so while Paul's message may have attracted a hearing, it did little more than tickle their ears. This was, after all, the cradle of Hedonism, Cynicism, Stoicism, and multiple other "isms" that dulled the ears to the truth and hardened the heart to the message of new life in Jesus. Some ignorantly took "Jesus" and "the Resurrection" to be two new gods to be added to their burgeoning collection.

"What is this blabbermouth talking about?"

"The council ought to be acquainted with his nonsense. Perhaps it's subversive."

So they took Paul to the council of Ares at the Areopagus up on Mars Hill, where he was required to explain himself. Paul realised that this was important, since it would be this body of city fathers who would either open the door for him to teach in their city or tell him to get out of town. Whatever the outcome, Paul gave it his best shot.

There was no sense in starting with a Scripture quote, since that would mean nothing to his audience. Neither were they turned on by the thought of "plentiful harvests, full bellies, and hearts full of joy," as had been the good citizens of Lystra. Religion and philosophy were the common denominators between Paul's message and where these people sat, so that is where he began his pitch.

"Gentlemen, I commend you for your religious broadmindedness, for in my brief sojourn in your fair city, I noticed an altar dedicated to 'An Unknown God.' Well, from today on, you have no further need to plead ignorance. For a start, the evidence of your eyes demands the reality of a creator. And if he is a creator capable of making the infinity of space above our heads and the earth beneath our feet, it would be gross arrogance to imagine that we could ever build him a house to live in or give him something he might be short of. He's the one who does the giving.

"It's clear from your smorgasbord of religions that we humans have long been reaching out in our quest to find God, no matter where we were born or in what culture we grew up. But the reality is that God is not far from any of us. Even the well-known poet Epimenides stressed just how very close he is to each of us when he wrote, 'In him we live, move, and have our being.' And even if that Cilician poet Aratus was right when he said of Zeus that 'we are all his offspring,' then surely it would be an insult to the human race to credit a lump of rock or even of precious metal with being the stuff from which we are descended. But since it really is true that we are all God's offspring, then it's time for us to turn away from all that ignorant religious superstition. It is by a man that God will judge the world, not by a carved rock. God has given clear evidence of this man's credibility by raising him from the dead."

Paul told them all about Jesus. The response was mixed. Predictably, the cynics sneered, since cynicism was the basis of their religion. Happily, a few did believe, but the upshot of the hearing was that the council tabled the matter for possible consideration at a later date. Paul and his talk of resurrection was a non-issue, to be treated with courteous contempt by his intellectual superiors.

Paul felt snubbed. To be tossed out of town on the cusp of a riot was one thing, but to be disdainfully ignored was a blow to his pride. Since he was now gagged till the matter would be resolved (if indeed it ever would be), there seemed little point in staying longer in Athens. He left town in low spirits and dragged his weary feet west towards Corinth. His body ached from the beatings he had endured. He was racked with worry about his friends in Thessalonica, who he feared he had abandoned to their fate. On top of it all, with no church full of generous new believers to send him on his way from Athens, he was flat broke.

His arrival in Corinth was a culture shock. From the stoic, sometimes ascetic culture of intellectualism in Athens to the materialistic nouveau riche, live-for-the-moment culture in Corinth was a mere forty miles. But it might as well have been on a different planet. This was a big city, twenty times the population of sleepy Athens. Ancient temples gave place to modern commercial buildings, and the hustle and bustle of business dispelled quiet contemplation. The economy was regularly boosted by the Olympic Games, which attracted a wave of athletes and fans every four years. Even religion itself was a thriving industry, with its surplus offerings sold off in the meat market and Aphrodite's temple prostitutes, who looted the pilgrims every night. Moral laxity was the fashion, the very name of the city borrowed by the Greeks as a pseudonym for fornication. This was a spiritually oppressive place, and Paul limped into town, depressed and fearful.

The Jewish quarter was in the poorer part of town, so that was where Paul headed. He found work through the local tent makers' association and fell in with a couple of fellow Jews named Aquila and Priscilla. Like him, they had recently arrived in town, having been kicked out of Rome by Emperor Claudius, and like Paul, they were believers. Paul was much encouraged to learn that a church had already been established in Rome, and the more he heard about it, the more he longed to go there. So new courage rose in his heart. He was no longer alone, and as Solomon had once observed, "By yourself you are vulnerable, but with a friend at your back you can defend yourselves. But better yet, a three-stranded rope can't easily be snapped."

Paul wanted to make some tangible expression of his recommitment to God now that his confidence had returned, so he took a Nazirite vow. This committed him to keep off alcohol and required him to refrain from having his hair cut for the duration. Like that of Samson, Paul's strength seemed to grow again, along with his hair.

Every Sabbath, Paul and his two new friends worked together to persuade the attendees at the synagogue that Jesus really was the Messiah. Finally, to Paul's enormous relief, Silas and Timothy caught up with him. They brought encouraging news of the church in Thessalonica, and they also brought financial support from their generous friends in Philippi. On the strength of this, Paul quit his job and concentrated full time on preaching.

This growing clique of Christians in their congregation irritated the Jews. First Stephanas and his whole family were sucked in by this new teaching, then Crispus, the president of the synagogue, caught the bug, followed by Gaius Titius Justus, a Gentile who lived right next door. Paul was baptising them all. This had to be stopped!

So the following Saturday, the elders stood up to oppose Paul, using abusive language.

"Very well," Paul said, rising from his seat and shaking the dust off his coat. "My obligations here are complete. From now on, we will concentrate on the Gentiles. Your blood be on your own heads!" So saying, he and the rest of the new believers walked out. But they didn't go far, just next door to the house of Gaius Titius Justus.

If the pattern of things in other cities repeated itself in Corinth, then it wouldn't be long before trouble would be brewing here, and they would be forced to move on. But that night, Paul dreamed of Jesus, who clearly told him, "Don't be intimidated, Paul. Just keep on speaking out, for I am right here with you. I have many people to claim as my own in this city."

So the home of Gaius Titius Justus became the address for the church in Corinth, and there Paul taught every day while many more new believers were baptised and joined the fellowship. Freed from the necessity to earn his living, and able to sleep in the same bed for more than a few nights in a row, Paul used his spare time to write letters.

After Paul had been in Corinth for some nine months, a new proconsul was appointed by Rome. He was a Spaniard by the name of Gallio, a most likable man with a sense of humour. Seizing the opportunity of a new broom that had the proverbial potential to make a clean sweep, the Jewish elders effected a citizen's arrest and had Paul dragged before Gallio in the public square. "This man is trouble," their spokesman Sosthenes accused. (He was the new ruler of the synagogue, since Crispus had turned traitor.) "He incites people to illegal expressions of worship."

Paul recognised this as a serious threat to the further spread of the gospel. If Gallio were to rule against him, then that would establish a precedent wherever Roman jurisdiction extended, branding Christianity an illegal religion. The church would be driven underground.

Paul was about to make his defence when the proconsul cut him short: "I am sick to death of you Jews arguing about words and the nitpicking little details of your precious law. You are wasting my time! I rule this matter to be outside the scope of Roman legislation. Settle your own squabbles!" So saying, Gallio indicated to his soldiers that the Jewish elders should be ejected from his court. This apparently anti-Semitic display delighted the crowd, who surged forward gleefully and started to rough up the wretched Sosthenes. But Gallio wasn't bothered. The Jews had made their bed, and they could lie in it.

God's promise to protect Paul while in Corinth was now guaranteed by the Roman proconsul, so Paul stayed put for a further nine months, and the church in Corinth was firmly established.

The time passed, and Paul became anxious to be back home in Jerusalem for Pentecost, so he bade the church farewell, promising to return before too long. Looking back from the stern of the ship towards Corinth as it slowly sank below the western horizon, Paul had a sense of accomplishment. Planted in the rotting soil of that corrupt city were the good seeds of the word of God. There was already tangible evidence of the first shoots of this new life: the church.

But when people are involved, nothing is ever simple. Paul would later receive a visit from three members of the Corinthian church, who filled him in on what happened after he left and shared with him a list of questions from the members. Paul immediately sat down to dictate a letter.

Disunity was his main concern. Apparently, factions were being formed in honour of various church leaders: Peter and even Paul himself. Paul was especially upset to learn that they were apparently bringing these divisions right to the communion table or taking them before the civil authorities for litigation. Also there was rivalry over different spiritual gifts and which gifts suggested that their holders were the most spiritual. And reportedly, there was immorality in the ranks. Well, that would need to be rooted out and quickly.

The questions they asked included the wisdom (or otherwise) of eating meat that had been previously sacrificed to idols, the relative merits and demerits of marriage for a Christian, and the question of whether divorce was ever appropriate. Paul used the natural to illustrate the spiritual, likening the great temples that he remembered in Corinth to the temple of the human body, and recalling the Olympics that were held not far from Corinth, he compared the marathon runner to the Christian.

Paul included an amazingly beautiful paragraph about the nature of love that never fails, words which doubtless first adorned the walls of the church in Corinth but have adorned those of countless churches ever since.

Finally, Paul underscored the importance of the resurrection of Jesus, listing the hundreds of people who had actually met Jesus after his resurrection and pointing out that, because he rose, they too could now look death squarely in the face with no fear.

Paul signed it appropriately, including greetings from Priscilla and Aquila. But it was with a degree of nervousness that he sent Timothy off to deliver it personally, conscious of the in-your-face style of what he had written.

Priscilla and Aquila sailed with Paul as far as Ephesus, where they disembarked with the intention of establishing a new branch of their tent-manufacturing business. So this was Ephesus, the great capital of Asia Minor. Well, the waterfront wasn't anything to boast about. Many of the warehouses were boarded up, and the place had a past-its-prime feel. The hills above Ephesus had been logged off some years previously, causing the exposed soil to be eroded and carried down in the runoff to silt up the approaches to the port. Now only shallow draft vessels could make it to the dock, and then only at high tide. The great trading ships had to stay away.

However, the rest of the city was still impressive. Most prominent was the temple of Artemis, much larger than the Parthenon in Athens. Around it was a thriving industry of artists and craftsmen, turning out replicas of the great lady of Ephesus to sell to gullible tourists.

But Paul didn't have time to be a tourist. He took the opportunity of the brief stop in Ephesus to meet the Jews in the local synagogue. This was the city he had set his sights on a couple of years earlier, just after leaving Galatia. Now he had but a few hours to gain a toehold. So he got right down to the heart of the matter. He would have stayed longer, but the ship was due to sail, and he dared not miss his ride.

"We'd love to hear more about this," the elders assured him.

"Then I'll come back as soon as I can, if God will let me," Paul assured them warmly. Then he was gone.

The ship eventually docked at Caesarea, and Paul travelled up to Jerusalem. He spent a month there, preparing himself for his big Nazirite sacrifice and touching base with the church. Then he returned to Antioch. Home at last, but with so many wonderful stories to share.

---— **21** ——---

The Distance

One Sabbath, not long after Paul had left them in Ephesus, Priscilla and Aquila were surprised to hear a visiting preacher at the synagogue. The man was clearly a scholar and a powerful orator, but best of all, he was speaking about Jesus. "Surely this is the one about whom John the Baptist spoke. Jesus must be the Messiah," he concluded. "So repent and be baptised. Get ready for the coming one." The congregation was stirred, and there were some who responded to his appeal.

But to Priscilla and Aquila, he had missed the best bit, the part about Jesus' death and resurrection and the coming of the Holy Spirit. Why would he stop short of the climax of the whole message? So after the service was over, they invited him to come to their home.

Apollos was his name. He was a long way from his home in Alexandria in North Africa and in the course of his travels, he had heard all about John and Jesus and so was passing on the little he knew. Apollos' face fell when his host and hostess told him that Jesus had been crucified, but lit up again when they shared with him the good news of the resurrection. They brought him right up to date, telling him all about Paul's travels and how the church was taking root in cities all over the empire. "We just got here after spending eighteen months in Corinth. Now that's a cesspool of moral depravity, but the church is growing like a rose on a dung heap."

Apollos was intrigued. "I must go there at once!" he announced, jumping up from the table. And he did. They sent him off with letters of introduction to their friends in Greece.

Not long after he was gone, Paul came back to town. He had travelled over land, visiting the churches that he and Barnabas had planted five years previously. His heart was more at peace now he had seen first-hand how well they were all doing, but he was unsettled at the thought that so many of the towns and villages he had passed by on the way were still in ignorance of Jesus – places like Colossae and Laodicea. "We have to do something to reach out to them," Paul told Priscilla and Aquila, with concern written all over his face.

Paul was quickly aware that something had shifted in Ephesus during the months he had been away. At the synagogue, he was surprised to find a new study group of around a dozen men, all believers in Jesus. Well, Paul was right there. This could not possibly be the result of his previous visit, which had been all too brief, so what had happened? Then it came out.

There had been this visiting preacher named Apollos who had told them all about Jesus and had even baptised them, just like John had baptised people in the Jordan. But something was not quite right. They believed in Jesus, all right. They had all the right words, but there was none of the joy and life that usually sparkled in a group of new believers. They had the form of godliness, but not the power of it.

"Did you receive the Holy Spirit when you believed?" asked Paul.

"The 'Holy Spirit'? What's that?"

"Tell me about your baptism." They described what had happened, and how it had been just like John had done it twenty-five years ago.

"John baptised people as an expression of repentance in preparation for the coming of Jesus," Paul explained. "You need to be baptised so as to become one with Jesus himself. As you go under the water, your old sinful self dies and is buried. Your former slave masters are drowned, like those Egyptians at the Red Sea. You become one with Jesus in his crucifixion, death, and burial. Then, as you are raised up again from the water, so you share in his resurrection by the glorious power of the Father. You begin a whole new life as free men, the yoke of slavery to sin forever broken. So when the Spirit who raised Jesus from the dead is living in you, then he is living his life in your bodies also."

There was no hesitation. The truth of John's message had once again paved the way, and now they were wide open to Jesus himself. Paul took them all down to the beach and baptised them, one by one, into the name of Jesus. When they were all done, Paul gathered them into one dripping wet huddle, laid his hands on them, and prayed. Then it happened, just like the day of Pentecost all over again. The whole group burst out in praise to God in language they had never before heard or spoken. The Holy Spirit of Jesus was in town and Ephesus would never be the same again.

Paul's welcome in the Ephesian synagogue lasted for a record three months. With coherent logic, he argued his point, but it was never to win the argument that he strove, but simply to persuade his audience of the arrival of the kingdom of God. Many believed, but there are always those to whom change is abhorrent. It was not so much that they couldn't believe, but more that they stubbornly refused to believe. Their intransigence turned to slander, so rather than be party to a slanging contest, Paul withdrew, taking with him half the congregation. He rented a lecture hall, named "Tyrant Hall," in memory of an unpopular former professor. There for two years, he hosted daily dialogues. Almost everyone in town must have attended at one time or another, and soon the goddess Artemis no longer had the monopoly of being the only tourist attraction in Ephesus. People came to the Tyrant Hall meetings from far and wide. Paul stayed put for those years, preferring to send others on missionary sorties. They travelled to the towns of the interior of Asia, places like Sardis, Thyatira, Philadelphia, Smyrna, Pergamum, and Laodicea. When Timothy eventually came back to join Paul, he proved an invaluable emissary on a number of occasions, notably accompanying Epaphras to Colossae.

Years later, while Paul was enjoying a stretch of accommodation at the emperor's expense, he wrote this new church in Colossae a letter. Though he had never met most of them, he assured them of his love and prayers. His letter reminded them all of the supremacy of Jesus and warned them against anything that might take their eyes off him. Loving unity should be central in their fellowship, he told them, and gave specific instructions on how they should relate to one another, both in the home and the work place. Paul added a PS, requesting that his letter be reread to their near neighbours in Laodicea, twenty miles up the road.

Included in the same envelope was another letter marked "Private and confidential" and addressed to Philemon. Paul had met Philemon in one of the many Tyrant Hall meetings and had introduced him to Jesus. Now it was time to ask a favour in return. It concerned a young runaway slave who Paul had encountered along the way and had also led to Jesus. Onesimus, this eager new believer, was doing much to relieve Paul's discomfort in jail, but that was no excuse for his breaking the law. Onesimus was, after all, a fugitive and could be arrested at any moment. He would have to go home to face the music. Just because he was now a Christian didn't mean he no longer owed allegiance to his erstwhile master. Jesus' freedom was one thing, but that didn't mean he could assume release from his slavery. So Paul wrote Philemon a letter. Having buttered him up appropriately, he asked him to welcome Onesimus home, no longer just as a runaway slave, but now as a brother. And Paul made the rash promise, on Onesimus' behalf, to repay any liabilities that might still be outstanding.

Those days in Ephesus were unusual. Extraordinary signs and wonders confirmed the truth of Paul's message, and since that message was radiating out to the dozens of little towns that were hidden away in the rugged hills of western Asia, people there also wanted to experience Paul's healing touch. Travel was difficult, so visitors would borrow some of Paul's personal items to carry home to their sick friends. Handkerchiefs and towels kept disappearing, and word got back that people were being healed just by touching them.

But Ephesus was that kind of place, rather touchy-feely, spells and potions. So this Jesus stuff rapidly became the flavour of the month, and soon everyone was trying on the old "in the name of Jesus" routine. There was a team of exorcists who went under the pretentious title of "the Seven Sons of Sceva." Sceva, they claimed, was a Jewish high priest. Nothing ventured, nothing gained, so they decided to give it a whirl. Next time they faced a client who was demonised, they addressed him: "In the name of the Jesus whom Paul is preaching, we command you to come out of this man!"

A strange voice responded, "I know who Jesus is, and I have heard of Paul, but who are you?" So saying, the man launched himself at them, knocking them flying, raining down kicks and punches till they were badly mauled. Their attempts to escape were frustrated by the man's tenacious grip, and only by abandoning their clothes and fleeing out into the street buck-naked were they able to get away.

Word of their embarrassing retreat spread all over town, and the name of the Lord Jesus was thereafter held in much higher honour. Indeed, many of the exorcists and sorcerers who had been trying it on were so terrified that they brought to the Tyrant Hall their magic books and spells. A huge bonfire outside in the street celebrated their repentance, and the smoke of thousands of drachmas' worth of nonsense rose to heaven like incense.

But the local tourist trade was in jeopardy. There were many artisans whose livelihood depended upon the continuing popularity of Artemis. This lady was a grotesquely deformed goddess, whose fall from heaven had inspired the temple that was widely regarded as one of the Seven Wonders of the World. The hotel and catering business was taking a beating since word had got out to would-be pilgrims that Artemis was being upstaged. And the silversmiths were suffering, since the invisible Jesus didn't lend himself to being replicated as a souvenir.

Demetrius, chairman of the union of silversmiths, resolved to put a stop to this nonsense. He convened a meeting of the entire chamber of commerce and then stood up to address the assembly:

"Ladies and gentlemen, we all share a common interest in protecting the trade that is generated by the worship of Artemis. Yet here's this fellow Paul, leading the people of Ephesus astray and spreading his poison all over the province. He is teaching that man-made gods are not gods at all. I tell you, it's bad for our business and bad for the temple and, if we are not careful, will discredit Artemis herself."

"Hear, hear!" someone shouted.

"Great is Artemis of Ephesus!" someone else yelled from the back row, and soon everyone took up the shout. Then they were all on their feet, shouting the slogan at the top of their voices. The meeting spilled out into the street and surged down the Arcadian Way, gathering momentum and people as they went. Someone recognised the bewildered Gaius and Aristarchus, a couple of foreigners who were in town to visit Paul. Assuming they were part of the problem, they were grabbed and swept along with the crowd right into the huge amphitheatre at the end of the street. There the crowd swelled till the place was pretty much filled with angry, chanting people. The truth was that most of them had no idea what was going on, but fun like this was not to be missed.

Paul was all for going in. What an opportunity to preach the gospel! Why, the whole city must be there. But his team restrained him, and even some of the city officials who were friends of Paul sent him a message, begging him to keep away.

Some of the Jews from the synagogue, however, were not so wise. Sensing an opportunity to have these wretched Christians kicked out of town, they pushed their way to the front, boosting their spokesman up onto the podium to make a speech. But the crowd quickly recognised him as a Jew, another of those cursed worshippers of an invisible god, and shouted him down. To most Ephesians, the difference between the Jewish religion and Christianity was indefinable. They were both as bad as each other.

Someone started the chant again, and soon twenty thousand voices were screaming in unison: "Great is Artemis of Ephesus! Great is Artemis of Ephesus!" They might have kept it up all night had not the city clerk intervened.

"My fellow Ephesians," he shouted. This was a face they recognised, so they quieted enough to hear what he was saying. "Everyone knows that we are the guardians of the temple of Artemis, and that it was here in Ephesus that her image chose to fall from the sky. Since this is unquestionably so, why all the fuss? You have dragged these two foreigners here [indicating Gaius and Aristarchus] for no crime of which I am aware. They haven't stolen anything or blasphemed our goddess, have they? If Demetrius has a grievance against anyone, he can bring it to the authorities in the prescribed manner, and if there are any other concerns that any of you have, then they can easily be settled in the regular legal assemblies established for that very purpose. But no more of this shouting! Why, we could be charged with rioting for today's shenanigans. Now, it's time to go home. If you would all please be so good as to leave the theatre quietly and in an orderly manner ..." And to his enormous relief, they did.

———————————

It was clear to Paul that his welcome in Ephesus had worn thin, so it was time to be moving on. In any case, he was worried about the church in

Corinth and the effect his very direct letter might have had on them, so he badly wanted to pay them a visit. A few months previously, he had taken the precaution of sending Titus to them as his personal representative. Titus was from Antioch and had accompanied Paul and Barnabas to the Jerusalem summit on circumcision seven years previously. So Titus had gone to Corinth with instructions, not only to pour oil on whatever troubled waters he might find, but also to encourage the Corinthians in their contributions to "the collection." Hearing that the church in Jerusalem was once again struggling financially and desiring to demonstrate to them the respect and love of Gentile believers all over the world, Paul had started to raise funds for their relief. He always referred to this fundraising drive as "the collection." Paul had sent word to Titus to meet up with him in either Philippi or Troas, so when his ship docked in Troas, Paul anxiously scanned the crowds for Titus, but to his disappointment, there was no sign of him. The seeds of the church had blown into Troas, and Paul was torn between staying to help them get established and moving on to Philippi in search of Titus. Such was Paul's concern for Titus that he opted for the latter course.

His passage across the Aegean Sea was spoiled by worry. What had happened to Titus? Had those Corinthians waylaid him? Had he made the mistake of bringing some of the collection with him and been set upon by bandits? "Conflicts on the outside and fears within" is how Paul later described his emotions on that voyage. But all that only served to make the reunion in Philippi the sweeter. There was Titus' smiling face, and the good news he shared of the state of things in Corinth brought enormous relief to Paul's jangled nerves.

"They really love you, you know," Titus assured him. "Yes, they were terribly worried about the matters you raised in your letter, but they have taken radical steps to put things right."

So relieved was Paul that he abandoned his plans to rush on down to Corinth, choosing instead to write them another letter, while himself remaining in Macedonia. But after he had checked up on the churches he had founded there and had rattled the can to get the drachmas rolling into the collection, Paul headed west on the Via Egnatia, all the way into Illyricum. He took Titus with him for company. This was brand-new territory and rounded off Paul's mission to fully proclaim the gospel from

Jerusalem to Illyricum and all stops in between. Titus proved a useful sidekick to Paul and was popular with the many new friends they made in that province. Years later, Titus would return there to continue his mission, but when the best part of a year had elapsed, he and Paul headed back through Macedonia and Greece, finally reaching Corinth.

Paul was relieved to see first-hand how well the Corinthians had responded to his letter. Gone were the squabbles over speaking in tongues, denominations, and cliques. To crown it all, the Lord's table had been restored to a place of unity and love.

Now that Paul was no longer worried about Corinth, he found his thoughts wandering farther west. Italy was just a brief boat ride over the sea from Corinth, and ever since he had heard of the church in Rome from Priscilla and Aquila, Paul had longed to go there. Possibly he could use the church in Rome as a staging post for extending his ministry through France and into Spain.

Paul used his spare time in Corinth to get down to some serious writing. He composed his magnum opus, a long and detailed treatise on the gospel of the grace of God. This would be useful in future to send to many of the churches he had founded. As soon as it was finished, he incorporated a copy of it into a letter to the church in Rome, in which he promised to pay them a visit in the near future, en route to Spain. Little did he then know that his visit to Rome would be en route to nowhere.

But after three months in Corinth, Paul decided to make a quick trip back to Jerusalem before resuming his mission to Rome and beyond. The collection was now a considerable sum, and he wanted to get it into the hands of the people for whom it was intended. His original plan had been to send it in the care of some members of the Corinthian church, but the more he thought about it, the more he worried about entrusting so large a sum to a group that had been plagued with arguments in the past. In any case, how much better that it be delivered by Paul himself, leading a procession of Gentiles representing every church that had contributed. Paul had in mind the triumphal processions that returning Roman generals led as they came home to Rome as conquering heroes. Not that he considered himself a hero or his Gentile followers as defeated captives, but he felt his heart swelling with gratitude to God, who always led his church in triumphal procession, spreading to the crowds that lined the streets the fragrant joy of knowing Jesus. Knowing Jesus, he felt, was like an aroma of life to those who joined the procession on the road to salvation (or the stench of death to others who refused to follow).

Paul had intended to travel by ship direct to Antioch and thence to Jerusalem, but a plot to harm him and steal the collection was uncovered, forcing him to change his plans. He travelled back along the road up through Macedonia, which was by now becoming so familiar.

His triumphal procession was getting quite long, since it now included representatives from churches in Corinth, Berea, and Thessalonica. To Paul's great joy, Doctor Luke joined the convoy in Philippi. Further down the road, they would gather up more representatives from Ephesus and several of the churches in Asia, and finally Gaius from Derbe and good old Timothy from Lystra would join the party. It was useful to be travelling with so large an entourage, since it was dangerous to have that much cash in their luggage.

But en route, they made a brief stop in Troas, which Paul had previously been forced to bypass because of his worry about Titus. Paul now had a ready entrée to the city, avoiding the need for the use of a Trojan horse, as had famously been required fourteen hundred years previously.

"We can stay for a week," Paul promised the tiny church, if indeed you could call it a church, since it was little more than a group of interested people. So Paul wasted no time before laying the foundations for the church of Jesus Christ in Troas.

He set the precedent of meeting on the Lord's day, now officially recognised as being Sunday, the first day of the week. "Never neglect regularly meeting together so that you can encourage each other," Paul instructed. "It's important to establish strong links with each other through regular fellowship."

Paul taught them the meaning of the bread and the wine and passed on to them the precise wording of the tradition he had inherited from those who had been present the night before Jesus was crucified. Next was the traditional teaching of the Apostles. To pass this on took a little longer and stretched way into the night. So much to say and so little time!

They were meeting in an upstairs room on the third floor, lit by many lamps that made the place stuffy. Some of the audience grew drowsy as Paul talked on and on. One young lad, sitting on a windowsill, fell fast asleep. Those nearest to him looked up just in time to see his legs disappearing out of the window. There was a gasp of horror, and then the whole room emptied as they all charged down the stairs to find poor Eutychus' lifeless body sprawled in the street. Paul, who had been farthest from the door, arrived last. Pushing through the crowd, he knelt down beside the lad. Eutychus was quite dead, and all because he had talked so long. Remembering the example of Elisha as he raised to life the son of the Shunammite woman, Paul stretched himself on top of the corpse. A moment later, the boy groaned, stirred, and then sat up. Everyone was completely amazed. Now they had seen it all. If ever there was a convincing demonstration of answered prayer and the power of the resurrection, then this was it. Everyone returned to the upstairs room, and someone produced refreshments. After that, they all got their second wind, and the lecture continued till the rising sun signalled that it was time for the audience to go to work.

And that was exactly what the church had always been about since day one. They were devoted to the Apostles' teaching, fellowship, the breaking of bread, and prayer. In just one week the foundations of a new church were all laid, so Paul announced that it was time to be moving on.

He wanted some time alone to pray, so he installed his team on board a ship with the money safe in the hold and then walked the thirty miles across the peninsula to Assos, where the ship was to dock next. Paul rarely had time on his own when he could pray out loud without others listening in. But there was a particular reason that he wanted this time alone. Over the previous few days, he had been getting a nagging feeling that the Holy Spirit was warning him of a big change coming down the pipe. So Paul walked and prayed, all the while keeping an eye on the laboured progress of the ship around the peninsula off to his right. That evening, they all met up in Assos in time to sail on together next day.

The end of the line for their ship was Miletus, where they all disembarked with their precious cargo and awaited a ship that was headed in the right direction. Paul's sights were set on being in Jerusalem in time for Pentecost, just four weeks ahead, so as much as he might have liked to, there was just not time to make the detour into Ephesus. In any case, to get involved with the many social visits that such an excursion might involve, not to mention the possibility of a further tangle with Demetrius and his silversmiths' guild – well, time simply did not permit. So Paul sent a messenger to the elders of the Ephesian church, inviting them to meet him in Miletus, and a couple of days later, they arrived.

It was a brief and tearful meeting, for Paul was now sure it would be their last. He reminded them of the core of his message: that people should turn to God in repentance and have faith in the Lord Jesus. He urged them as elders to keep careful watch over the church in their care.

"The Holy Spirit has told me that trouble awaits me in Jerusalem. But that's okay, since I don't value my own life that highly. But sadly, I have to tell you that we will never meet again." With that, he bade them all kneel down with him as he committed them to the grace of God. They were all in tears by the time he finished. He embraced them each in turn and then walked up the gangplank onto the coastal freighter that would take them on the next leg of their journey. The ship slowly drifted on the current away from the quay and was lost to view as it rounded the point and then turned south.

They sailed across the north-eastern corner of the Mediterranean. Sailing close to Cyprus, Paul was reminded of the time ten years previously when he had visited the island in company with Barnabas and Mark. That's where the adventure had all started. Now what did the future hold? There was so much land yet to be possessed, but would he ever get out of Jerusalem alive?

Next day, the ship docked in Tyre to trade its cargo for a new one. The captain estimated that the unloading and loading again would take about a week, so the team made the most of the opportunity to meet with the local church.

"Whatever you do, don't go to Jerusalem," the members begged them, but Paul's mind was made up. The whole church turned out to wave them good-bye when the ship sailed the following week. A further stop in Ptolemais facilitated another brief visit with the church there, and then it was on to Caesarea, the end of their voyage. There to meet them was a friendly face: "Philip, the evangelist," as he was now known, rather than "Philip the caterer," as he had started out his ministry. In recent years, Philip had settled in Caesarea and concentrated on raising a family. He had four daughters still at home, each of whom had the gift of prophesy. Probably the food was terrible, since none of them seemed prepared to major in the culinary arts. But despite that, the team stayed there for the best part of a week.

One strange incident stands out from that stay in Caesarea. A prophet named Agabus came unannounced into one of their gatherings. Without a word, he walked up to Paul, untied the belt round his waist, and then wrapped it round his own wrists and ankles, hobbling himself on the floor at their feet. Silence fell as he was accomplishing this contortion, and only when he was trussed up like a chicken did he speak for the first time: "Thus says the Lord, 'The owner of this belt will be bound by the Jews in Jerusalem and handed over to the Gentiles.'"

This was nothing new to the team, but nevertheless they joined in the protests of the local Christians, who were shocked by the warning.

"You are breaking my heart!" Paul said in mock sorrow. "I am quite prepared, not only to be bound, but even to be killed in Jerusalem."

"God's will be done!" they all conceded, resignedly.

22

The Arrest

Next day, they set out on the sixty-five-mile walk to Jerusalem. Some of the local Christians from Caesarea accompanied the convoy, but the hope that it would be a triumphal procession into the city turned out to be wishful thinking. Paul leading a troop of a dozen Gentiles at the beginning of the Pentecost celebration was not designed to bring cheering crowds of Jews into the street; in fact, rather the opposite. That they were carrying with them a fortune in Greek and Asian currency made no difference. They were offered cramped accommodation in the home of an old believer named Mnason. He was a Cypriot who had been brought to faith during that very first visit Paul and Barnabas had made to his island home.

First thing next morning, they all set off, a little nervously perhaps, to meet the big guns at headquarters. But their fears were ungrounded. James, Jesus' brother, greeted them warmly, as did all the elders.

Paul introduced each of his followers in turn, explaining exactly where each man called home and telling of the church that flourished in their towns.

Then they opened their treasure chest. "This is a token expression of how grateful these Gentile believers are to you all and how deeply they love you," Paul explained to the amazed elders. The Gentiles looked on with veiled smiles, as do those giving a precious gift to a loved one. The Jews hesitated in their gratitude, uncertain how they ought to react. Paul held his breath. This was a touchy moment. To accept the gift, Paul realised, would be for the elders to give unreserved approval of his mission to the Gentiles. To take all that money might even appear to put Jews in the debt of Gentiles. On the other hand, to reject it would cause such a rift between the Jewish church and their Gentile brothers and sisters as might never be healed. Paul had expressed his concern in his letter to the church in Rome: "Please pray that the believers in Jerusalem will accept the relief contributions I will be taking, in the spirit in which it is being given."

So Paul let out a sigh of relief when James' face creased with smiles as he expressed profound gratitude to Paul and his delegation. All the elders joined in, sharing hugs all round with their Gentile brothers.

Later, James shared with Paul another concern: "While you have been gone, thousands of Jews have become believers, which, I feel sure you will agree, is wonderful news. However, word has come back to Jerusalem down the grapevine that everywhere you have gone, you have been telling the Jews you encounter that they no longer have to keep the law of Moses or circumcise their children. We know that this is not the case, but how do we convince others that it is only the Gentiles you are relieving of the obligation to conform to the law? And now here you are in company with a dozen Gentiles, so their worst fears appear to be confirmed.

"So here's a possible way forward. We have in our company four Jews who have made a Nazirite vow, as you yourself recently did. So why don't you take some of this cash and pay their expenses and officiate personally at their sacrifice. That would send a clear signal that you are a practicing Jew who upholds the law of Moses."

Well, that seemed like a reasonable strategy, especially in view of the fact that the thirty days of preparation for the four candidates were already passed. It only remained for Paul himself to meet with the priest in charge and then undergo the required week of purification rights for himself as a Jew returning from travel abroad.

The plan appeared to be working well for the first few days, but then trouble came in spades. Some pilgrims, Jews from Ephesus who were in town for the festival, recognised Trophimus, one of Paul's Gentile delegates from their own hometown. To make matters worse, they also recognised the man in whose company he was walking through the city, Paul: the troublemaker responsible for the silversmith's riot over Artemis. That day, they contented themselves with whispering and pointing, but when they saw Paul again the following day, this time in the Holy Place of the temple, being purified by the priest, they could keep quiet no longer.

"Help! Sacrilege!" they shouted. "This is the man who has been causing trouble all over the world, stirring up anti-Semitism, inciting rebellion against our laws, and threatening this temple. And now, to crown it all, he has brought Gentiles into this holy place and defiled it!" Of course, they hadn't actually seen any of Paul's Gentile friends in the temple, but assumptions are a powerful motivation.

The temple was divided by a clearly defined wall that prohibited non-Jews, on pain of death, from entering the section described as the Holy Place. "No foreigner is permitted to enter the sanctuary beyond this balustrade. Whoever is caught will have only himself to blame when he is killed," the welcome notice read.

On reflection, Paul thought it ironic that it would be this wall of division between Jews and Gentiles that would prove the flash point for his arrest and confinement for the years that were to follow. Some four years later, when Paul would still be in prison as a result of this false accusation, he would yet be mulling over this irony when writing a letter to his friends in Ephesus. "There was a time," Paul would write, "when you were excluded from all the promises and privileges that Jews enjoy, especially that of knowing God. But now Jesus has come and destroyed the barrier that separates Jews and Gentiles, broken that dividing wall by taking all that hostility to himself on the cross and shedding his own life blood to make us one – one with each other and one with God."

But now, incensed by this apparent outrage, a mob quickly formed as people ran from all directions. They grabbed Paul and hauled him out of the Holy Place, and the great doors of separation slammed shut behind him. Once in the court of the Gentiles, the mob proceeded to punch the lights out of the man who had preached peace to all the nations for whom the temple was intended to be a house of prayer. And they might well have killed him had not a squad of Roman soldiers from the Antonia Palace next door intervened. At the sight of these well-disciplined soldiers, the mob fell back, leaving the crumpled figure of Paul on the ground. The soldiers roughly pulled Paul to his feet and snapped handcuffs on him.

"What's going on here?" barked Claudius Lysias, the commander. "Who is this man and what's he done?"

A chorus of contradictory shouts was the response. "Take this man to the barracks!" the commander ordered his men. But the mob wasn't going to let public enemy number one get away that easily. They surged forward once again, clawing at Paul and shouting, "Kill him! Kill him!" In the end, the soldiers had to carry Paul shoulder high to tear him away from the ferocity of the mob. They fought their way up the steps to the door leading to the Antonia Palace, but just as they reached the top, Paul found himself right next to the commander himself. "Excuse me, sir," Paul said in educated Greek. "Might I have a word?"

"How come you speak Greek?" the surprised Roman asked. "I took you for that Egyptian terrorist we've been out to arrest."

"I'm no Egyptian," Paul assured him. "In fact, I am a Jew, native of the great city of Tarsus. I was wondering if I might be permitted to say a word to the people?"

This obviously well-educated man didn't look like trouble, and hearing what he had to say might help him understand the nature of the riot, so the commander gave him permission to speak.

The steps he was standing on offered Paul a natural podium, so he just stood there, holding up his still-manacled hands till the crowd quieted down.

"Ladies and gentlemen," he started in Aramaic. That immediately gained the attention of the people, who were wondering what kind of strange speech this Gentile lover might use. "Let me tell you who I am. I am a Jew, born in Tarsus in Cilicia, but raised right here in Jerusalem. I studied under the great Gamaliel and have always been as zealous for God as you all are showing yourselves to be today." Now they were all straining to hear every word he had to say. This was not at all what they had expected. He told them how he had been a persecutor of the Way and how, years ago, he had been headed to Damascus with the sole intent of imprisoning Christians. "Then everything changed!" Paul told how he had encountered Jesus, who had commissioned him to be his witness to the Gentiles. The people had been listening, enthralled, till Paul mentioned the Gentiles. Instantly, there was a growl of disapproval and someone shouted, "Let the world be rid of him! He's not fit to stay alive!" The next moment, the crowd went mad, tearing off their coats and flinging dirt into the air.

The soldiers backed up through the door to their barracks, dragging Paul with them.

"Interrogate him!" ordered the commander. "Find out what this is all about."

The shirt was torn from Paul's back and his chains attached to a pulley, by which he was hoisted from the ground in readiness for the lash. It was obvious from his scarred back that this was by no means the first time he had suffered this kind of indignity. Just before the torture began, Paul just had time to ask the centurion in charge of the inquisition, "Excuse me, but are you sure it's legal to flog a Roman citizen without first giving him a fair trial?"

"Stand down!" the centurion ordered the man with the lash. Leaving Paul hanging there, he went out to find the commander. "Begging your pardon, sir, but it has been brought to my notice that the prisoner is a Roman citizen."

The commander smothered an oath and hurried out to where Paul was suspended. "Is it true that you are a Roman citizen?" he demanded.

"I am," wheezed Paul.

"To become a Roman citizen cost me a fortune."

"I was born one." Paul managed to convey a modicum of pride through his discomfort.

"Unchain this man," the commander said quietly, clearly distressed at the realisation that he had unlawfully bound a citizen of the great city and very nearly committed a crime against his person.

Nevertheless, he kept him in custody overnight till he could discover what had so upset the Jews. Feeling himself to be unqualified to cross-examine Paul on the niceties of Jewish law, he resolved to leave the matter to the world's experts: the Jewish Council. He had the manacles removed, enabling Paul to present himself before so august a body with greater dignity than would have a chained detainee.

When asked how he pleaded, though not yet accused of any specific crime, Paul addressed the Council: "Brothers, I stand before you today with a clear conscience."

One of the councillors rapped out an order: "Punch him in the mouth!"

Before Paul could dodge, he found himself reeling from an unexpected blow. Shocked and hurt, Paul fired back through the blood: "God strike you too, you hypocrite. How dare you accuse me of breaking the law while you yourself break the very law you claim to be upholding."

"Watch your mouth," growled the security man who was now holding Paul. "That's God's high priest you are addressing."

"My deepest apologies," Paul said contritely. "I didn't recognise you, sir. The Scriptures clearly teach that we are never to speak disrespectfully to our rulers."

There was a lull in the proceedings while Paul's apology was accepted. Paul took the silence as an invitation to continue. "Brothers, I am a Pharisee and the son of a Pharisee. The only crime of which I can imagine being accused today is that of upholding the traditional Pharisaic doctrine of the resurrection from the dead."

"Divide and conquer" has long been a familiar tactic in war or argument, and Paul recognised that the Council was made up of half Pharisees, who taught people to anticipate an afterlife, and half Sadducees, who taught that when you're dead, you're dead, and that's an end of it. Suddenly, Paul was all but forgotten in the furious if clichéd theological debate that erupted. It was not clear to the commander exactly how Paul figured in the fight, but he resolved that he ought to be removed for his own protection.

Back in his cell that night, Paul had another of those experiences that qualified him to be an Apostle. He saw the risen Lord Jesus: "Take courage, Paul. You have borne witness to me here in Jerusalem. Now you will do so in Rome."

God's agents for saving life are sometimes very young, and it was one such who chanced to overhear a covert conversation on the following morning. It may have been the foreign accents that attracted the lad's attention, or it may have been the use of his uncle's name, but Paul's nephew was suddenly all ears as he walked through the market square. He moved closer to the huddle of out-of-town Jews and pushed his way into the circle. No one paid any heed to a stray child. What he heard made his blood run cold.

He ran straight to the barracks where he knew his uncle Paul was being held. He hardly knew the man, but blood is always thicker than water, and family is family when all is said and done. Undaunted by the forbidding building and intimidating guards, the boy pushed on in till he found the cell where Paul was being held.

"Uncle Paul!" he called through the grill, and when he had his attention, he related what he had overheard. "There's a huge group of Jews with strange Asian accents who have vowed not to eat till they have killed you."

"How do you think they are planning to do that, since I am safe in here?"

"They seem to be in league with the high priest to have you brought back to the Council for further questioning and are planning to ambush you on the way there."

"Guard!" shouted Paul. "Please take this young man to the commander. He has some important information to give him."

Commander Lysias had a soft spot for children and, sensing the boy's nervousness, took him by the hand and led him to a bench, where they sat down. "So what's this important information you have for me, eh?"

The story came tumbling out, till finally the lad concluded emphatically, "Whatever you do, don't give in to them! They are just waiting for you to give the word so they can murder my uncle."

"Okay, young man. I believe you. Now let's keep this conversation between us two. Don't say anything to anybody, or your own life could be in danger. These are not nice people we are dealing with."

That night, Paul was escorted out of the city by a detachment of nearly three hundred soldiers, and the following evening, he was delivered to Governor Felix in Caesarea with a letter from Claudius Lysias in Jerusalem. In it, he explained how he had rescued a Roman citizen from the murderous clutches of a mob of Jews (omitting the part about his having nearly given him a flogging). The important bottom line was: "I detect in him no crime worthy of imprisonment, let alone death." That letter would have stayed in Paul's file all the way to Rome, had it not suffered water damage on the way.

Paul was kept in Herod's coastal palace till his accusers could catch up with him. As it happened, they wasted little time in getting there, and less than a week later, there was Ananias, the high priest himself, flanked by a bevy of elders and ably represented by a high-priced lawyer by the name of Tertullus. He earned his fee by prefacing his accusation with some blarney about how much they all appreciated the peace that Felix had administered since his arrival in their province. Everyone knew that was a barefaced lie, since history would later brand Felix as a "master of cruelty and lust who exercised the powers of a king with the spirit of a slave."

Sensing that he may have laid it on a bit thick, Tertullus got to the point.

"This man is a proven troublemaker the world over. He is a ringleader of the pernicious sect of the Nazarene and was arrested in the very process of desecrating the temple." A chorus of "Hear, hears" from his backing band confirmed his words. It was indeed a brief speech but sufficient to appeal to Felix' propensity to crucify such troublemakers.

Paul was next invited to present his own defence and proved himself just as adroit with the blarney as had been the prosecution, but he was wise enough to keep it short: "I freely admit that I serve the God of our fathers as a follower of the Way, which my learned prosecutor vilifies as a mere 'sect.' I believe the same Scriptures, share the same faith in God as do they, and have a clear conscience before God and man. Twelve days ago, I came to Jerusalem bringing gifts for the poor and to present offerings to God. I was ceremonially clean when they found me in the temple, peacefully worshipping God. There, a group of Jews from the province of Asia accosted me. It is they who ought to be here to present their complaints before you, Governor Felix. Or else let those who are present accuse me of any crime of which they may have found me guilty at the meeting of the Council last week. I contend that they have nothing against me, except perhaps that I stated my belief in the resurrection. That seemed to offend them for some reason."

Governor Felix adjourned the case till Commander Lysias could bring his report personally on his next visit to Caesarea.

Felix knew all about the Way and so realised that Paul represented no security risk. While he was kept in custody, he was given minimal restriction, and his friends were free to visit as often as they wished.

Paul wasn't sure what to expect when a few days later, he was once again summoned to the governor's presence. To his amazement, this was no austere judicial gathering but rather a relaxed family affair, with the governor's young wife, Drusilla, sitting next to him. They chatted about this and that, but Paul wasn't going to allow an opportunity like that to be missed, so he soon turned the conversation to faith in Jesus Christ. Paul, ever the preacher, waxed eloquent about righteousness, self-control, and coming judgement.

He was perhaps skating on rather thin ice, since Felix was known to have seduced his much younger wife from the arms of her former husband, the king of Homs in Syria. It was well known that John the Baptist had lost his head while preaching a similar sermon some years previously.

After a while, Felix became uneasy. "We'll call it a day for now," he said, dismissing Paul. But a day or so later, he got up his nerve to call for Paul once again. Dursilla was noticeably absent on this occasion, probably offended by Paul's moralistic ranting. This happened several times over the following two years. Paul had a sneaking suspicion that Felix was fishing for a bribe to let him go, but nothing was ever said.

Two long years of frustration dragged by. The only breaks in the overcast for Paul were the frequent visits from his good friends, Doctor Luke from Philippi, Aristarchus from Thessalonica, and Timothy from Lystra. On their arrival in Jerusalem, the delegation from the Gentile churches had hovered in the background while events unfolded. When Paul had been moved to Caesarea, they had followed him and once again gladly accepted the hospitality of Philip the evangelist and his four prophetic daughters. But as days turned to weeks and weeks to months with no end in sight, several members of the group had been forced to head for home. Families beckoned and businesses demanded. Luke, Aristarchus, and Timothy, however, stayed.

Paul, who spent much of every day in prayer for his many friends in the congregations he had planted on his travels, was hungry to know how his prayers were being answered. He used Timothy as his special representative, sending him here and there to convey his greetings and to bring back to Paul first-hand accounts of the status quo. So Timothy was gone as often as not.

Aristarchus' cheerful company did much to keep up Paul's spirits, while the good doctor's medical expertise enabled him to keep a lid on Paul's mystery ailment. Paul never talked about it, and Luke, to his chagrin, never came up with a clear diagnosis. They simply referred to it as Paul's "thorn in the flesh."

After a while, when waiting became routine, Luke got down to the serious business of writing. At first, he wrote a record of Paul's travels by extrapolating extracts from his personal journal. Clearly, the parts when Luke himself was present tended to contain much more detail than the other parts, when he only had Paul's own sketchy account to go on. When that was finished, he resolved to research and write an orderly account of the life of Jesus right from the beginning, just as the facts had been handed down to him by those who from the first had been eyewitnesses. He started his writings in the form of a letter that he addressed to "Dear Theophilus," a generic he though appropriate for all lovers of God. He wanted people to have an accurate record of all that happened, one they could really trust. But it went way further than a letter, and before he was finished, he had written a whole biography.

Governor Felix, however, did not make the same good use of those years. Rather, he excelled himself in high-handed cruelty, quelling riots between Jews and Greeks in Caesarea. In desperation, a Jewish delegation was eventually sent to Rome, resulting in Felix being recalled by Emperor Nero. He was never heard of again.

Porcius Festus, Felix' successor, was cut from an altogether different cloth. Just three days after his arrival in Caesarea, Festus headed to Jerusalem. There, a long agenda was presented to him, which included the charges against Paul. "We would like this man transferred to Jerusalem for trial here," was the demand. Festus immediately smelled foul play, which was smart, since there was indeed a plan to ambush Paul en route.

He did, however, set Paul's case high on his agenda when back in Caesarea. The usual gaggle of priests and lawyers showed up, spewing their confused charges, all of which were thin on evidence and high on rhetoric. Paul once again protested his innocence.

"Are you willing to answer these charges before me in Jerusalem?" asked Governor Festus.

"No, sir, I am not!" Paul said emphatically. He knew that to make such a journey would be the end of him. "I stand here on trial in this Roman court. You and I both know full well that I have done nothing wrong. Yes, I am willing to die if indeed I am guilty, but since I am most certainly innocent and these Jews are planning to kill me unjustly, I decline to be handed over to them. I appeal to be tried by Caesar." There was a sudden buzz of conversation around the court at this unexpected development. Festus turned to consult with his legal advisors and then rapped on his desk for silence. "You have made your appeal to Caesar, so to Caesar you will go." Angry and frustrated, the Jerusalem delegation shuffled out of court.

A few days later, Festus received a state visit from King Herod Agrippa II. He was the last in the line of Herods, which now extended five generations since Herod the Great. With him was his younger sister, Bernice. There was something odd about their relationship, which some even suspected of being incestuous. But none of that bothered their host.

Felix, realising that King Agrippa was something of an expert in all things Jewish, shared with him his dilemma over Paul. "The thing is," he explained, "the man has appealed to Caesar, but I have no idea what to write to the imperial court about the official charges against him. It's all theological mumbo-jumbo and some talk of a dead man called Jesus, whom Paul insists is still alive."

"I would be most interested to hear what this man has to say," the king said, to the enormous relief of the governor.

"Then you shall, this very tomorrow."

The friendly chats Paul had enjoyed with Governor Felix were not to be repeated with his successor; quite the opposite, in fact. The great hall was packed with important people from the city, all anxious to see the new governor in company with their king. Then a hush fell, and everyone stood as an impressive procession entered the room: officers in full uniform, leading men of the city in their robes, finally the governor in company with King Agrippa and his sister, Bernice. These three took their seats on a raised platform, and then everyone else was seated. Finally, a door at the back of the room was opened, and in came two soldiers, leading a chained man between them. He was led to the middle of the room and then halted, with all eyes fastened on him.

"This is the man," Festus announced in a clear voice addressed to King Agrippa, but that everyone could hear clearly. "The whole Jewish community wants him dead, but I find nothing in him deserving of punishment. So, by his own appeal, he is to stand trial before Caesar. I need your help in writing the charges against him. King Agrippa, I hand the proceedings over to you."

Without hesitation, the king addressed the prisoner: "You have our permission to speak."

If Paul was intimidated by his audience, he gave no sign of it. He addressed his remarks directly to the king, expressing confidence that since Agrippa was well versed in Jewish customs and controversies, he would appreciate what Paul was about to say. Paul started at the beginning, telling of his religious upbringing as a Pharisee, his belief in traditional Jewish doctrine, and his hope of the resurrection of the dead.

Then he moved on to talk of Jesus of Nazareth, how in his Pharisaic zeal he had persecuted Jesus' followers till one day, on the road to Damascus, he had been stopped dead in his tracks. You could have heard a pin drop as Paul described how he had met Jesus that day.

"How could I have disregarded this heavenly vision, King Agrippa? Ever since then, I have preached that people should repent and turn to God. My message is nothing more and nothing less than what the prophets ever since Moses have been saying: that the Christ would die, then rise again to proclaim light and life to Jews and Gentiles alike."

"Humbug!" Festus could restrain himself no longer. "You are out of your mind, Paul. All your studying has driven you mad."

"Most excellent Festus, I am not mad. What I am saying is both true and reasonable. The king knows what I am talking about, since all this is common knowledge hereabouts. You believe the prophets, don't you, King Agrippa?"

The king was taken aback by so direct an appeal. "Do you imagine for one moment that in such a short time you can persuade me to be a Christian?" replied the king.

"Long time or short, my prayer is that not only you, oh king, but all who are here today will become as I am. Except, of course, for these," added Paul, rattling his chains. Laughter filled the room.

At that, the king got up and led the platform party out of the hall.

"Quite extraordinary!" he said when they were back in the privacy of the governor's house.

"He's not guilty of anything, so far as I can see," said Festus.

"I agree. He could be set free, if only he had not appealed to Caesar," concluded the king.

23

The Voyage

It was late summer before passage was arranged for Paul to be sent to Rome. A centurion from the Imperial Regiment by the name of Julius was in command of a century of soldiers charged with the transfer of Paul and a few dozen other prisoners. Paul already knew Julius, since the soldier had enjoyed conversations with the educated man in the otherwise rough company of the army barracks. He made no objection to Paul's personal physician, Luke, and his "servant," Aristarchus, travelling along with them. Timothy was away when they left, so he missed the boat.

As they boarded a coastal trader, there were tearful farewells from Philip and the other members of the church in Caesarea. First stop was Sidon, and to Paul's great joy, Julius permitted him a few hours ashore to meet with the church in that city. It was a disappointment that the ship was not scheduled to put in at Seleucia, where he might have met some friends from Antioch. Instead, the ship headed out to sea for what turned out to be a slow passage. The wind was against them, so they tacked this way and that. For a while, they made use of the wind shears that Cyprus offered but then sailed north to hug the coast of Cilicia and Pamphylia, hoping that the occasional off-shore breezes might compensate for the prevailing westerlies.

Eventually, they reached the port of Myra, where they disembarked.

The option of continuing on round the coast and then marching over land was abandoned in favour of a less arduous and more direct sea voyage. Paul and his two companions were sad to see their ship sailing away towards so many cities they knew and loved.

As luck would suggest they had it, Julius found a large grain vessel en route from North Africa to Rome. Their new ship was slow and sluggish, heavily laden as it was with grain. To make matters worse, the westerlies persisted, losing them yet more time as they wrestled their way along the coast to Cnidus, a port at the south-western tip of Asia Minor. From there, it should have been but a hoop and a holler over to the tip of Greece and thence to the boot of Italy; however, that westerly wind forced the captain to opt for a long tack south down to Crete for what letup that island might offer. The vessel rounded the eastern point of Crete just south of Salmone and, to their disappointment, encountered the same contrary wind on the south coast of the island as had dogged their progress ever since leaving home. They crept along the shore of the island till they came to Fair Havens, a bay that offered a modicum of shelter and a temporary anchorage.

It was already well into October, and their hopes of an Indian summer were long since abandoned. There was now no way they were going to reach Rome before the winter, so it was time to find a port to hole up till spring. Fair Havens offered some protection, except from winds directly from the south.

That evening, Paul and the paying passengers sat together with the captain and officers for the evening meal. What to do next was the topic of conversation. There was little enthusiasm for staying put, not only because of the questionable anchorage, but also because Lasea, the nearby village, had little to offer 270 stranded passengers and crew in the way of provision or entertainment for a whole winter.

Less than fifty miles west on Crete was the port of Phoenix, an altogether much more attractive alternative, well protected and adequately serviced. The captain was all for going just that little bit farther, and his first mate agreed with him.

"Gentlemen," Paul interposed, when there was a lull in the conversation, "I hate to disagree with the expert opinion of our captain; however, I predict that this voyage will prove to be a disaster. It will end in the loss of the ship, the cargo, and even loss of life." There was an awkward silence, during which everyone looked down at his plate.

"Well, that's going to depend on the weather tomorrow morning," the captain said, relieving the awkwardness.

First light next morning revealed a gentle south wind, perfect for a westerly course, so they weighed anchor and set off along the south coast of Crete in high spirits. Their enthusiasm, however, was short lived, for scarcely had they left the shelter of the bay when the sky to the north, which had previously been hidden to them by the bulk of the land, suddenly grew black. The southerly breeze gave place to a terrifying wind that screamed down at them over the island, driving them out to sea.

"She's a nor'easter," one of the sailors yelled in alarm. Before they could pull it down, the sail was ripped to rags that thrashed and writhed in demented frenzy beyond the desperate grasp of the crew. Four men threw their combined weight on each of the great beams of the two steering oars in a vain attempt to bring the ship round into the wind, but to no avail, so the ship was carried along, with the waves beating her stern. The motion of the ship and the protesting of her tortured timbers were alarming, so ropes were looped over the bow, then the ends worked along the two side rails till the ropes were round the belly of the ship. Then they were cinched tight in the hope that they would lessen the likelihood of the whole structure splitting apart by the violent motion of the towering waves.

Land was sighted not long after the storm struck. There were fears that they would be thrown up on the rocks on the windward shore, but to everyone's enormous relief, they passed harmlessly by what they assumed to be the island of Cauda. Once they had passed to the lee side of the island, they used the slight shelter that it afforded to bring the lifeboat on board. It was swamped with water and a dead weight, but they dared not let it go, since it might represent their final hope. Eventually, they had it emptied, hauled aboard, and lashed down tight so it would not blow away into oblivion.

The speed at which they had come up on Cauda indicated to the crew the terrifying pace at which they were being driven south. "We are going to be on the sandbars off North Africa before we know it," someone yelled. A large square of sailcloth, tied at the corners, was thrown over the stern. Once in the water, it bellied out, holding the stern of the boat into the wind and slowing their deadly progress.

The gloom was so deep that they barely noticed nightfall, and the arrival of the following dawn did little to brighten their spirits. In any case, there were no horizons to be seen, just endless gray, flying spray that stung the eyes and numbed their skin. Mountains of water endlessly thundered under their tortured hull.

The inevitable process of jettisoning the cargo began when it was light enough to see a hand in front of your face. If the grain stayed in the hold and got wet, it would swell and split the ship open like a coconut. Next, all the spare tackle joined the cargo in the sea. The ship now rode higher in the water, with the happy result that they were no longer swamped each time a wave passed them. But the endless monotony of getting the water out of the bilges and back into the sea where it belonged went on and on. They took it in shifts, everyone being required to take their turn at the backbreaking toil, even Paul.

The shrieking ferocity of the storm went on unabated, day after day, night after night. Sleep was almost impossible till people were so tired they could barely stand up. Hot meals were but a distant memory. Any hope of navigation was impossible since there had been no sign of sun, moon, or stars for days. They had no idea where they were or where the storm was carrying them. Finally, all hope of being saved was abandoned, and each man resigned himself to his own private misery.

A good two weeks of this must have passed when Paul stood unsteadily to his feet and, clinging to a spar for support, shouted to get the attention of as many of the ship's company as were in earshot. To the irritation of some, Paul started by saying, "I told you so! You would have saved yourselves so much grief if only we had never left Fair Havens in Crete." Any fool can have 20/20 vision in hindsight! "But now I have something to tell you. The bad news is that the ship is going to be lost, but the good news is that not one of you is going to die."

"And just how do you know that?" growled someone from the gloom.

"I know it because last night an angel from God came and told me not to be frightened any more. He assured me that not only will I get safe to Rome to stand trial before Caesar, but that the lives of everyone else in the ship will also be spared."

There were murmurs of approval, but the expressions on the faces of the men were hard to read. Scepticism perhaps? Or was that a flash of hope?

"You don't have to believe it," said Paul. "The point is that I believe it. I have faith in God. It will happen exactly as he promised. So take courage!"

There was something contagious about Paul's confidence. He had once said something similar that they had all but ignored: "I am absolutely convinced that nothing will be able to separate us from God's love – death, life, angels, demons, or all the powers of hell. Today or tomorrow, neither the sky above our heads nor the ocean depths below our hull, nothing in all creation will ever stop God loving us." Previously, that had all sounded just like so much religious talk, but now Paul's specific confidence was like a ray of hope in the darkness of their despair. They might have questioned his faith when all was plain sailing, but now in the depths of this storm, every man on board desperately hoped that what Paul was saying would prove true. They *wanted* to believe it.

Around the middle of the following night, the sailors' sixth sense told them that land was near. They threw a weighted string over the side and touched bottom less than a hundred and twenty feet below. A few minutes later, they tried again, and now the water was but ninety feet deep.

"We are going to run aground!" someone shouted in fresh alarm.

Anchors were dropped from the stern of the ship to arrest their perilous advance.

"Don't worry!" shouted Paul. "We are going to run aground on a sandbar. But we'll be okay."

But they were not okay. Sometime during the night, the sailors all moved to the bow of the ship and began loosening the lifeboat. "What are you doing?" bawled Julius.

"Begging your pardon, sir, but we sailors know what we are about. Just setting some more anchors up for'ard."

Land-bound soldiers may not have recognised the irrationality of setting anchors downwind, but Paul had spent many days aboard ship and had even suffered shipwreck on at least one previous occasion. He knew that no sailor would contemplate such absurdity. "They are planning to take the lifeboat to save their own skins," Paul shouted in the soldier's ear. "If they don't stay with us, we don't stand a chance."

Julius barked some orders, and his men rushed forward and, using their swords, hacked through the ropes the sailors were using to lower the lifeboat, dropping it into the sea.

Dawn was turning the sky grey, and every man was straining his eyes to see if there was land. Once again Paul called for everyone's attention: "Listen up, guys. No one has eaten a square meal in over two weeks. You are weak and worn out, but now you are going to need to get your strength up for the final challenge. Not one of you is going to drown today. Here," he said, holding up a hunk of bread. "Breakfast time!" Then he looked up: "Thank you, God, for this good food." So saying, he tucked in. Soon, everyone regained his appetite and was enjoying what couldn't have been better, even if it had had jam on it! Two hundred and seventy men ate their fill, and when they were done, they tossed the leftovers into the boiling sea.

It was about then that they saw the land. Nobody recognised where they were, but there was a bay with a sandy beach before them. Well, that was good news. No rocks!

"We'll run her aground on yonder beach!" pronounced the captain. The anchor ropes from the stern were slashed, and the foresail was hoisted up what was left of the mast. Immediately, the ship surged forward.

Paul noticed a brief but furious discussion between Julius and his sergeant, which Paul discovered later had been to save his life. The soldiers wanted to kill the prisoners to prevent any of them from escaping, but Julius refused.

They were halfway to the beach when the boat gave a sickening lurch and slewed sideways, listing steeply to port. "She's aground!" Now the waves slammed into the exposed hull, and the stricken vessel was engulfed with spray. Judging from the sounds of splitting timbers, she was literally being pounded to matchwood.

"Every man for himself!" yelled Julius.

The deck was canting at an impossible angle, and they all slid down into the boiling maelstrom. Those who could swim struck out for the beach. The others grabbed hold of anything that would float and let the waves hurl them as they would. But they made it, every last man of them, coughing and spluttering as they staggered from the surf up the blessed firmness of land.

It wasn't long before people started emerging from the trees. At first, they kept their distance, caution tempering their curiosity. But when they perceived the pitiful state of their uninvited guests, natural kindness kicked in. The refugees were cold and wet, teeth chattering, nerves shot as they sat in the sand with that wretched wind still blasting the cold November rain into their faces. Communication may have been limited, but the language of compassion spoke eloquently when someone produced a flint and started a fire. Soon everyone joined in the hunt for driftwood to build up the blaze.

Paul grabbed a pile of sticks and was just making his contribution to the fire when a snake, whose home Paul was about to burn, registered its disapproval by sinking its fangs into his hand. Paul, still wearing the iron cuff that identified him as a convict, was instantly suspected by the islanders of being a murderer. He might have escaped the ravages of the sea, but justice had caught up with him, just the same.

When Paul nonchalantly shook the snake off into the flames, they watched him suspiciously, expecting his arm to start swelling or him to fall down dead at any moment. But when time passed and nothing happened, they were impressed: "Perhaps he's not a murderer, after all. Maybe he's a god!" Ah, how fickle the opinions of man!

Not far from the sandy bay at which they had made their grand arrival was a fine Roman villa, and it was thence that the locals led the ragged procession of castaways. It turned out to be the home of the chief man on the island, which they were told was Malta. Publius, as their host introduced himself, was amazed to find 276 bedraggled men on his doorstep but quickly remembered his manners and had his servants organised into laying on hot drinks and then food and shelter for his guests. Publius turned out to be a most congenial host who for three days did his best to dispel the horrors of their disastrous Mediterranean cruise by lavishing hospitality and kindness on them.

It soon became apparent that Publius was a worried man. His old father, who shared his home, was dangerously sick with a high fever and dysentery.

"Would you permit me to look in on your father?" Paul asked politely.

"By all means," said his host, who took him into the sick room and introduced him. Paul's bedside manner was unexpected. Having made the usual small talk, he then knelt down beside the bed and started to talk to someone neither Publius nor his father could see. After a couple of minutes, Paul got back to his feet, leant forward, and put his hands on the old man's head and chest: "Jesus Christ heals you."

A big smile spread over the man's face, then he sat up and swung his legs over the side of the bed. "I'm starving," he said. "When's lunch?"

Word of this miracle was all over the island in no time, and soon sick people started arriving in droves. Paul gave them all the same treatment.

Gradually, the former ship's company was billeted out to homes around the island, and the grey months of winter passed much more comfortably than anyone could have imagined. Paul used the time to tell them all the good news about Jesus and his resurrection.

The erstwhile captain of the wrecked ship discovered to his great joy a vessel from his homeport of Alexandria. Its captain had been smart enough to put in at Malta for the winter before the weather had turned sour. Julius was pleased too, since this ship was on its way to Rome just as soon as spring would show a smiling face.

February brought warmer weather and a westerly wind. The ship weighed anchor with 276 extra passengers, each laden with gifts and supplies from their new Maltese friends. It was not without some misgivings that they saw the land disappearing over the stern rail, but the ship's twin figureheads of Castor and Pollux, patron gods of all sailors, leant some reassurance to the superstitious members of the crew. Paul, Luke, and Aristarchus, however, enjoyed their quiet confidence in the God who had promised a safe arrival in Rome. But everyone was glad to see land when before nightfall, they sighted the southern tip of Sicily, and a short time later, they dropped anchor in the port of Syracuse. Three days later, they sailed a further eighty miles north to the strait between Sicily and the Italian mainland. After just one night in the port of Rhegium, the captain was pleased to see the wind had backed to the south, facilitating a comfortable two-day sail north to their final destination in the Bay of Naples: Puteoli.

It was with mixed feelings that they disembarked: relief to be safe on land at the conclusion to a dangerous six-month voyage, but sadness at leaving a company that had grown close through shared adversity.

But first, they had to wait for a week in Puteoli for arrangements to be made with Rome for the arrival of this fresh batch of prisoners. Julius graciously permitted Paul to pass the time with some Christian brothers, who miraculously materialised soon after their arrival. Then they set off on the final leg of their journey, a 150-mile hike along the impressively constructed roads that, like all roads, led to Rome. Not far out of the city, they encountered a group of Christians who were looking for Paul, having heard that he was on his way. This brief encounter proved an enormous encouragement to Paul as he faced the uncertain justice of the emperor.

The entrance to the greatest city in the world was, perhaps, an anticlimax. While others may have been impressed by the magnificent buildings, Paul saw beyond the evidence of his eyes. Just as Jesus had encouraged his Disciples to see past the great stones of the temple, and just as Abraham had lived all his life ever looking forward to the city whose architect and builder would be God alone, so Paul was looking for greater things than those which presented themselves to his travel-weary eyes. Around the time Paul was marched into Rome, foundations were being laid for a great amphitheatre where thousands of Paul's fellow Christians would lose their lives: stoned to pulp, slashed to death with blades, ripped apart by wild animals.

Julius proved to be a real friend to Paul. The report he gave to the commandant of the Praetorian barracks was such that Paul was released to await his trial under house arrest, with just one soldier to guard him. So Paul, Luke, and Aristarchus all shared a rented house near the barracks.

Paul wasted no time but immediately invited the leaders of the Jewish community to meet with him. He was unsure what kind of reception to expect. Would they be hostile or friendly?

"Brothers, I don't know what you may have heard about me, but it is precisely because of the hope of all Israel that I am here in chains," Paul explained, holding up his manacled hands.

"We haven't heard a word about you from Judea, good or bad. But we have heard plenty about this sect you represent. We would be most interested to hear your views on the subject."

So Paul told them all about Jesus.

As it turned out, prison did nothing to hinder Paul's ongoing mission; in fact, as he wrote to the church in Philippi, "I want you to know that my imprisonment has actually served to advance the gospel." Paul probably touched more lives through what he wrote in those final years in prison than he had in all his years of freedom.

While under house arrest, Paul enjoyed a constant stream of visitors, amongst them John Mark, with whom he had maintained a strained relationship ever since his very first mission to Cyprus. Mark turned out to be a huge encouragement to Paul, bringing him news of Barnabas and the churches in Antioch and Jerusalem. He proudly told Paul that he had just finished writing a biography of Jesus. "Peter helped me," Mark confessed.

Timothy finally caught up with Paul there in Rome and proved invaluable as both a courier and a companion, faithful right to the end. In fact, shortly before his death, Paul wrote a note to Timothy: "The time of my end is close. I have fought well, finished the race, kept the faith, and soon I will receive the crown of righteousness which the Lord himself will give me."

24

The Correspondence

Paul's letters were many: a baker's dozen at least.

Details of Peter's travels don't figure much in the story; however, like those of Paul, Peter's letters from prison, following his inevitable arrest, survived the disintegration of time. He wrote to the churches he had recently founded, encouraging them to live holy lives and prepare for tough days ahead.

"The end of all things is getting close," he wrote, "my own demise in particular, so I am writing to ensure that after I am gone you won't forget all I have told you. Cynics are bound to multiply, scoffing about the coming judgement. 'Whatever happened to Jesus' promise to return?' they will ask. It was cynics like these who were caught out once before when the flood drowned them all, but next time it will be fire rather than water. Time in God's economy is very different than it appears for us. To God a thousand years is gone in what seems like a day. So it isn't that God is slow at keeping his promise, rather he is patient – waiting till we are all ready, since he has no wish for anyone to be caught out. On that day, everything will be destroyed by fire, but it will be replaced by a new heaven and earth, a home for righteousness. So think carefully about the kind of lives you should be living."

Jesus himself never wrote a letter, but his half-brothers did. James wrote to the Jewish Christians who had been scattered abroad in the persecutions that harassed the church in Jerusalem. His concern was to redress a possible imbalance that Paul's many letters may have caused by his emphasis on salvation being received by faith alone, in no way being earned by good living. Some were twisting this truth out of all proportion, teaching that doing good was no longer important since God would give salvation to anyone, regardless of how they lived. So James wrote to emphasise that any faith that did not result in doing good was not genuine faith at all, but just a fraud: a waste of space.

Jude, another half-brother of Jesus, shared James' concerns. He wrote a brief note of warning about infiltrators into the church who were seeking to misuse the grace of God as a license for immorality. These same people were going so far as to deny the identity of Jesus Christ, who Jude proudly owned as his Sovereign and Lord – quite something for a younger brother who once mistakenly accused his big brother of being mad.

John, one of Jesus' very closest Disciples, wrote three brief letters describing how a genuine Christian could be distinguished from a fraud. "The first thing to look for is a person's life style," John wrote. "Since when Jesus returns we will be just like him, it is logical that real Christians will already be purifying themselves in preparation for his arrival. People who don't live right are obviously not genuine children of God."

John had heard Jesus saying that people would be able to recognise his followers by the love they would have for each other. So he wrote, "Anyone who does not love is not a genuine child of God. God is love, so it stands to reason that his children will display the family likeness: love. God's ultimate expression of love was to give Jesus as a sacrifice for our sins. It follows, therefore, that since God loves us that much, then God's genuine children will be recognisable by the loving way they lay down their lives in the service of others. Real love is not just a feeling, but obedient action in response to what God has commanded."

John remembered that day in Caesarea Philippi when Jesus had asked them what people were saying about him. It had been on that occasion when Peter had for the first time, acknowledged Jesus as Lord. "That is the key that will unlock the kingdom!" Jesus had said.

So John continued his explanation by writing, "Genuine children of God will acknowledge Jesus for who he is: the Son of God. Those who refuse to do so are the very opposite: anti-Christ. But there's no mistaking the presence of the Holy Spirit living in a person's heart. It is the Spirit who gives God's own personal assurance to a man or woman of the right to call God 'Father.' That is the final evidence of the real thing: right in the heart, the inward witness of God himself."

———————————————

The prize for all the letters must go to John for his last letter, for this tells the final chapter of the story. John wrote the letter while he was passing some of his senior years on an island reserved by the Romans for the exclusive use of enemies of the state. The Isle of Patmos was one of the many broken islands off the coast of Asia, some sixty miles west of Ephesus, where Paul had spent so much time.

His letter starts by addressing itself to seven churches on the mainland of Asia, not far from where John was currently residing, churches that Paul had established during his time in Ephesus. There was a personal message that John was relaying from Jesus himself for each of these churches individually. Judging by what the messages contained, some of them were doing better than others. The highest praise was given to those who had endured suffering and persecution without compromise. "The Lord has set before you an open door of opportunity," John wrote.

Those lower down the ratings were the churches that had compromised the purity of their beliefs by taking on board false teachers that led their members into sin. To one church, John relayed a disturbing condemnation: "You have a reputation for being alive, but in fact you are dead. Get back to obeying what you were originally taught. Wake up!"

Perhaps the saddest of them all was the one addressed to the church in Ephesus. Having acknowledged their hard work and perseverance, John confided in them Jesus' profound disappointment: "You have forsaken the love you once had."

The list concluded with a message to the church in Laodicea: "I fear that your love has become tepid. It's no longer palatable to me: neither hot nor cold. You claim to be rich and have everything you need when in fact you are bankrupt. But I am here to offer you genuine riches. Because I love you so much, I will challenge your self-satisfied complacency by giving you trouble. So smarten up and repent. It's me knocking. Trouble is my way of getting your attention. So just open the door, and I'll come in to share your life with you, and you can share mine."

The last time John had seen Jesus was on that occasion when he had ascended into the sky from the top of the Mount of Olives. John had enjoyed the closest of relationships with Jesus during those final days, so much so that he always thought of himself as the Disciple whom Jesus loved. Jesus had even hinted to Peter that John might survive till Jesus returned in the clouds, but by the time John wrote this last letter, all the other Disciples were already dead. John alone remained, still looking forward to the day when he would see Jesus again.

So one Sunday, John was startled to hear a voice he recognised coming from behind him. John whirled around to find himself face to face with a terrifying being. To say that he was a man would be to stretch the word, but that was the closest description that John could find. He was dressed in a long robe, tied at the chest with a gold sash. His hair was shining white, his eyes blazed like fire, and his face shone as brilliantly as the sun. His feet were like bronze glowing in the heat of a furnace. His voice had the thunder of a mighty waterfall. From his mouth protruded a razor-sharp double-edged sword.

John was paralysed with fear and fell to the ground like a dead man. Next thing he knew, there was a hand on his shoulder, and the voice speaking gently to him: "Don't be frightened, John. It's me. I am the First and the Last, the Alpha and the Omega, who was, and is, and always will be – the Almighty. I was dead, but now I am alive forever. I hold the keys of death and hell."

Some kind of a door swung open into heaven. "Come on up, John. Come take a look into the future," Jesus beckoned. John stepped through the door.

The first thing that he saw was a throne set on a crystal-clear expanse of glass. The appearance of the One on the throne must have been too much for John to describe, probably beyond the scope of human language. Colour was the impression that stayed with him, colours that sparkled like precious gemstones, jasper red at the centre, then orange like carnelian, and, surrounding that, emerald green. A rainbow, from which sparked flashes of lightning, encircled the throne.

Closest to the throne were four beings, four creatures, for you couldn't describe them as animals or as men or even as angels. One looked like a lion, the next like a bull, the third like a man, and the fourth like an eagle in flight. Surrounding these were twenty-four elders, all dressed in white and wearing gold crowns. They were each seated on a throne.

Next, John saw that a Lamb was standing right next to the great throne. It looked as though this Lamb had already suffered the pain of sacrifice yet was standing tall.

John noticed an amazing phenomenon. It started closest to the throne with the four beings, then moved out like a ripple. The four beings fell on their faces and sang, "Holy, holy, holy is the Lord God Almighty who was, and is, and is to come."

Immediately, the twenty-four elders responded by falling prostrate from their thrones, removing their crowns and reverently laying them before the one great central throne. They took up the refrain from the four beings: "You are worthy, Lord God, to receive glory, honour, and power since you are the Creator of all things."

But then the wave moved further outward, and the song swelled into the amazing harmony of a great chorale, thousands upon thousands, ten thousand times ten thousand, all of them angels singing the music of heaven. A great swell of worship came from this angelic choir: "Worthy is the Lamb to receive all power, wealth, wisdom, strength, honour, glory, and praise."

Then, what at first seemed to be but an echo arose from behind and beyond the angels, an innumerable multitude of people from every nation, each wearing a white robe and carrying a palm branch. They moved forward through the ranks of angels to take their position directly in front of the throne. Their song took on the harmonious refrain: "Salvation is from God, who sits on the throne, and from the Lamb."

But then the music broadened out till it came from every direction all at once, as the infinity of all creation joined in one great song of praise: "To him who sits on the throne and to the Lamb be all praise, honour, glory, and power, forever and forever."

"Amen!" agreed the elders and the four creatures. Then everyone fell flat on their faces. "Amen," they all agreed. "Blessing and glory and wisdom and thanksgiving and honour and power and might be to our God, forever and forever … Amen!" All creation shook with the resonance of its complete and united agreement.

―――――――――

What John saw next was difficult to describe and almost impossible to understand. It was an epic of horror and wonder, as the hosts of heaven vanquished the forces of evil. But finally, John saw a series of scenes that brought all things to closure.

Riding through the open gates of heaven, he saw Jesus, but not the gentle Jesus whom John had seen riding into Jerusalem on a donkey. Now he was mounted on a white horse. His eyes blazed like fire. From his mouth came a sword, and he wore a crown on his head. "Faithful and True," they called out to him. "Word of God! King of Kings and Lord of Lords!" Behind him rode the armies of heaven.

The next scene was a countless throng of people awaiting justice before a great white throne. Life's great journals were opened, and each man was judged by what the records showed he had done. It was doubtful that any would be found to have measured up to the required standard of perfection. But then another book was opened, the Book of Life, and it was that book that decided the ultimate destiny of every man.

The next scene was of a pristine new heaven and earth, with a city of glorious splendour. "God is now making his home with man," announced a herald. "He will wipe away every tear from their eyes and banish death, grief, and pain forever." The city shone with the glory of God, shimmering like crystal. There was something unnatural about the light. It didn't come from the sun, for that would have cast shadows, but the light was the glory of God. Even the street was like transparent gold. Down the middle of this grand avenue flowed a river, the water of life, which bubbled up from the throne of God and the Lamb. Along the banks of the river was a grove of trees: the tree of life that produced life-giving fruit year round. Even the leaves were good for you and offered healing to the nations.

John heard the voice he loved speaking directly to him: "Everything is finished, John. I started it, and now it is done. I give to anyone who is thirsty a drink from the spring of the water of life."

John had a flash back to a Samaritan woman beside a well long ago.

"John, tell the people to come! Whoever is thirsty, tell them to come to me for the free gift of the water of life. I will be their God, and they will be my children."

As though in response, a great cry of yearning arose from all around, as of a bride calling out to her groom: "Come, Lord Jesus!"

"Yes," he answered. "I am coming very soon."

In case you missed the first half of this story...

TO MAKE AN OLD STORY NEW
The Epic Saga of the Bible's Old Testament Retold with Colour and Warmth

Human history is traced from our once-upon-a-time origins, through the great disaster that nearly wiped the human race from the planet. From an insignificant family of displaced nomads, kings and poets arise who will shape human destiny. Fascinating characters, fast moving action and sparkling humour track the thread of the original Bible story, allowing the narrative to live afresh today.

CONTACT JUSTYN REES:
www.justynrees.com
jrees@upstream.ca

About the Author

Justyn Rees is a lifelong student of the Bible. His deep understanding of the book enables him to make its profound truths accessible to ordinary people. He is a storyteller whose ability to keep audiences of all ages on the edge of their seats has taken him to several continents as he tells the greatest story ever.

Born in the United Kingdom, Justyn uses his many British dialects to lend colour to the characters he portrays, while his sense of humour brings the truth he relates to street level.

Justyn's career has included directing a conference center near London, England; serving as pastor for one of Canada's largest churches; leading a team of musicians and actors across Canada on a five-year mission of reconciliation; and facilitating a delegation of church leaders from a dozen denominations to Rwanda. He has authored several books and is in demand as a speaker at conventions and conferences on both sides of the Atlantic. Justyn now lives in the province of British Columbia in Western Canada with his wife Joy.